12⁵⁰

The Barbed-Wire College

The Barbed-Wire College

REEDUCATING GERMAN POWS
IN THE UNITED STATES DURING
WORLD WAR II

Ron Robin

PRINCETON UNIVERSITY PRESS

PRINCETON, NEW JERSEY

Library of Congress Cataloging-in-Publication Data

Robin, Ron Theodore.
The barbed-wire college : reeducating German POWs in the
United States during World War II / Ron Robin.
p. cm.
Includes bibliographical references and index.
ISBN 0-691-03700-0
1. World War, 1939–1945—Prisoners and prisons, American.
2. World War, 1939–1945—Education and the war.   3. World War,
1939-1945—United States.   4. World War, 1939–1945—Psychological
aspects.   5. Prisoners of war—Germany—History—20th century.
6. Prisoners of war—United States—History—20th century.
7. Education, Higher—United States—History—20th century.
8. Social sciences—United States—History—20th century.
9. Education, Humanistic—United States—History—20th century.
I. Title.
D805.U5R63   1995
940.54'7273—dc20   94-21161

This book has been composed in Sabon

10   9   8   7   6   5   4   3   2   1

Contents

List of Illustrations

Preface and Acknowledgments

THIS STUDY of one of the many government-sponsored intellectual enterprises of World War II began as a somewhat predictable attempt to assess the success of indoctrination efforts among the 380,000 German POWs incarcerated in the continental United States during the war years. I rapidly discovered that my attempts to formulate objective measurements of the program's accomplishments were of little significance. Claims for the profound cultural transformation of German POWs during World War II were suspect and unsubstantiated. Moreover, many historical examples, from the United States and elsewhere, provided ample evidence that the very concept of reeducation was an elusive if not ineffectual political weapon.

Not wanting to devote an entire book to damning American reeducation officials for being presumptuous or misleading, I have, instead, attempted to understand why they would claim success for this manifestly ineffectual project. The answer appears to be that these mobilized professors believed that they had accomplished an assignment that was far more important than the formal military mission of democratizing a benighted enemy. The transformation of the original mission of reeducation into a more personally meaningful task is, then, the subject of this historical investigation.

In writing this book I have benefited from the kindness and knowledge of colleagues, friends, and anonymous readers. Many years ago Gunther Barth taught me the craft of writing history; he is partly responsible for my interest in the study of reeducation and German POWs. Richard Hill and my father, Eli Robin, were early readers and exacting critics. William L. O'Neill pointed out some crucial weaknesses in the original draft of this book. Winfried Fluk and Haim Shatzker guided me toward a broad understanding of German culture at mid-century. I gained much perspective from conversations with Paul Flemer and Andy Heinze. Willi Paul Adams, James Long, and Daniel Krauskopf, were, as always, supportive and helpful. Yariv and Leora Zultan provided indispensable aid in deciphering some of the torpid German prose I came across. I owe a special debt to two individuals whom I have never met, Arnold Krammer and Judith Gansberg. Their pioneering studies on the German POW experience in the United States provided me with background, and much food for thought. While wandering around the United States in search of archival material, I enjoyed the hospitality of many friends, in particular Fred

Paxton, Sylvia Malizia, Jean and Jim Collin, Daniel and Judith Bloom, Susan Levine, Peter Barta, and Lyda Beardsley.

Lauren Osborne, my editor at Princeton, proved once again to be an exceptional person. Throughout the course of this project she managed to balance heavy doses of encouragement and constructive criticism. Her exacting demands improved the quality of this manuscript immensely. Bill Laznovsky's careful editing saved me from making numerous embarrassing mistakes.

I have been extremely fortunate in receiving both financial and logistical assistance for this project. Sheldon Rothblatt and the staff of the Center for Studies in Higher Education made my stay at the University of California, Berkeley, a most productive experience. Sheldon was both a gracious host and an encouraging critic of my work. A CEIS grant from the Fulbright Foundation and the United States Israel Educational Foundation allowed me to spend this important summer sojourn in Berkeley. A mini-grant from Haifa University's faculty of the humanities provided funds for research assistants and photo duplication.

As always, my family has offered a nurturing setting for my work. My parents, Eli and Shani Robin gave both encouragement and advice. My partner in life, Livi Wolff Robin, endured with good humor my obsession with this project. Our children, Gal, Sivan, Noa, and Matan have constantly reminded me that there are many more important things in life than writing history. Whether they like it or not, I dedicate this book to them.

Abbreviations

AEO	Assistant Executive Officer
EDP	Edward Davison Papers, Beinecke Library, Yale University
NCO	Noncommissioned Officer
NFSO	National Sozialistische Fuehrungs-Offiziere (morale officers)
OPMG	Office of the Provost Marshal General
OSS	Office of Strategic Services
OWI	Office of War Information
PMG	The Provost Marshal General
POW	Prisoner of War
POWD	Prisoner of War Division, Foreign Office, Great Britain
PWD	Psychological Warfare Division
RG 389	Record Group 389, Records of the Provost Marshal General, National Archives, Washington, D.C.
SFP	Stephen Farrand Papers, Hoover Institute, Stanford University
SHAEF	Supreme Headquarters, Allied Expeditionary Forces
SPD	Special Projects Division, Office of the Provost Marshal General
WRA	War Relocation Agency
WSP	Walter Schoenstedt Papers, Special Collections, University of California, Davis

The Barbed-Wire College

Introduction

DURING the course of World War II over 430,000 prisoners of war (POWs) embarked on an unforseen journey to the distant, alien land of their most powerful enemy. Upon surrendering to advancing Allied troops, many German, Italian, and Japanese prisoners were removed from the various war theaters and shipped to the continental United States. The largest group of these accidental tourists—some 380,000— were Germans. The sudden and massive presence of enemy captives on American soil led the Pentagon to breach both prevailing military etiquette as well as the Geneva Convention by establishing a reeducation program for these soldiers of the Third Reich. The program's ultimate objective was to provide ideological alternatives to National Socialism for the cross section of the German nation represented in the prison camps.

The enemy POW experience in the United States is by now a dim memory, conjured up occasionally to illustrate a host of other issues. In *V Was For Victory*, John Morton Blum's seminal study of American society in the war years, the POWs are invoked as an illustration of the irrationality of segregation, when a group of African-American soldiers are denied access to a Kansas diner, while German POWs enter the establishment freely.[1] A recent story in *Reader's Digest* describes the meeting between an American family and German prisoners as an illustration of the importance of forgiveness in Christianity.[2] Such typical vignettes of POWs in the United States make no mention of the ambitious indoctrination program for enemy captives; reeducation appears to have no part in the public memory of the home front.

To a certain degree, as Barry Katz suggests in his study of another of the war's academic enterprises, the fading of this footnote to the global conflict is understandable. The mobilized humanists who ran such scholarly wartime endeavors "did not engineer a secret weapon, nor can they be said, by any stretch of the imagination, to have made a decisive contribution to the war."[3] When measured narrowly as just another sideshow of World War II, the reeducation of enemy POWs was of little lasting significance.

Such an assessment of this intellectual venture is however, misleading. To be sure, reeducation neither altered the course of the war nor affected the immediate future of postwar Germany. However, the historical relevance of reeducation does not lie in the field of military accomplishments, but in its illumination of the intersection between scholarship and government policy in modern America. In addition, the documentary records of reeducation provide insights into the pivotal institutional and cultural battles of American academia during an important period of transition.

This study has, then, two primary objectives. The first is the reconstruction of prominent professional concerns and crucial political struggles within American universities during the 1940s. Reeducation officials were, for the most part, mobilized professors from the humanities. Their assumptions of reeducation were fundamentally linked to two central aspects of university life in the 1940s: the decline of the liberal arts and the beginnings of the anticommunist university purges that became so prevalent in the 1950s.

The second task of this inquiry is the tracing of American concepts of enemy reeducation, as formulated by mobilized academics and adapted by military authorities. When compared with British strategies for the enlightenment of German POWs, and when placed within the context of other American projects—the reeducation of Communist POWs during the Korean War as well as the attempt to indoctrinate American citizens of Japanese descent in the relocation camps of World War II—the reeducation project for German POWs reveals a complex and uniquely American relationship between academic, pedagogical presumptions and the policies adopted by government clients.

The mobilized humanists charged with uplifting the enemy had a vested interest in proving that true and profound conversion could be achieved through intellectual discourse; their formula for achieving such an objective was quite predictable. As humanists, the idea of behavior modification was anathema to them; they advocated, instead, a rational learning process. The "knowledge" that they sought to impart to the prisoner-students had a distinct binational slant. As Americans, they advocated that spreading an awareness of their nation's own special political system would benefit the postwar world, in general, and a new Germany, in particular. As students and admirers of nineteenth-century German culture, they argued that exposure to the underlying liberalism inherent in that golden age would soothe the Nazi beast.

This somewhat pedestrian prescription for reeducation was formulated by a group of scholars who were recruited at a very late stage of the war. By the time the architects of reeducation began seeking personnel, they faced an acute shortage of suitable candidates. The superstars of the liberal arts, including the most prominent experts in German culture, had already been pressed into the service of other intellectual enterprises. With the exception of Harvard Professor Howard Mumford Jones, the members of the reeducation staff were not on the cutting edge of their respective fields. They were, if I may stretch a military metaphor, the troopers of the academic profession. To be sure, these scholars in uniform, like their more prominent colleagues, traded in ideas, but they produced few intellectual innovations. They showed a marked tendency to follow well-worn paths rather than break new ground.[4]

Reeducation officials had pressing personal reasons for treating their assignment as a simple exercise in rational persuasion. They were unfamiliar with, and suspicious of, alternative strategies. They were teachers, not soldiers; their military experience ranged from nonexistent to negligible. Few staff members had ever worked outside of the classroom and, of course, they were unacquainted with the dynamics of prison life. Predictably, these educators fell back on a conventional formula: they reconstructed the milieu of their colleges. Their student body was of course quite unsuited for this academic framework. The irreconcilable differences between National Socialism and democracy were perhaps, reason enough to expect limited success. But beyond this ideological obstacle lay a more mundane reason for the faulty dialogue between German soldiers and American educators. Once settled in the camps, these captive soldiers behaved much in accordance with the standard conduct of the prison inmate. The teacher was the warden, and, by implication, he was the enemy. At times the inmate would demonstrate varying degrees of acquiescence; but accepting the worldview of the warden was out of the question.

THE American attempt to create a college behind barbed wire occurred in the wake of the successful Allied campaigns in North Africa and Italy which brought American forces face to face with overwhelming numbers of captured enemy troops. Hastily constructed makeshift enclosures in service areas behind battle lines proved unwieldy. The proximity to the actual battle arena provided potential incentive for the bolder element of the POW population to escape. Moreover, the technical difficulties of catering to the needs of this ever-growing population of enemy soldiers placed an undue burden on the Allied logistical efforts. The lack of adequate food and medical attention, and the diversion of much-needed troops to patrol these enclosures, hastened the removal of POWs from the theaters of war.

The American solution to the POW problem was ingeniously simple. The Liberty Ships transporting supplies and troops to the war zones usually had no defined mission for their return journey. American authorities could easily fill the empty hulls with captive enemy troops and channel them to the United States. Here the logistical problem of dealing with this sudden presence of hostile enemy captives could be handled more expediently. The geographical expanse separating the United States from Europe was bound to discourage any rash of escape attempts. The vast majority of the some five hundred U.S. POW camps scattered throughout the United States were located in isolated rural areas, a fact which further dampened any dreams of fleeing captivity.

The establishment of these prisons in rural areas addressed pressing economic needs, too. Agriculture, more than any other segment of the American economy, suffered from the nationwide shortage of manpower. The backbreaking, poorly paying manual labor required by this sector made it difficult to find ready replacements for those who were either inducted into the military or lured to the city in search of financially attractive industrial occupations. As late as February 1945, congressional representatives of farm states were still pressuring the War Department to ship over at least another 100,000 German POWs "to relieve the farm labor shortage."[5] Tens of thousands of POWs, then, fulfilled a vital economic role in rural areas where the War Manpower Commission of the War Food Administration had certified that labor was scarce. Farmers and food processors paid the government the going civilian rate for the labor of the prisoners "to avoid unfair competition" with those agriculturists and businesses who used "free civilian labor." It is safe to assume that the very presence of a POW labor pool kept civilian wages artificially low in these labor markets. POWs received 80 cents per day in canteen coupons for their labor. The remainder of their wages went toward paying for the routine operation of the camps, as well as a variety of other POW-related needs within these prison enclosures. In 1944 alone the government earned $22,000,000 through this employment scheme. The same year the War Department reported additional savings of $80,000,000 by using POWs in a variety of service activities in military installations.[6]

Most of these prisoner-laborers were Germans; at one point or another 378,898 German soldiers had been incarcerated in the United States. Italians made up the second largest group—51,455 men. The smallest group, and the latest arrivals in the United States, were the Japanese; the War Department reported that only 5,435 were brought over to the United States.[7]

This large presence of belligerents dispersed throughout the United States could not, of course, be kept a secret. Indeed, once apprised of this vast network of enemy prison camps within their midst, both ordinary citizens and influential journalists inundated military authorities with advice and complaints regarding the POW problem. The most common public grievance was that the army was pampering the prisoners, lavishing on them excellent food and easy work, even as American boys were laying their lives on the line. Military authorities rejected these accusations, by claiming mere adherence to the Geneva Convention.

In actual fact, American POW policy was definitely affected by popular sentiment. Well-ingrained prejudices and preconceptions guided the development of different policies for each of these three national groups of captives. Thus, the bulk of the Japanese POW population, small in number and encumbered by a particularly pernicious stereotyped image, was tucked away for the duration of the war in two camps: Camp McCoy, Wisconsin, and Camp Clarinda, Iowa. American military authorities were primarily concerned with security measures and the isolation of this seemingly incorrigible, supposedly fanatical group of enemy captives.[8]

Italians, by contrast, basked in their image as happy-go-lucky, reluctant soldiers. Throughout the war, the American press described the relaxed atmosphere of Italian camps and the contentment of easy-going, sometimes sloppy, and always cheerful Italians.[9] Such accounts had little to do with reality. The Italian camps experienced bitter and often quite violent political struggles among a variety of factions. The number of escape attempts serves as a partial indicator of significant turmoil within the Italian ranks. Military statistics reveal 2,827 escape attempts among enemy POWs held within the continental United States. Of these, 2,222 were Germans, 604 were Italians, and one was Japanese. Relative to the number of prisoners, Louis Keefer notes in his history of Italian POWs in the United States, "the Italians seemed twice as prone to escape as the Germans: 1.2 escapes per thousand versus 0.5 escapes per thousand."[10]

These facts notwithstanding, U.S. military authorities encouraged congenial portrayals of Italian POWs, because of the War Department's plans to dismantle most Italian POW enclosures and organize the prisoners into auxiliary service units. The military proposed to utilize this seemingly harmless group of prisoners for a variety of tasks, mainly in ordnance and supply units. About thirty thousand Italians joined these service units. The rest were either rejected for technical reasons or were "non-cooperators," meaning those who refused assignments for political reasons.

As for German POWs, both military policy and public sentiments were affected by images that were significantly more complex than the uncomplicated portrayals of amiable Italians and fanatical Japanese. Negative attitudes toward Japan—the enemy closest to home—were already part of the public discourse prior to America's engagement in the war. By contrast, public opinion polls indicated profound ignorance, if not lack of interest, concerning Germany's global policies, and their potential impact on the safety and security of the United States. According to a Gallup Poll in October 1943, only 34 percent of the American public believed that

Germany "is our main enemy." By contrast, 53 percent identified Japan as the country's primary foe.[11]

Upon their arrival in American POW camps, German military captives did not appear to be as incorrigible as the supposedly fanatical Japanese. However contemptible their wartime actions might have been, the American public did not demand that these POWs, as representatives of the German nation, bear full responsibility for their deeds. "In the war with Germany, who do you think our chief enemy is: the German people as a whole or the German Government?" Seventy-four percent of the respondents to this November 1943 Gallup Poll query placed the blame squarely and exclusively on the shoulders of the German government.[12]

The sheer numbers of German POWs demanded, as well, a response quite distinct from the benign neglect of Italian prisoners or the policy of strict incarceration applied to their Japanese counterparts. A War Department booklet published for supervisors of German POW laborers underlined the possibility that "these prisoners will, as a group, have a strong influence in future German affairs, and their conceptions of our form of government may determine to a great extent Germany's postwar relations with the United States." As such, the War Department warned labor personnel to avoid behavior and expression of opinions that the enemy could interpret as dissatisfaction or weakness. "Careless talk about the uncertainty of the future, our racial problems, our national leaders both civil and military, our relations with the rest of the Allied nations and even the mild complaining most of us do naturally, does have an undesirable effect on the opinions the prisoners hold with regard to American life and ideas."[13] While the Japanese could be written off as intractable fanatics and inscrutable orientals, this pamphlet hinted that German political deviancy was not the result of irredeemable personality or racial defects. Given a correct and selective presentation of American values, the POWs could conceivably be transformed from adversaries to disciples.

These were not idle thoughts or mere speculation. Beginning in the fall of 1943, the Office of the Provost Marshal General (OPMG), the military police authority charged with managing POW camps in the United States, began preparations for an ambitious program of "intellectual diversion" for German POWs.

The program began as a covert effort. A cadre of university professors joined forces with a small group of "safe" prisoners in preparing material for this secret operation. A monitored diet of reading material provided the main tool for this phase of reeducation. For the most part, the reeducation program, known officially as the Special Projects Division (SPD), relied on a newspaper edited by prisoner-collaborators as well as on a series of great literary works that had been banned by the Nazis. Toward the end of the covert phase, which lasted until the spring of 1945, the SPD reluctantly began using a slim diet of movies, the only element of mass culture in the program.

Reasons for secrecy were varied. To begin with, the SPD sought to avoid blatant defiance of the Geneva Convention, which forbade indoctrination. The potential threat of retaliatory measure against Allied captives in German hands weighed heavily on the minds of War Department officials. The SPD faculty also assumed that the POWs would, out of pride or conviction, reject any obvious attempt to reshape their political beliefs.

By the spring of 1945, following V-E Day and in preparation for the imminent repatriation of the POWs, the SPD initiated a new phase of its program. After sifting through the prisoners in search of the most politically reliable element, the SPD launched a series of crash courses in democracy. The ultimate aim was the preparation of a significant bloc of trustworthy Germans to spearhead change in Germany itself. The twenty-five thousand graduates of these various courses were indeed shipped back directly to Germany, even as their comrades were being sent to France as forced laborers.

The underlying didactic approach to both phases of reeducation was colored by a fascinating set of inconsistencies. Most senior members of the SPD staff were not experts on contemporary German culture. With four exceptions, none had any meaningful command of the German language. Their aides, a select group of German POW assistants whose task it was to provide some insight into the culture of their peers, were marginal men, quite alienated and intellectually distant from the mainstream of German society. Moreover, few of the architects and planners of reeducation had had any significant military experience. Such issues as military mentality, the regime of camp life, and the unique pressures associated with captivity never seemed to engage their attention. A deliberate exclusion of behaviorists and other social scientists from the SPD staff further shielded reeducation officials from an understanding of the tensions affecting the lives of their wards.

It would be quite a simple task, then, to dismiss the reeducation program as a misconceived effort riddled with fundamental errors, and managed by an incompetent staff. However, such an assessment implies that, given a more informed approach to reeducation, these German prisoners might have left the camps as new, democratically oriented men and advocates of an enlightened American political philosophy.

My own view is that no plan for reeducation would have made any meaningful difference. Reeducation master plans and schemes for the ideological indoctrination of Germans played a marginal role in the transformation of German institutions and political attitudes. The magnitude of defeat, the carving up of Prussia, the decimation of the Junker class, and the division of the country into two distinct ideological camps

are but some of the more convincing explanations for the rapid dissipation of National Socialism and the acceptance of Western values in significant portions of German society.

These issues notwithstanding, the SPD's approach to reeducation still
raises some important questions. The most intriguing enigma of the program, and a key to understanding the worldview of the educators, was
the seemingly poor choice of strategies for reeducation. Of all the possible
approaches available for devising the program, SPD educators deliberately and wilfully chose the least plausible course of action. Irrespective of
the somewhat irrelevant background that they brought to the mission,
these educators were surely aware of the weaknesses of their designs.

In choosing their course of action, the educators consciously ignored
the rank and file. Knowingly, and not by accident, they chose to re-create
the familiar milieu of the American college campus, and to focus most of
their attention on a marginal and numerically insignificant intellectual
subculture within the camps. The SPD offered the prison population
reading material of a highly intellectual and abstract nature. Such material meant little to the average prisoner of war. The SPD-sponsored newspaper was basically a literary journal, which consistently disregarded demands to incorporate light reading. In response to pressure from the field,
the newspaper's staff grudgingly published the occasional news item from
Germany. News from home remained, however, sparse and marginal.

As for the crash-course phase of the program, the model here was that
of a freshman undergraduate semester in the liberal arts. The program
offered core courses in German history and American civilization, and a
variety of other activities modeled after the undergraduate seminar. Language, literature, and history provided the basis for this phase of reeducation. These crash courses offered no meaningful insights from the social
sciences, due, in part, to the deliberate exclusion of social scientists from
the teachers' roster.

Rather than dismissing this strategy from the comfortable, yet intellectually precarious vantage point of hindsight, I hope, instead, to explain
here the compelling reasons for adopting this academic format for reeducation. My argument is that SPD educators had ulterior motives for devising such a seemingly unsuitable program.

My search for the hidden agenda of reeducation officials is based upon
a variety of different sources, each with a somewhat different portrayal of
the program. This study is derived, to a large extent, from archival collections of SPD documents as well as the unpublished in-house histories of
the different divisions within the SPD which were written prior to the
dismantling of the program in the spring of 1946. In sifting through this
material I have confronted significant contradictions between the documentary record and the SPD's monographical accounts.

The internal monographs state, for example, that the primary obstacle facing the successful implementation of reeducation was the presence of a strong, and at times aggressive Nazi hard core within the camp. The archival files of the SPD suggest, by contrast, faulty communication between educators and prisoners as the main impediment. Perhaps the most important discrepancy between documents and monographs was the declaration that, despite the perceived Nazi threat, reeducation was at least partly successful. These claims, which appear throughout the monographs, are not supported by the documentary record, in particular the internal polls of POWs which registered no meaningful change in the worldview of the vast majority of internees.

Many important technical details in these monographs contradict the actual archival records as well. Thus, the monograph of the film branch of the SPD depicts a strategy that has little to do with what actually transpired. The thrust of the movie program, according to the monograph, was to present good wholesome entertainment and educational material, and to avoid at all costs any film glorifying violence and sex. However, the actual records of films prepared and screened before POWs was replete with violent movies, all of which served, of course, a didactic purpose. Moreover, the film monograph reveals little of the efforts of powerful figures in the SPD to dismiss mass culture as a tool for reeducation. Of course, none of the SPD's histories mentions internal rivalries or the ideological clashes among the faculty. Most significant, the in-house monographs ignore the Red Scare and hunt for Communist sympathizers that shook the program during the summer of 1945.

Inconsistencies and selective recollections are prevalent in other material as well. The personal accounts, memoirs, oral histories, and articles written after the fact by educators and prisoners, have produced other significant contradictions of the official record. Members of the German auxiliary staff of the national POW newspaper recalled American narrow-mindedness and censorship when the Germans dared express unpopular views. However, the newspapers themselves, as well as a variety of other documents, suggest that the Germans' complaints were far from accurate.

American personnel have also produced very selective recollections of reeducation. The memoirs of many reeducation officials state that the program never sought to Americanize its wards. While "it was quite natural that many object lessons were drawn from American history and civilization," one of the senior staff members of the reeducation program recalled in an article published shortly after the dismantling of the program, "the teachers never intended to identify the ideology and practice of democracy with one particular state or its culture."[14] The actual curriculum found in the files of the OPMG suggests otherwise.

In pointing out these inconsistencies, I do not suggest that there was a conspiracy of sorts to produce an unfaithful record of the reeducation program. Final documents are often eulogies rather than autopsies; invariably there are few candid criticisms in such material. It appears, as well, that many of the protagonists demonstrated a selective recollection of events because, in their minds, the SPD was merely a metaphor for much broader issues, such as the significance of the war, freedom of expression, or the meaning of education in modern society. As such, rather than hunt for misrepresentations of events in order to merely clarify "the facts," I have attempted to understand the reasons for the sometimes selective, sometimes mistaken reconstruction of circumstances.

I have, as well, resisted the temptation to conduct an oral history of my own, mainly because I have no desire to "straighten out" the record. I have sought to comprehend the protagonists' representation of events rather than challenge it. The many personal accounts that already exist were written without the prompting of a questionnaire. As such, these autobiographical recollections provide the best possible insights into the participants' own comprehension of historical development, their part in the reeducation project, as well as their interpretation of the significance of World War II. This study attempts, then, to understand the protagonists' version of the truth, in particular the motives and convictions underlying their selective reconstruction of what actually transpired.

In so doing, I have not written an intellectual history, but, rather, a social history of an intellectual endeavor. In contrast to some of the exemplary histories of mobilized professors during World War II, I have focused more on the social dilemmas of reeducation officials than on their intellectual interests. I have sought to understand their mundane, yet fascinating personal preoccupations. The mobilized academics appear in this book as ordinary people rather than as intellectual mandarins. Such features as status anxiety, professional rivalries, conceit, deceit, as well as a very irresolute stand on the issue of academic freedom, are as important as the enumeration of contemporary intellectual trends for understanding the development of reeducation policy.

A university, Robin Winks has argued in his study, *Cloak and Gown*, has many of the trappings of a nation-state. "A university will have a national anthem . . .; it will have a flag . . . a set of well-sung heroic leaders—largely athletic though at times academic—and a sense of national boundaries, which define the 'campus precincts' sometimes as sharply as any rising national state in nineteenth century Europe." The SPD experience suggests that crossing the border separating this secluded intellectual domain from the national state was not unlike immigration to a foreign land. Upon leaving the familiar world of the college campus, reeducation officials did assimilate some of the concerns of their new surroundings. At the same time, they remained preoccupied with the culture and politics of the academic land they had left behind; they strove to re-create intimate landscapes, little enclaves reminiscent of home. The following pages will attempt, then, to reconstruct the concerns of these intellectual sojourners and their search for familiar points of orientation in the politically and culturally confusing world of the 1940s.

PART ONE

The Mobilization of
Liberal Arts

CHAPTER ONE

The Genesis of Reeducation

WHEN FORCED to handle the occasional contentious cabinet meeting, President Woodrow Wilson would often relate his recollections of a Princeton faculty gathering which was riddled by such discordant views that agreement seemed impossible. And yet, Wilson marveled, having committed themselves to a process of dialogue and rational discussion, the members of this splintered and quarrelsome group were able to reach a common solution. "To Wilson," historian Emily Rosenberg has observed, "Princeton might have been the country or the world. Its conference rooms offered realistic lessons about conflict: consensus was possible if rationality prevailed. . . . National and international interests could be harmonized as thoroughly as the different academic factions in Wilson's Princeton anecdote."[1]

Wilson's university parable was more than mere rhetorical flourish. The United States was, after all, a nation of immigrants, in which the social and political acculturation of newcomers was often approached as a pedagogical enterprise. Such representations of political objectives in educational terms were by no means restricted to domestic issues. Beginning in the latter half of the nineteenth century, the school as a political symbol appeared prominently in the country's first hesitant forays in foreign policy.

Driven by a mixture of evangelism and power politics, altruism and imperialism, a series of privately endowed yet government-sanctioned American colleges sprang up in various corners of the globe ranging from India to Egypt. These educational institutions abroad symbolized what the American political establishment viewed as the fundamental difference between American expansionism and old-world imperialism. Americans sought to enlighten rather than conquer, persuade rather than subdue. Even though government endorsement of international education was never more than a token reminder of American aspirations, it reflected a widely held assumption that moral influences and persuasion could eliminate the need for naked power in the management of global affairs.[2]

The harsh realities of twentieth-century world politics did not, at first, destroy resilient convictions in the benefits of marketing American political objectives through educational projects. Global conflict merely suggested the need for greater government coordination and involvement in such enterprises as the international exchange of scholars and students, as well as support for American schools abroad.[3] Of course, endorsement of the genteel exchange of ideas had explicit limits. The school as microcosm of the world lost much of its luster when applied to the great ideological clash underlying World War II. Never before had modern Americans witnessed such active displays of hostility, such vicious attacks on their way of life. The Fascist worldview appeared intractable and quite resistant to change; the idea of rational persuasion inherent in the concept of school as a tool of diplomacy seemed superfluous. There appeared to be little hope for the redemptive approach to global politics.

Predictably, as the first wave of German POWs entered the United States, the Roosevelt administration dismissed recommendations for using these captives for anything beyond solving the agricultural labor crisis in the country's farming sector. Enlightening and educating this fast-growing enemy population seemed unwarranted, basically a waste of time. The enemy seemed too bitter and the clash of cultures so pronounced; there appeared to be no hope for any form of reconciliation. Instead, the United States and its allies planned to destroy physically the Fascist infrastructure, thereby rendering the enemy quite incapable of maintaining its old worldview.

American strategy during the early war years never envisioned any winning over of selective segments of the German population, either elite groups or captive soldiers. A fundamental premise of the American war effort was that unmitigating annihilation would strip the German nation, once and for all, of the destructive illusion of omnipotence. "The realization of utter defeat brought about by unconditional surrender and total destruction was all that mattered," notes historian Lothar Kettenacker in his discussion of Allied policy. "No room was to be left for another stab-in-the-back legend which would allow the myth of military invincibility to linger on."[4]

The most important weapon of this policy was the Strategic Bombing Campaign. The psychological rationale for strategic bombing—a euphemism for methodical and indiscriminate destruction of the enemy's civilian infrastructure—was that "severe shock" would "break up well-established attitude or behavior patterns so that new influences can operate."[5] Contemporary supporters of decimating bombing aspired not only to destroy political and military authority, but also to deprive ordinary Germans of "the symbols of status" and, by implication, all previous compliance with aggressive national policies. "It seems safe to assume that most Germans will find it difficult in the future to think of war in romantic terms as the greatest glory of the super race," advocates of the annihilation approach argued.[6]

Supporters of the "punishment and deprivation" strategy received powerful patronage from the highest echelons of government. Throughout the early stages of the war, it was President Roosevelt himself who steadfastly rejected the notion that the German people could be transformed without resorting to drastic measures. In his youth, Roosevelt had spent many a holiday in Germany and, in the early spring of 1891, was placed by his parents in a local school, where he recalled having experienced firsthand the pervasive militarism of German society. During his brief studies there the nine-year-old Roosevelt endured compulsory courses in map reading and military topography, in addition to a strict nationalistic interpretation of history, all of which left unfavorable impressions in his mind. He emerged from that experience with harsh views concerning the German national character.[7]

Roosevelt readily accepted the advice of his confidant and Secretary of the Treasury, Henry Morgenthau, to approach the German issue as a pathological problem, the only solution being a veritable eradication of contemporary German society and, thereafter, rebuilding from scratch. Morgenthau had devised a master plan for the dismantling of the extant German economic and political infrastructure, and the subsequent "pastoralization" of the soon-to-be vanquished Third Reich. By incapacitating Germany's industrial capabilities, and by dismembering the state, Morgenthau proposed "returning the Germans to their primeval agrarian origins to start all over again."[8]

The President categorically rejected an alternative strategy proposed by his secretaries of State and War. They had urged the establishment of a policy to differentiate between Nazis and ordinary Germans who, according to their interpretation, had been coerced into collaborating with Nazism. Their appeals fell on deaf ears. Roosevelt and other critics of the lenient approach to Germany strove to avoid what they considered to be the primary error of 1918. Under the guidance of President Wilson, the United States had then urged separate approaches to the German people and their leadership. The Allied forces of the Great War had not planned for a fundamental restructuring of German society beyond the disbanding of the ruling class which had propelled a supposedly unwitting German nation into war. According to the Wilson vision, the elimination of an imperial, class-ridden government clique would automatically lead to the introduction of democratic frameworks that, in turn, would encourage the basically positive German populace to take control of its destiny.[9]

In the early 1940s there was little tolerance in the Oval Office for rehabilitation of the German people along Wilsonian lines. The "theory of accident"—the assumption that random bad luck had twice placed the fate of a basically positive German population in the hands of a megalomaniacal oligarchy that governed the people against their will—found an unappreciative audience in the President's inner circle. Roosevelt's views on the incorrigible nature of Germans and his rejection of reeducation were supported by a wide variety of scientific research, some government sponsored, some purely academic. These research projects, the works of sociologists and other behaviorists, credited pathological characteristic traits and deviant behavioral patterns as the primary reasons for German aggression. No magic formula could change the nature of German society, they implied; there was an intrinsic need for a basic upheaval in German culture before any significant transformation could come about.

Typical of this approach was a widely publicized book by the psychiatrist Richard Brickner, *Is Germany Incurable?* (1943). Brickner's thesis was that an accurate analysis of Germany's problems could be found "not among experts on world affairs, but in the doctor's office." The German nation, he asserted, was suffering from the classical symptoms of paranoia.

> The paranoid is the megalomaniac, treating his environment exclusively as a device for his own aggrandizement and glorification. Grandiose mystic notions of the cosmos that nobody can refute because they have no basis in everyday life crop up in him, huge world-embracing thoughts that make the thinker feel as big as the universe. He often develops a belief in Destiny or the Wave of the Future or a personal divine mission. . . . Others' failures to cooperate with his divine mission, meaning that everybody else is in a gigantic conspiracy to sabotage his self-aggrandizing programs, give him a "persecution complex." He is the "they" man—"they" have it in for him, "they" whisper behind his back, "they" are the malicious schemers who make sure that no job, deal, career, marriage or project of his ever succeeds.[10]

According to Brickner, the symptoms of paranoia were not restricted to the country's leadership; they were endemic to the culture and could be traced back "throughout at least five generations of German history." He argued that Germany's current rulers, "like some of their predecessors," were "mere transient leaders of a type that a paranoid culture will inevitably seek or produce."[11] Under these circumstances, he implied, neither political concessions nor reasoning would be of any avail. Only drastic, long-term treatment, including a dramatic restructuring of German society, from the level of the family to its highest political institutions, could revive Europe's perennially problematic nation. No purely political solution or political dictate could accomplish the mission. Brickner envisioned a long, drawn-out therapeutic procedure involving "experts in a dozen different fields—anthropology, law, sociology, nutrition, transport, propaganda, psychology, economics, as well as psychiatry."[12]

Brickner's exposition received lavish praise from the River Gods of the social sciences, including Margaret Mead and Ruth Benedict, who not only endorsed his thesis, but also his solution. Of course, not all accepted his premise. Psychoanalyst Erich Fromm accused Brickner of using shallow analogy instead of thorough analysis.[13] But Brickner's thesis struck a responsive note in government circles, where empirical studies commissioned by the military in the United States and Great Britain—mostly the works of academic personnel who had been mobilized for the purpose of psychological warfare and intelligence—had a distinctly similar ring about them.

Henry Dicks, a psychiatrist of the Freudian persuasion serving in British military intelligence, reported on a correlation between personality traits and political attitudes among German prisoners of war in the early phases of the war. Dicks, who had achieved some notoriety for his psychiatric examination of Rudolph Hess, claimed that "Nazis or near Nazis were likely to be men of a markedly pre-genital or immature personality structure" caused by "a repression of the tender tie with the mother" and a strong love-hate relationship with an "extra-punitive" father figure. Such pervasive patterns of child rearing, which Dicks claimed were responsible for the typical Nazi character, could not be changed with a hasty reeducation program aimed at adults whose personality had already acquired irreversible, pathological traits. In the Wehrmacht, there "was never less than 35 per cent of active carriers" of National Socialist ideology, which Dicks claimed was the result of faulty early childhood development. In order to change such a pattern, he stated, German society would have to undergo a fundamental transformation of "parent-child relations, educational policy, and social mores."[14]

Dicks's conclusions were supported, by surveys of the Intelligence Section of the Psychological Warfare Division of Supreme Headquarters, Allied Expeditionary Force (PWD, SHAEF). The American sociologists and psychologists employed by SHAEF were charged with monitoring the resilience of German forces in Europe. They reported that German soldiers' confidence in Hitler's leadership "held at an amazingly constant level" during a long period of steady German retreat.

> Whereas average confidence in Hitler was about 60 per cent when Germany still held the larger part of Italy and all of France, 14 months later when all these territories had been lost, not to mention the catastrophic developments on the Eastern Front and the destruction of German cities from the air, confidence was at the same figure of 60 percent.[15]

These findings among German soldiers, interrogated immediately upon surrendering to advancing Allied forces, could not be explained away as some temporary phase that would disappear as the realities of captivity and defeat sank in. Preliminary surveys among German soldiers in POW camps in the United States demonstrated an obdurate ideological stance even after many months of captivity. Of the twenty camp newspapers published by POWs in the early months of 1945, eight advocated National Socialism. An additional twelve papers were of a moderate "less imbued" Nazi stance, or tried "to be tolerant to both sides." Only one camp newspaper, published in Camp Indianola, Nebraska, was unambiguously anti-Nazi.[16] Censors' reports revealed also little remorse or change in a robust Nazi subculture among the prisoners. American news reports from the camps concurred. They documented an arrogance as well as an unrelenting belief in the tenets of Nazism among the prisoners.

Aside from these very negative academic assessments of German national character, there were equally compelling political reasons for rejecting reeducation in the POW camps. Powerful military figures, in particular within the Air Force, opposed reeducation because it appeared to contravene the Geneva Convention and might have conceivably led to reprisals against American POWs in Germany. This outmoded, romantic code of behavior governing the etiquette of war had been written before the tempest of World War II. As such, the Convention was accordingly vague and inappropriate for this new bout of global warfare. The concept of reeducation posed a problem because the Geneva Convention prohibited the exposure of POWs to propaganda, without ever defining the term clearly. At the same time, the Convention did allow for something loosely defined as educational projects.

One of the most important opponents of reeducation was Major General Allen W. Gullion, the Provost Marshal General (PMG) who was charged, among other duties, with administering the affairs of enemy POWs in the United States. In a letter to his commanding officer, the Chief of Staff of Army Service Forces in the continental United States, Gullion listed many of the commonly held fears among the military concerning reeducation for German soldiers. He too felt that such a program might legitimize a countereffort by Germany. He reminded his superiors of the wording of the Geneva Convention, the prohibitive price in physical setup and manpower, as well as the detrimental effect of relinquishing POW working hours to the classrooms. However, his overriding concern was with the uselessness of such an endeavor. "Enemy prisoners of war are, for the most part, not children," he wrote. "Those who have sufficient intellectual capacity to be of value to a post-war world have already built the philosophical frameworks of their respective lives. Those whose minds are sufficiently plastic to be affected by the program, are probably not worth the effort."[17]

The War Department did not indeed relish the idea of increasing the taxing burden of the PMG. Hampered by the poor quality of officers and enlisted men available for the mission—mostly rejects and castoffs from other units—the PMG cringed at the thought of an indoctrination campaign that might trigger dissent among the prisoners, thereby making the already onerous task of running the camps all the more difficult. Camp authorities relied heavily on cooperation from the POWs, in particular their officers and NCOs, in maintaining discipline within the ranks. Reeducation, as a challenge to the internal military infrastructure in prison compounds, was liable to jeopardize such comfortable arrangements for command and control of the prisoners.

A reeducation program promised to raise severe bureaucratic obstacles as well because the distribution of authority over POWs was quite chaotic. "In contrast to our principal allies and enemies we have no centralized prisoner of war administration," a State Department document observed in March 1944.

> At present, general policies with regard to prisoners of war are determined in the Office of the Assistant Chief of Staff, G-1; intelligence questions and certain other phases of prisoner of war activities are controlled by G-2; and the Office of the Provost Marshal General has supervision, but not direct control, over the operation of the prisoner of war program. Direct control of the prisoner of war camps is exercised by the Corps Area Service Commands. The War Department can address no instruction directly to camp commanders but must issue them to the Service Commands.[18]

For those not entirely convinced by the military angle of the problem there was, of course, the nagging fear that a massive reeducation effort would pry open the proverbial Pandora's box. Any creditable undermining of the German worldview raised the uncomfortable specter of pushing the disoriented and disabused towards Communism. Such a prospect, in the eyes of many, was infinitely more dangerous than allowing a seemingly discredited Nazi doctrine to die a natural death. Noted sociologist Talcott Parsons warned that "the view so common among Americans that it is 'conversion' to democratic values which is the key to bringing Germany 'around' is one of the most dangerous misconceptions currently in the air." He argued that political reorientation "by propaganda or other means of indoctrination would almost certainly intensify a tendency to ideological reaction," and perhaps even "bring a communist ideology to a commanding position."[19] This lack of enthusiasm for reeducation in military, political, and academic circles appeared to remove the issue from the national agenda.

By the middle of 1944, however, the proposals for reeducation were resurrected by the Departments of State and of War. Both departments had become increasingly apprehensive about the fortunes of the Morgenthau plan to dismantle and "pastoralize" Germany. The President and his

Secretary of the Treasury had been able to win the support of Churchill, and the program seemed on the verge of moving to an operational phase. Somewhat annoyed by the poaching of Morgenthau, Secretary of War Stimson, Secretary of State Hull, and his successor Henry Stettinius lobbied strenuously for a rehabilitative approach to the German problem.

Their interdepartmental solution to the German problem was a pragmatic, if not highly selective, reading of the information at hand. Neither department appeared apprehensive about persistent and recurrent German militarism and its impact on global destabilization. "To Stimson," Warren Kimball notes, "the war was simply another chapter in power politics." There was nothing inherently abnormal about the German nation. Moreover, Stimson argued that American interests would not be served by a policy of vindictiveness against the entire German population; nor would the deindustrialization of the country aid plans for new geopolitical arrangements based on economically interdependent American-style republics. The Secretary of War advocated that the best policy was to make over the German people in the American image, thereby assuring German support in all future struggles in the international arena. In addition, Secretary of State Hull argued that the Morgenthau approach adopted by the president amounted to little more than "blind vengeance." "It was blind because it failed to see that, in striking at Germany, it was striking at all of Europe. By completely wrecking German industry it could not but partly wreck Europe's economy, which had depended for generations on certain raw materials that Germany produced."[20]

In addition to the dangerous economic implications involved in dismantling the German nation, both departments of State and War were concerned that the punitive approach to Germany was not accompanied by positive reinforcement, or a rehabilitation program. Up to this point, the war effort had concentrated on devising a harsh negative strategy of "dismemberment," destruction, and forced de-Nazification; but alternatives had to be presented lest the Germans seek comfort in other totalitarian doctrines. Any attempt to produce rehabilitative solutions for Germany would have to wait, of course, until an Allied victory. In the meantime, the two departments raised the option of a pilot project, a reeducation initiative for the ever-growing POW population.

The cause of reeducation received welcome support with the arrival of a new PMG. Major General Archer Lerch could claim a certain familiarity with the role of education in the service of national interests. Since joining the service in 1917, Lerch had spent a significant portion of his military career as a faculty member of ROTC programs at his alma mater, the University of California, Berkeley, and at the University of Florida. Consequently, Lerch was no stranger to the idea of merging martial arts with liberal arts. The new PMG was also an ambitious person. He apparently hoped that the addition of a high profile and somewhat exotic program to the rather drab duties of his military police corps would provide a springboard for his future career in the army. In direct departure from the position of his predecessor, Lerch offered enthusiastic support for the program.[21]

In light of the changing political circumstances and military assessments of reeducation, the State Department's Special War Problems Division, in conjunction with the War Department, presented on March 2, 1944, a joint strategy for the "indoctrination of German Prisoners of War." This plan remained fundamentally unchanged throughout the years of reeducation.[22] A basic premise of the master plan was that instead of discrediting National Socialism, American authorities should foster respect for the American alternative. The plan revealed a hypersensitivity about the image of America as a haven for lowbrows. German POWs, like most Europeans, regarded "this country as an uncultured, materialistic nation inferior to any European country." Therefore, the document recommended that "an indoctrination campaign should endeavor to reach the Germans by presenting to them in so far as is possible in the circumstances the best aspects of American life and institutions."[23]

The most intriguing portion of the document dealt with the description of the German nation. Germany appeared as a land of high culture. Germany's pathological political culture, by contrast was deliberately downplayed. The document stated that the vast majority of POWs were neither "confirmed or fanatical Nazis," nor a servile people. Germans were described as proud patriots with intense political awareness and a refined culture. Indeed, their most common attribute was that "their standard of formal education is high."[24]

The men who had written this joint proposal for reeducation were undoubtedly aware that their description of German culture was simplistic and that their correlation between the number of years spent in school and "education" was fundamentally deceptive. German youths did indeed spend on average a significant portion of their childhood and adolescent years in educational institutions. However, the system was rigidly divided between a small elite group who received a secondary education, and the great majority who spent most of their schooling years in a variety of vocational institutions. As historian James Tent observes, Germany offered its youth "two separate and distinct types of education, with little or no provision for transfer between them."[25] Formal education began with a four-year common school, the *Gemeinsame Grundschule*. At the age of ten, a small 10-percent minority passed on to a stream of elite secondary schools, while the rest spent the remainder of the formal years of education in a separate, elementary *Volksschule* system. Thus, for the vast majority of German youth, formal education lasted for eight years, followed by a period of vocational training. The Nazis had introduced few fundamental changes in the school system. Aside from politicizing an already nationalistic secondary school curriculum, James Tent notes, the "Nazis had made no attempt at integrating elementary and secondary education into a common educational ladder, despite much noise about creating a new egalitarian society." The educational system produced a small cadre of highly educated, highly nationalistic secondary school graduates, and a vast common class of unpoliticized, undereducated mechanics, artisans, and laborers.

The misrepresentation of German education and culture in the proposal for reeducation served, of course, a political purpose. The wording of the document hinted at strong disapproval of conventional strategies of psychological warfare. Whether motivated by a fear of transgressing the Geneva Convention, or perhaps prompted by an aversion for the techniques of propaganda, the authors of this document sought to discourage the use of conventional forms of indoctrination by presenting Germans as a nation of intellectuals. Bernard Gufler, head of the State Department's Special War Problems Division, and John Brown Mason, a peacetime professor of political science at Stanford, and at the time the State Department's liaison officer for the reeducation program, argued repeatedly and strenuously that "any attempt to reorient them [the POWs] away from Nazi ideals and convictions was bound to fail if the attempts were made on the basis of frontline and combat psychology." These State Department officials contended that the reeducation of a cultured nation would most likely succeed if it was based on written treatises and logical expositions of the virtues of American culture and politics. As such, they insisted on a "a battle of mind designed to improve the attitudes of the prisoners rather than to incapacitate them."[26]

Instead of attempting to manipulate the minds of the POWs, the blueprint for reeducation proposed a campaign of truth in which the facts would speak for themselves. Quite predictably, then, the program aimed to "utilize the desire of numerous prisoners to have contact with American educational institutions." There, in the Groves of Academe the prisoners would discard both the notion of American vulgarity as well as the misconceived endorsement of National Socialism. Given the explicit aims of logical persuasion as well as cultivating a positive image of American society, the reeducation blueprint paid little attention to popular culture. Of course movies could be an asset, but these would be for the most part "scientific and educational films." Only the very last sentence in the section on film—almost an afterthought—mentioned the possibility of showing "from time to time good non-political Hollywood productions."

Guided by demands to avoid open transgressions of the Geneva Convention and fearful of unrest in the poorly staffed camps, the proposal's authors envisioned a covert project, "not an obvious campaign designed to turn the prisoners against their country." The plan called for the creation of a centralized prisoner of war administration that would include specialized personnel for the purposes of edifying the German captives. Through reading materials, selective use of visual aids, and the creation of a newspaper written by cooperative POWs rather than by clever propagandists, the plan for reeducation aspired to attract POWs to the American Way. In sum, instead of lecturing on the deficiencies of Nazism and running the risk of antagonizing the POWs, the program planned to present a positive, attractive alternative to the harsh, uncompromising ways of National Socialism.

The State and War departments circulated this joint proposal for reeducation at a particularly opportune time. Growing public criticism over the lack of initiative in uplifting the prisoners had attracted the attention of Eleanor Roosevelt. Deeply disturbed by reports of rampant Nazism in the camps, and after personally interrogating Major Maxwell McKnight, then chief of the Administrative Section of Prisoner of War Camp Operations in the OPMG, Mrs. Roosevelt apparently urged the President to reconsider his position on reeducation.[27]

There is little to suggest any change of heart in the President's basic mistrust of reeducation and his skepticism regarding the rehabilitation of the German nation. Perhaps he hoped that by approving the program he might appease the chagrined secretaries of War and State who had, at this stage, made little progress in their attempts to scuttle the Morgenthau plan. Most probably, Roosevelt's change of heart was related to growing concerns of political liability. The management of POW camps in the United States was beset by highly unfavorable press reports.

Charges in the popular press ranged from the typical "mollycoddling" to more serious accusations of fostering the rise of enclaves of Nazism in the heart of the United States. In a typical article on camp life the *New York Times* informed the American public that their enemies did not even have to suffer the mild deprivation of rationing. "I saw piles of juicy hams, plenty of butter, steaks and sausages," F. G. Alletson Cook reported. "There is only one limit on what the men eat—their individual capacity. They get absolutely all they can stow away of whatever dish is on the menu, rationed on the outside or not."[28]

All press reports, irrespective of their political slant, expressed frustration over lost opportunities. Here was a unique occasion to prearrange alliances for future conflicts. A common complaint, registered in a pair of articles first published in the *Atlantic Monthly* and later reprinted in *Reader's Digest*, contrasted the Russian solution to that of the United

States. The incarceration of POWs without the benefit of political rehabilitation was a fateful mistake, noted James Powers in his section on the
"American muddle." With his eye cast fearfully toward the future, the
foreign desk editor of the *Boston Globe* suggested that "slight pressure
from one side or the other at this time may result in final crystallization of
social and political attitudes among large numbers of these men, who will
be citizens of the Germany of tomorrow."[29] Powers claimed that the decision as to whether these men would be friend or foe lay in the hands of
American POW authorities.

> Shall we send these prisoners home with a clearer understanding of this
> country's decision to stand no more of their nonsense, or with an indul-
> gent notion that we are simpletons, against whom a third try will suc-
> ceed. To blame the strictures of the Geneva Convention is idle. The
> British get results under that identical Convention. . . . England no
> longer plays with her deadly foes.[30]

In his section on the "Russian Solution," Henry Cassidy noted that the
United States would do well to copy the Soviet Union's reeducation of
German POWs which, he predicted, would allow America's ideological
adversary of the future to gain control of Germany without even having
to fire a bullet. By means of a skillful combination of intimidation and
indoctrination, the Russians had enticed growing numbers of prisoners of
war to join a front organization for the German Communist Party. In
fact, the whole process of reeducation in Soviet camps had been placed in
the hands of converts, mostly POW officers who used the prestige of their
rank to garner new recruits. The Russians had craftily recruited to their
cause some of the Wehrmacht's highest ranking and respected generals;
the rank and file, Cassidy reported, dutifully followed. Only the Russians
realized how to use the prisoners as an investment for the future, he
added. "Their finished product—education made available to the prisoner, and propaganda tools put in his hands—deserves a place in the
future military machine of any country, signatory to the Geneva Convention or not."[31]

The consensus among press reports was that the misguided politics of
POWs in the United States could be changed only if the politicians would
do the right thing. "Until the Germans realize where the awfulness of the
crimes . . . cultivated by the Nazis . . . [had] led them," they would not
change. As such, an article in *Life* pointed out, it was the duty of the
American to both "subdue" as well as "cure" the cross section of the
German nation in the camps.[32] America would do well to cease its gentle
treading around the Geneva Convention and, instead, use this fleeting
historic moment to shape the future. The POW camps in the continental

United States could play a role in the transformation of the German enemy into a made-to-order ally.

Given this deluge of unfavorable accounts of inaction in the camps, the acceptance of a reeducation program was a small price to pay for removing such a politically sensitive issue from the public eye. Indeed, as the veritable inundation of German POWs suggested, the fall of Germany was imminent; fears of German reprisals and the contravening of the Geneva Convention were no longer relevant.

It was under these circumstances of immense public pressure to uplift the enemy, government resistance and skepticism, as well as infighting in the president's inner circle, that the American military authorities were authorized to begin reeducating German POWs, not by psychological manipulation, force, or fear, but through logic persuasion. The endorsement of reeducation was not derived from any meaningful assessment of the task at hand; it was a political decision based on domestic considerations. The format of reeducation by rational persuasion represented a victory for those government officials who, for a variety of reasons, disapproved of the rehabilitation-through-annihilation plan of Secretary Morgenthau. Ostensibly the issue was the uplifting of a foreign enemy; in actual fact, the program was a reflection of domestic power struggles. The obvious fact that the regimented surroundings of a military camp and the political culture of totalitarian regimes were quite immune to barrages of logic was of little significance. The internal political virtues of the chosen strategy for reeducation far outweighed its manifest unsuitability for the task at hand.

CHAPTER TWO

The POW Camp and the Total Institution

"America," whispered Grundmann.
Gühler said nothing. He looked at the country that stretched
before him into the distance, empty and monotonous and dotted
with hills. The trees on the hills stood base beneath the heavy,
leaden sky. . . . The morning wind blew cold across the sea, making them shiver. But they only stared out into the wide, flat
country that seemed to them endless and full of mystery.
                                        —Hans Werner Richter[1]

THE BLEAK, spartan barracks, planted on the forbidding terrain of an
alien country, had a curiously uplifting affect. After months of milling
around in makeshift enclosures, deprived of adequate food, and ritually
humiliated at every temporary camp along the way, these stark enhut-
ments which made up the POW camp for Germany's military captives in
the United States signaled a return to a familiar routine.

For Germans captured during the course of allied offensives in Italy
and North Africa, surrender had taken a heavy emotional toll. The humil-
iation of defeat could be rationalized, of course, as a mismatch between
an outnumbered and exhausted German army, on the one hand, and the
fresh, well-stocked American fighting force. But a far more onerous psychological burden was the captives' loss of fundamental frames of reference. They were soldiers, a calling based upon a rigid etiquette which had
governed their lives since induction. Captivity destroyed all remnants of
their predictable routine and hurled the surrendering troops into a mael-
strom of disorder, uncertainty, and disgrace.

The destruction of group identity and exclusive military frames of reference was hard to bear because rigorous initiation had erased previous
pristine civilian concepts of self. Relentless training and harsh manifestations of authority were all part of the soldier's rites of passage. Military life reproduced the Total Institution, Erving Goffman's seminal
definition for a tightly controlled, culturally sealed world in which an
individual's previous experiences were forcibly erased.[2] Upon entering
military life, the German recruit, like any other inductee into a modern
military regimen, was exposed to constant attempts to destroy his civilian

"self." This process which Goffman called "mortification," was a crucial stage in producing loyal, reliable soldiers. By demolishing the recruit's sense of past and individual self-esteem, the army as Total Institution could more easily mold idiosyncratic civilians into its own unique behavioral modes.

This "stripping process," the "mortification of self," followed a fairly predictable pattern: the removal of civilian clothes, the shearing of hair, the issue of common drab clothing. Subsequent stages would focus on a process of hazing in which disoriented recruits endured endless, senseless drills, spread throughout the day and night, in order to heighten confusion. "Stunned" recruits emerged from this experience dazed but "psychologically held together by the symbols of common uniform and haircut, . . . and by the new equality of hazing" which had erased their previous eclectic self.[3] "The routine of military life, the repetition, drill, and uniformity of response, work to dampen and dull any individual intensity of awareness," sociologist Glenn Gray noted in his recollections of military life during World War II. The soldier swiftly learns "to suspend thoughts that unfit him for his appointed mission. . . . Thinking tends to become not only painful but more and more unnecessary," he observed.[4]

The primary task of the training mechanism of the army was to render the novice mentally incapacitated outside of the familiar military frames of reference, thereby ensuring his undivided loyalty to the institution. Within the isolated subculture of the military unit the soldier learned to identify exclusively with the group; he accepted a privilege system that reinforced his allegiance to the military social system and cultivated an "inmate culture" within the introverted world of the camp perimeter. Thus, efficient mortification produced individuals who felt worthless and confused outside of the Total Institution.[5]

Captivity, in its initial stages, had a potent destructive affect on the "inmates" of the military Total Institution. Their rigorously controlled world had crumbled, with no other social structure to compensate for its loss. The dispirited men, now reduced from being members of a tightly controlled organization to the stressful predicament of being nonentities, tramped sullenly and aimlessly through hastily erected temporary stockades. The faceless captives had lost all familiar points of bearing. Dishevelled strangers-in-arms rubbed shoulders uncomfortably; sailors and soldiers, tank crews and infantry, glared warily at each other. Lacking familiar frames of reference, such as well-defined units and daily schedules, their dominant sentiments were suspicion, alienation, and self-pity. Endless days were consumed slowly with listless attempts to pass the time. Life was reduced to scavenging for cigarettes, a preoccupation with food, battling the lice, and devising strategies for dodging the swarms of flies infesting the stockades. "Imagine ten thousand men milling about from morning to night: chatting, sullen, seeking out lost comrades, bartering cigarettes, exchanging rumors, and staking out a place to sleep," recalled former German POW, George Gaertner. "One never knew the politics or the motives of people around you"; therefore, there was a tendency "not to form deep friendships with any other POWs."[6]

A gnawing and constant hunger further eroded all sense of self-worth during these initial disorganized stages of captivity. Helmut Hörner, a German infantry sergeant who kept a diary of his daily experiences described the "shameful" loss of "the famous German discipline" among the hunger-stricken men in their jostling for food. When ordered by their American captors to line up for the distribution of tin cans, the half-starving prisoners reacted "like a scared herd of sheep chased by a fierce dog. Instead of lining up, they fight to get to the front while the weaker ones are run over without any consideration. . . . We watch the shameless action by the Americans as they beat the German prisoners mercilessly with their red-lacquered sticks after they [the prisoners] try to use force to get to the boxes."[7]

At every stage of the arduous journey from the temporary stockades in Europe and Africa to POW camps in the United States, the prisoners were systematically deprived of all remaining symbols of their past, pride, and identity. At countless checkpoints along their odyssey, German captives were pounced upon by triumphant American soldiers seeking souvenirs—medals, military insignia, weapons, army booklets. The noncombatant support troops in the rear were especially zealous in stripping the battle-weary captives of anything that could even remotely pass as regalia. "I try to bring some order to my thoughts while I stare at my field blouse, robbed of all decorations and badges," a despondent Helmut Hörner scribbled in his hidden diary. "Where my national insignia was sewn, there is now a hole through which the white of my undershirt can be seen. On my left wrist is a band of white flesh where a short time ago my wristwatch kept the skin from becoming tanned."[8] The aggressiveness of the searchers heightened as the distance from the front increased; the spirits of the captives sank accordingly.

The once stable world of the soldier-turned-prisoner was further unsettled by initial impressions of American society and its military. First encounters clashed quite distinctly with the distorted preconceptions of the average German soldier. The United States did not appear to be the flabby and morally weak nation of German propaganda. American soldiers displayed the self-confidence of the well-fed; they had about them the secure demeanor of the victor. Most disconcerting and quite puzzling were the glimpses of American life seen through the cracks and windows of railroad cars shunting prisoners from debarkation points toward their isolated camps. At times the train would slow down to allow the POWs, indeed to compel them, to see the total absence of war scars and the great abundance of the land that lay before them. The bright lights of cities and villages, the omnipresent car parked outside the most ramshackle of homes, demonstrated wealth and power that contradicted the myths and disinformation of German propaganda.

Eventually the train ride would come to an end, and the shocked cargo of vanquished troops would stumble off the trains into the uninviting terrain which would be their home for the duration of the war. Swiftly, however, their fortunes appeared to change. Almost immediately, familiar frames of reference resurfaced within the confines of their camps. Aided and abetted by their American guardians, the disoriented captives resurrected their familiar social structures. Both the landscape of the camp and the prescribed rules and regulations of the American captors encouraged this reincarnation of the POWs' previous sense of belonging, in particular their military identity.

The typical prison compound, designed according to the specifications of the Office of the Provost Marshal General (OPMG), was divided into two distinctly segregated sections, almost two separate camps (fig. 1). The management and coordination of camp activities, as well as most of the security arrangements were centered in the headquarters encampment where central warehouses, staff barracks, and staff recreational facilities were situated.

The POW enclosure stood apart, separated physically from camp headquarters by barbed wire and a buffer zone of sports fields. Within the prison compound, standardized barracks, in groupings of four, formed a semicircle around the main hub of activity, featuring a dining hall, prisoner canteen, and recreational facilities, as well as a small administrative facility from which a staff of prisoners under minimal supervision ran the daily life of the inmates. For all practical purposes, the POW camp had the comfortable and familiar arrangement of a typical and "normal army training center," a former inmate at POW Camp McClean recalled.[9]

The presence of Americans within the prison compound was sparse at best. The understaffed OPMG's formula for running the camp was to avoid contact as much as possible and rely, instead, on a "perimeter system" of vehicle patrols and watchtowers monitoring the barbed-wire boundaries. The distance between prisoners and captors was increased by the language barrier. Due to the virtual absence of German-speaking personnel among the OPMG's staff, camp personnel were reduced to communicating with prisoners through the medium of a camp spokesman. The American guardians made no meaningful attempt to choose the POW spokesmen. This task was left to the inmates who, in turn, used this tool to reinforce old frameworks. This spokesman was invariably a trusted delegate of the internal prisoner power structure.

Much of the daily routine and running of the camp was left to the inmates, in particular the *Unteroffiziere*—the NCOs. In accordance with the dictates of the Geneva Convention, officers and enlisted personnel were incarcerated in separate camps. However, each camp of enlisted personnel had direct access to at least thirty of its own officers and numerous NCOs. Absolved from work duties by the Geneva Convention, the camps' NCOs devoted most of their energy to what they knew best: the reassertion of military discipline and, by implication, their special status as enforcers and keepers of the flame. The strict disciplinary code of the NCOs was sanctioned both by prisoner officers and by American guardians who were quite grateful for the relative quiet and predictability of the inmates' very military behavior.

The division into companies and the authority of POW NCOs and their supervising officers made the re-creation of a familiar military regimen complete. "The first thing that struck me as I entered Camp Hood, Texas," a newly arrived POW belonging to the Afrika Korps recalled, "was that German discipline re-created itself right away, with its orders, its commands. The Afrika Korps was a disciplined force where everybody obeyed as one man; . . . they let us develop right away a parallel hierarchy which took the prisoners in hand. *I had come home*," he added.[10]

POWs reinforced this quasi-independent social system through subtle adjustments of their daily routine. Lacking any basic combat duties, the military regimen focused mostly on ceremony; officers inspected living quarters, encouraged esprit de corps through team sports, and cultivated a ritual of contempt for the enemy. A liturgy of toughness, team spirit, and loyalty was played out ceremoniously on the camp's extensive playing fields. A fanatical devotion to intramural soccer matches built character, and served as a rallying point for group solidarity.

Unable to express this energy on the battlefield, the POWs waged symbolic war by defying and taunting the enemy in a variety of ways. Battling the enemy was carried out both by individual soldiers and by larger formations, too. The individual soldier's duty was to humiliate the American wardens—the equivalent of sniping. A common tactic was to praise American guards for fair treatment and adequate food, promising them that they would be remembered and rewarded after the ultimate German victory. Larger formations and, at times, the entire camp launched more concerted attacks against the enemy, ranging from the singing of Nazi marching songs to the occasional work slowdowns. Ultimately, scorn for the enemy was demonstrated by an elaborate panoply of symbols: the use of the Nazi salute both among themselves and upon confronting an American officer, and the conspicuous and defiant display of Nazi regalia, such as the waving of homemade swastika banners when prisoners passed through American towns on their way to work details. Defiant celebrations of Nazi festivals were another common form of waging war by other means. In numerous camps throughout the country, prisoners held *Morgenfeier* celebrations honoring the ideologue of National Socialism, Alfred Rosenberg. Nazi holidays, including Hitler's birthday, were celebrated routinely in the early stages of captivity. These ceremonies continued secretly after American officials banned them.[11]

The one major difficulty in maintaining a defiant and disciplined re-creation of the German military establishment within the camps was the issue of enforcement. The German hierarchy had no legitimate means of implementing what was basically a voluntary adherence to its military code. The entire mechanism of prisoner autonomy within the camps hinged upon the development of a system of sanctions aimed at the rebellious few who dared question its legitimacy. There was, of course, no official or legal tool for punishing subversive behavior. Nevertheless, a covert system of enforcement soon materialized. "Deviant" activities first elicited threats from enforcer squads. Recalcitrant offenders were subjected to kangaroo courts, "Holy Ghosts"—beatings by vigilante POWs—and in extreme and very rare circumstances summary executions.[12]

The type of offense which led to such internal disciplining was usually of a military nature, although in some rare cases, in those camps with a strong presence of committed Nazis, this vigilante system punished purely political offenses as well. And yet, most accounts of the German POW experience have dismissed the issue of military discipline while assigning, instead, exclusively ideological motives to the internal POW justice system. The typical prison camp is often described as a microcosm of the totalitarian Nazi State rather than a typical manifestation of the military subculture.[13]

Such assessments are based on problematic sources of information. To begin with, a code of silence kept enforcers from revealing their true motives, even when caught in the act. Whether motivated by fear or acquiescence, rank-and-file camp inmates also routinely refused to divulge information. Most information emanated from apologists and collaborators, all of whom had strong personal reasons for insisting that the vigilante justice system within the camps was basically a symptom of Nazi terror and unadulterated National Socialist coercive tactics. By presenting disciplinary offenses as political acts, informers hoped to receive special treatment from their wardens.

The poor quality of American intelligence within the camps meant that authorities had no means of verifying these claims. Lacking any meaningful information network within the POW enclosures, and confronted by a formidable language barrier, American authorities invariably accepted the argument that Nazi ideology was behind inmate violence. This interpretation supported, and was supported by, prevailing preconceptions concerning the hypnotic grip of National Socialism. The cold-blooded violence of the most notorious instances of actual lynching gave credence to these convictions. All in all, fourteen vigilante POWs were convicted for six internal executions and two forced suicides. All the accused, according to Judith Gansberg, "argued to the last that they were merely carrying out their duty because the victim in each case was a 'traitor.' "[14]

The American authorities accepted these incidences as plain manifestations of Nazism. "As soon as the Nazis are established in camp, a system of supervision and control is organized," a War Department pamphlet noted.

> They [the Nazis] are old masters at that game. Believing, and in some cases not without foundation, that the camp authorities are willing to depend on them, they establish a Nazi hierarchy to take things into their own hands. The result is a continual political domination over other prisoners. If the hierarchy, which meets secretly, is particularly strong or contains Gestapo or Political Commissar elements, the results may even be worse. Whenever a "Kangaroo Court" or an "Honor Court" (Ehrengericht) has been in session, a system of blackmail begins. Sometimes a prisoner is found dead near the dumps.[15]

This depiction of most institutionalized violence in the POW camps as incorrigible Nazism was, however, flawed. To begin with, the sources were impressionistic, if not anecdotal, and were derived from slanted second-hand accounts. A poll of departing prisoners of war indeed suggested that reports on Nazi terrorism were exaggerated. Only 16 percent of the polled prisoners reported that they were afraid to express "anti-Nazi" opinions in their respective camps.[16] Moreover, the only systematic study of the tensions between ideology and military discipline within the ranks of German POWs—Edward Shils's and Morris Janowitz's seminal research for the Psychological Warfare Division of Allied Forces in Europe—produced a different and equally plausible explanation for the endurance of group solidarity and ostensible Nazism among vanquished units of the Wehrmacht.[17]

Shils and Janowitz claimed that tenacious solidarity and defiant displays of Nazi symbols even after defeat were the result of neither fear nor of strong political convictions among the rank and file. They argued that visible expressions of ideological loyalty were by no means signs of successful and profound political indoctrination among the troops. On the contrary, the rank and file endorsed such "secondary symbols"—ranging from the swastika to ritual exaltation of the leaders—as demonstrations of military discipline. Unquestioning and elaborate incorporation of Nazi symbols signified complete and unwavering loyalty to the military creed. "Identification with the stern authority associated with the symbols of State power" Shils and Janowitz observed, "was a means for ordinary soldiers to re-affirm their acceptance of the code of military honor, but should not be seen as an endorsement of the political system which it upheld."[18] Their study contended that external circumstances—even such traumatizing events as captivity—had little effect on cohesion as long as the soldiers received primary psychological "nourishment" from the military social system. When confronted with "affection and esteem from both officers and comrades," soldiers remained loyal to their social systems, a loyalty which they displayed through unwavering acceptance and instinctive, indiscriminate display of national symbols.

Shils and Janowitz implied that the relative unimportance of political convictions within the confines of military life was not a uniquely German phenomenon. As far as they were concerned, efficient modes of basic training in most modern armies punctuated the average soldier's detachment from publicly pronounced, justifying ideologies of the state. Manifestations of public values within the armed forces were mere veneer; the colors of a flag could, in theory, be changed without any profound impact on the effectiveness of soldier and unit.

Of course, these theories were articulated by behaviorists who predictably discounted the power of faith and demonstrated little tolerance for ideology as a motivating factor in the behavior of nations. As far as Hitler's army was concerned these explanations oversimplified the issue at hand; it makes little sense to ignore the impact of the culture of totalitarianism and the burden of history on the minds of young German recruits. Military historian Omer Bartov contends quite convincingly that "the obedient and uncritical participation of millions of soldiers in 'legalized' crimes . . . reflected the moral values these young men had internalized before their recruitment."[19] Nevertheless, when compared to the POWs of other nations—both Allies and enemies—there is little doubt that the reactions of German POWs in the United States were well within the boundaries of typical military conduct associated with captivity.

Thus, the diary of German captive, Helmut Hörner, registered a common reaction among POWs of all nations to instinctively deny the enemy the satisfaction of eliciting ideological recantations from their captives.

The American wants to know today exactly what we think. But we do not permit him this favor. . . . Now we are separated from our former companions and stamped as Nazis. What nonsense these kinds of interrogations produce. Do the Americans seriously believe they can separate the wheat from the chaff?. . . It was possible for each one to tell the interrogators what they wanted to hear. But we voted for comradeship and did not worry ourselves about the unknown purposes of the American interrogators probing our ideology.[20]

A remarkably similar description of the military mind in captivity appeared in the memoirs of an Italian soldier incarcerated in the United States during the war. In his recollections of his refusal to collaborate with American authorities, Armando Boscolo emphasized the relative unimportance of ideology and, by contrast, the compelling pull of group loyalty.

I believe that a prisoner of war is always a loser, a loser who feels discomfort and remorse for not having given enough for his country, for not having fallen in battle, for not having avoided the humiliating captivity behind barbed wire, a man who feels the sting of having left his comrades alone to defend the flag. To have the respect of those still fighting, the prisoner must face captivity with total dignity—dignity, which unfortunately, neither American nor English detainers would respect and allow. . . . To collaborate with the Allies . . . would be like being a football player who switches sides when he sees his team is losing, an unheard of thing, which if it were to happen would result in the player being thrown out as a traitor. . . . Grossly mistaken, as well as speaking in bad faith, are those who say that the non-collaborationists were all Fascists. . . . That is a huge error and a terrible lie, because while the non-collaborationists included some Fascists, they also included many "collectivists" with Socialist and Communist-like ideas. Above all, the great majority of prisoners of war were simply not politically aligned, and those who refused to collaborate did so on the grounds I have mentioned—that switching sides mid-way through a war was morally and ethically incorrect.[21]

Allied captives expressed similar views. The relative unimportance of ideology in POW camps, even among Allied troops, was immortalized in Pierre Boulle's *The Bridge over the River Kwai*, where two apparently divergent ideologies were represented in the diametrically opposed personalities of the haughty, principled Colonel Nicholson, and his Japanese captor, the hysterical and harsh Colonel Siato. Both were able to turn the construction of a strategic bridge into a common goal, the Japanese commander driven by the urge to obey and fulfill the orders of his superiors, the British officer beset by the obsession to prove the superiority of his troops. Driven by these demons, neither Colonel Nicholson, nor his staff, nor any of the troops whose overriding concern was to demonstrate to the enemy an unyielding esprit de corps, was willing to acknowledge the implications of their actions. A lone medical officer, the narrator of the story, was the only detached observer of this curious phenomenon in which Nicholson drove his troops to the brink of death, and even collaborated with the enemy to avoid the destruction of the bridge. It is here, within the confines of the military Total Institution, that the narrator observed: "Perhaps the conduct of each of the two enemies, superficially so dissimilar, was in fact simply a different, though equally meaningless, manifestation of the same spiritual reality. Perhaps the mentality of the

Japanese colonel, Siato, was essentially the same as that of his prisoner, Colonel Nicholson."[22]

Irrespective of their very different personalities, and the distinctive political systems that they represented, both captor and warden shared a strikingly similar "sense of duty, observance of ritual, obsession with discipline, and love of a job well done"; both were obsessed with the "common demon" of military life: loss of face.

In one very important aspect, of course, Boulle's re-creation of the Allied POW experience differed from the German camps in the U.S. Colonel Nicholson did not have to resort to extreme measures to uphold discipline. His men unquestionably accepted his most bizarre orders. Nevertheless, vigilante terror was not a uniquely German phenomenon. There was nothing exceptional about the disciplinary framework, the type of victim caught up in the system, or the harsh forms of punishment. In fact, analogous developments appeared among Allied POWs in Germany as well.

The definitive history of Allied POWs in Germany has yet to be written, but the present state of the literature presents numerous examples of Allied enforcement of the POW code of honor. The German Luftwaffe, which ran the camps for captive Allied airmen grappled with many of the same concerns of the U.S. Provost Marshal General. Lacking an appropriate staff to maintain order within the camps, the German captors permitted the establishment of "Home Rule," which, for all practical purposes, meant POW autonomy and control over their lives in all internal affairs. But even among air crews, the cream of Allied fighting forces, the POW military hierarchy experienced occasional difficulties in maintaining a voluntary acceptance of a military regime behind barbed wire. Colonel Delmar T. Spivey, Senior American officer in such a camp, recalled that

> not all men were willing to do their part and many believed the authority of the SAO [Senior American Officer] was fictitious and could not be enforced. Some believed they owed no allegiance to the will of the camp as a whole nor did they consider what inconvenience the camp suffered as a result of their individual actions. . . . These mavericks in our otherwise disciplined herd had to be treated as individuals and if the barracks commander couldn't take care of the situation the man was brought to me; if I couldn't reason with him he became the ward of the strong-arm squad of his barracks. . . . They weren't averse to manhandling a boy who wouldn't obey camp orders.[23]

In extreme cases it appears that collaborators with German captors were subjected to executions and lynchings, much like their German peers in POW camps in Allied countries. This sensitive subject is often shrouded in euphemisms, but there are occasional breaches of what is essentially a conspiracy of silence. A well-known account of Allied POWs, *Stalag Luft III*, mentions briefly that a British officer was condemned to death by his peers for suspected collaboration with camp authorities.[24] Doug Collin's recollections of his POW experiences documents the beating to death of an inmate who had informed on his comrades' escape plans.[25]

These close parallels between the Allied and German experience in POW camps suggest a universal code of military life in captivity that transcended the idiosyncrasies of the different civilian political systems. The psychological strains of captivity, in particular the unrelenting burden of shame, could be softened by maintaining solidarity and avoiding, at all costs, a loss of faith.

It is a moot point, then, whether the internal punitive system of German POWs supported a Nazified code of honor. Punishment functioned first and foremost to enforce military discipline rather than ideological adherence. Moreover, fear of Nazi terror squads cannot explain the overwhelming acquiescence of the rank and file, nor can the unyielding acceptance of Nazi symbols be seen as evidence of profound indoctrination. Both tacit acceptance of the harsh punitive system within the camp as well as widespread manifestations of Nazi symbols represented an act of defiance, an expression of contempt for the enemy, a gesture of internal solidarity. Allied prisoners in German hands could express their defiance through relentless escape attempts. German prisoners, by contrast, were separated from home by thousands of miles of sea and sand; escape was not a viable option. The frequent brandishing of Nazi symbols served, then, as an alternative for harassing the enemy. Any breach of the code of honor—such as questioning the propriety of these symbols—was a threat to group solidarity. Therefore, the reaction of the keepers of the flame was unyieldingly harsh.

American authorities charged with the management of POW camps approached their mission uninformed on these matters. A severely pressed OPMG suffered from an acute shortage of career military personnel and, like many other service branches, had filled its ranks with hastily trained civilians-turned-soldiers. Lacking knowledge and experience of the dynamics of military life, these officers accepted intellectually weak but emotionally convincing explanations for outbreaks of institutionalized violence within the camps and the apparent unwavering endurance of National Socialism among the prisoners. Lacking an experience of military life in general, as well as knowledge of the manner in which soldiers contended with stress and duress, these military laymen charged with directing the affairs of POWs maintained that National Socialism thrived within the camps due to the lack of any competing ideological alternative.

They assumed that removing the Guidance Officers and other Nazi monitors from the camp would destroy the impenetrable subculture of the POWs. In actual fact, the removal of fanatic Nazis to special camps merely strengthened the cohesiveness of the rank and file. The transfer of politically motivated prisoners reinforced, by default, the prestige of the traditional guardians of military discipline, the junior officers and NCOs.

The OPMG stuck to its interpretation of the camps as microcosms of Nazi Germany and focused its efforts exclusively on dismantling a supposedly robust Nazi infrastructure by weeding out the ideologically motivated from the rank and file. Hard-core Nazis were isolated in separate camps in order to remove the threat of intimidation and political pressure on middle-of-the-road prisoners. Ardent anti-Nazis were placed in separate enclosures too, ostensibly for self-protection. In practice, the OPMG sought to isolate potential Communist sympathizers as part of this same effort to remove intimidating forces from the camps.

This fundamentally narrow understanding of group cohesion within the prison compounds produced, of course, disappointing results. Identifying the ardent Nazi was a simple enough process. The agents of National Socialism within the armed forces did little to disguise their identity and loyalties; Gestapo agents and zealous Nazis were quickly dislodged. American authorities paid particular attention to the isolation of the ideologically committed Indoctrination Officers—*National Sozialistische Fuehrungs-Offiziere* (NSFOs). During the latter stages of the war these new functionaries in all units had received sweeping powers to encourage and enforce the Nazification of the armed forces. However, as Edward Shils and Morris Janowitz argued, these political police had little positive impact on group solidarity within the German armed forces. Their contribution was negligible if not negative. The NSFOs were treated as outsiders, basically "a joke," according to Shils and Janowitz. The Morale Division of the Strategic Bombing Survey reported similar findings. German frontline troops, according to the sociologists of the Morale Division, were quite cynical about political pep talks, and usually slept through the "orientation sessions" of the NSFOs.[26] Consequently, the American separation policy had no lasting effect on dismantling the internal hierarchy of camp life.

American authorities attributed their failure to undermine the internal cohesion of the POW subculture to faulty criteria for distinguishing devoted Nazis from the silent majority. An additional explanation cited German ignorance of the very creed they espoused. POWs embraced National Socialism, according to this explanation, because they knew nothing of its darker pathological side. The OPMG's own surveys provided ostensible evidence that Germans had yet to learn the real meaning of Hitler's vision. During the course of an anonymous survey of POW views at Camp Atlanta, Nebraska, 72 percent of the prisoners claimed that they had never read Hitler's *Mein Kampf* and 83 percent claimed they had not been motivated by, in fact had never heard of, Pan-Germanism. They identified National Socialism with its expansive social welfare program, and the "just" redemption of Germany's lost honor.[27]

Most prisoners, according to this explanation, were unfamiliar with the dark side of Nazism and unaware of humane Western ideological alternatives. As such, the OPMG approached the battle for control of the camps as primarily a struggle of ideas and only marginally as an issue of social dynamics. The solution, then, was to devise a program for instilling competing ideas, in addition to the removal of hard-core National Socialists from within the ranks.

It is difficult to criticize American authorities for their preoccupation with the mesmerizing power of Nazism. After all, many of their prisoners had presumably committed unspeakable barbarities, and, given their ideological justifications for such atrocities, they appeared to suffer little remorse. Nevertheless, the solutions offered by the OPMG were extremely narrow. Constrained by the inability to manage the camps without the cooperation of the POWs' internal chain of command, the OPMG arbitrarily determined that leaving the prisoners' military identity intact would not hamper a reeducation effort. Guided by a combination of cultural preconceptions and administrative limitations, the OPMG quite deliberately avoided a sociological approach to its problems, preferring instead to hand over the project of reorientation to experts in ideas: humanists, poets, and professors of the Liberal Arts.

Having narrowed the task to one of moral persuasion rather than the dismantling of a social system, neither the OPMG nor its civilian overlords were prepared for anything other than an ideological crusade. Thus, with few apparent misgivings, the OPMG knowingly sent the wrong troops into this battle for hearts and minds. These idea warriors would, in turn, ignore the battle at hand and invent, instead, a war more attuned to their own weapons and training.

CHAPTER THREE

Professors into Propagandists

IN THE early winter of 1938, as America looked on from afar at the still-distant war, Harvard scholar Howard Mumford Jones startled the readers of *Atlantic Monthly* with an unusual analysis of the pervasive hold of totalitarian regimes. In anticipation of Antonio Gramsci's prison notes on cultural hegemony, the Harvard professor of English literature argued that the success of Fascism lay not in the ruthless deployment of repressive political tools, but in "the efficient creation by the dictators of a glamorous mythology." The aesthetically attractive myths of Fascism endowed the "downtrodden subjects" with appealing images of their collective past and a communal sense of self-worth which no longer existed in democratic societies. "We used to have Glamour in this country," Jones added somewhat sadly but it had been destroyed by " 'progressive' educators, the debunking biographer, and social historians." Jones urged his readers to learn from Fascist successes. His proposal called for mobilizing the liberal arts for the purposes of creating attractive democratic myths and resurrecting an engaging version of America's past.

Jones argued that it would make little sense to try to prove that the mythological figures of totalitarian cultures were "fake heroes." Whether the romance of totalitarian patriotism was derived from actual historical events or was pure fabrication was beside the point. The objective of the humanist and cultural historian was not to verify facts but to understand the lure of myths, to comprehend why people chose to believe certain legends. If Fascist regimes controlled their peoples primarily by producing an attractive collective history, American humanists who had "debunked too much" now had the mission to produce a usable and inspiring past for the impending battle for hearts and minds. The "only way to conquer an alien mythology is to have a better mythology of your own."[1]

Jones would be given the opportunity to practice his preaching a few years later upon joining the staff of the POW reeducation program. As fate would have it, the plans for reeducating German POWs were placed in the hands of a personal friend, one Lt. Colonel Edward Davison, who somewhat predictably would seek the services of reliable acquaintances.

Edward Davison, university professor, minor poet, and an obscure officer in the Morale Division of the Army Service Corps, was probably surprised to be informed of his nomination as director of the Special Project Division (SPD), a newly formed branch of the Office of the Provost Marshal General (OPMG) charged with the reeducation of German

POWs. Davison's nomination for this very sensitive position was quite curious. He was neither a typical American officer nor did he possess any particular knowledge of his potential "students." Davison was a recently naturalized American citizen with no academic or professional experience in the study of German culture; in fact he had no meaningful command of the German language at all. Moreover, his political convictions were quite ambivalent.

Born in Scotland in 1898, Davison dropped out of school at the age of twelve; four years later he joined the Royal Navy, where he had served as a paymaster. After establishing a reputation as a man of letters in London's literary circles of the 1920s, he moved to the United States in 1926 with his American wife. He subsequently taught at Vassar, at the University of Miami, and at the University of Colorado, Boulder, before joining the U.S. Army in 1943.

Davison's writings revealed serious doubts about the cause he was supposed to represent. His poems expressed irresolute assessments of the Allied stance, as well as a certain skepticism concerning the ideological divisions of the Second World War. Davison, a kind critic observed, was preoccupied with "the harsh predicament of twentieth century man, buffeted by the uncontrollable, often incomprehensible currents that have been unloosed since 1914."[2] In fact, his overtly political poems distinctly avoided an endorsement of the creed that he would have to advance as head of the SPD. The most significant political opinion to emerge in his writings was the assumption that global insecurities were caused, in large part, by the unfettered materialism of western nations. In his "Decline and Fall" (1937), Davison was particularly blunt in blaming capitalism for the catastrophic crises of the twentieth century.

> England Farewell! And you, America, you
> Who might have saved the spark that was divine,
> Go down! Morgan and Ford and Hearst and all
> The dollar gods you trusted, they are through,
> And what you signed upon the dotted line
> Has now become the Writing on the Wall.[3]

In "Kill or Get Killed" (ca. 1943), Davison's most powerful political poem, he struck out at the callousness of western nations, suggested that there were only negligible differences between power structures in either of the two war camps, and even expressed strong pacifist views:

> A soldier lay dead in the Kasserine Pass
> His eyes to the stars and his back to the grass,
> They buried him later amid prayers for grace
> And noted the look that he wore on his face.

It was, they reported, a look of amaze,
He fought unbelieving and died in a daze,
Till death rode him down and the grasses ran red,
He doubted that anyone wanted him dead.

This soldier, they tell me, was more than a fool,
Why, he had been trained in a very tough school!
His generals had warned him, his captain had shrilled:
"It's your choice hereafter: you'll kill or get killed!"

.   .   .   .

At home there were strikes as men struggled for gain,
Some people went hungry: the hogs got the grain.
But this stuff was never his business at all,
His duty was clear: keep your eye on the ball.

And so he met Death in the Kasserine Pass,
They gave him a cross and they metter "Alas,"
"He might have survived: he was certainly warned,"
"Dear soldiers, your lessons should never be scorned."

But on my face, too, there's a look of amaze
That peace-loving nations have such deadly ways.[4]

One can only assume that, as the danger of Germany and its allies became more apparent, Davison was able to sharpen his understanding of the contrast between Fascism and Western capitalism. In any case, this irresolute democrat began studying the problem of democratizing German POWs as early as 1943. Davison and two other colleagues from the Morale Division were sent on a study mission to Canada, where they confronted an alarmingly obdurate POW population. Their diagnosis of the Canadian problem focused on the need for educational remedies to soften the manifest power of Nazism within the camps.[5] A year later, when the OPMG was eventually called upon to implement a reeducation program of its own, Davison was the only officer left from the original task force and, therefore, the obvious nominee for the new job; the OPMG was unwilling to consider an outside candidate.

Davison, as his background and writings suggest, was a believer in the power of words and ideas, an advocate of intellectual leadership in a distinctly anti-intellectual global climate. In many of his poems he stated that the scourges of modern times could be controlled if intellectual leaders of altruistic vision would take charge.[6] Consequently, it was inevitable that his highly sensitive reeducation project would become an exercise in persuasion rather than a campaign in psychological warfare.

In constructing the framework for the reeducation program, Davison was assisted by Major Maxwell McKnight, the only senior staff member who had been part of the OPMG's Prisoner of War Division prior to the inception of reeducation. McKnight, a graduate of Yale Law School and member of New York's society set who had received part of his education in France, was quite at home in the intellectual milieu of the reeducation program. As the assistant director of the program, McKnight fulfilled an invaluable administrative function, thereby freeing Davison to take care of the educational content of the program.

Davison's efforts to seek an appropriate officer for curriculum director among the existing staff of the OPMG did not produce similar results. By late 1943, when the OPMG began organizing the reeducation program, the pool of suitable candidates for this mission was quite limited. Most Americans with relevant training in German culture had already been recruited by other branches of intelligence and psychological warfare. And yet, the need for at least one officer with an intimate knowledge of Germany and its culture was imperative. Acutely aware of his nonexistent command of German language, culture, and politics, Davison sought a guide whose knowledge of Germany was neither second-hand nor acquired. His choice was Captain Walter Schoenstedt, a former associate editor of the liberal newspaper, *Das Berliner Tagblatt*, and an exiled German novelist of moderate fame. Davison found Captain Schoenstedt, a recently naturalized American citizen, in the army's Morale Division, where he had been writing "Know your Enemy" pamphlets for the armed forces. Schoenstedt was probably the most crucial of all of Davison's choices. In addition to serving as Davison's ears and eyes during the initial stages of the program, the novelist-turned-soldier organized the first and most conspicuous attempt to reorient the POWs, the production of the division's POW newspaper. He was responsible for its content, as well as for the selection of anti-Nazi POWs for an editorial staff.

Schoenstedt's recruitment was in many ways an unorthodox choice. To begin with, in his youth he had been an ardent Communist; one assumes his superior officers were aware of this fact. In 1933 Schoenstedt had left Berlin for Paris where he was active in the Socialist-oriented International Writers' Organization. The son of a Berlin blue-collar worker, the young Schoenstedt had joined the *Rote Jungfront*/Red Youth Front, and eventually made a name for himself as a gifted proletarian writer. His novels of the early 1930s all dealt in one way or another with the oppression and plight of Berlin's working-class youth. Schoenstedt's greatest asset, and presumably one of the reasons for his choice, was his abrupt discarding of the Communist creed and his espousal of American liberalism; this occurred after his arrival in the United States in 1935. His militant aversion to both Communism and National Socialism earned him prominence and respect in the army's Morale Division; it also provoked the disdain of his former comrades, who would later accuse him of having become "a traitor to the working class."[7]

Schoenstedt brought to the program many of the classic disaffections of the exiled German writer. These men of letters epitomized the weaknesses of German intellectual resistance to National Socialism. To begin with, the vast majority of these intellectuals were either unable or unwilling to translate their calls to action into the language of ordinary people. Their cries for another Germany remained buried in their literary works or ensconced within the pages of journals of limited distribution; they appeared resigned to talking to themselves and preaching to the already-converted rather than addressing the lay public. Moreover, in a world governed by concentrated political forces, the writers were ineffective because of their unwillingness to discard individual expressions for more effective collective forms of protest. Their impact as dissenting voices was of marginal consequence due to their consistent refusal to work within recognized political frameworks. "With few exceptions," Egbert Krispyn notes, they attempted "to influence the course of events from a strictly private standpoint. They based their arguments purely on their own moral authority instead of working through the established structures of political life."[8]

It was, perhaps, quite unrealistic to assume that an introvert literary movement, however well-organized, could galvanize popular opposition to a totalitarian regime. Nevertheless, American authorities had great expectations from this select group of exiles. Many of these intellectuals had endorsed democracy and repudiated publicly the socialist leanings of their youth, thereby encouraging American authorities to bandy them around as role models. Exposure to the unique political circumstance of the United States had induced the erosion of prewar political creeds and the subsequent conversion to a distinctly American brand of liberal politics.

Walter Schoenstedt was very much the typical exiled writer. He was a strict believer in the mobilization of the German literary spirit in exile and a convert from a youthful Communism apparently brought about by his exposure to American society. In *Das Lob des Lebens/In Praise of Life* (1938), the first of his semiautobiographical novels to be translated into English, Schoenstedt documented the essence of his political convictions, in particular, the beginning of his conversion from Communism to American liberalism. The novel, which traces the life of Peter Volkers—presumably a character representing Schoenstedt himself—describes the resilience of Berlin's working class exposed to the hopeless conditions of unemployment, an oppressive educational system, and a militarist oligarchy. Somehow, the main character and many, but not all, of Volkers's friends are able to keep their humanity intact due to a resilient class-consciousness and a fervent belief in justice, which overrides the populist cant of National Socialism.

The villains in the novel are quite clearly identified. They are the political and cultural elites of Germany, creators of the unholy alliance between expansionists, militarists, and industrialists who, by clinging to old power structures even during the Weimar years, thwart Germany's brief experimentation with democracy. Above all, Schoenstedt leveled his criticism at Germany's petite bourgeoisie, the small businessmen, students, and professionals, who willingly fell in line with the country's antidemocratic forces, thereby ensuring the failure of Weimar. As far as the working classes were concerned, Schoenstedt was more understanding. He attributed their support for National Socialism to the cumulative effect of countless disappointments, deceptions, emotional deprivation, and debilitating poverty which eventually destroyed body and soul. "The German people have starved too long, they've been betrayed too often, and they weren't strong enough to take the freedom that had been promised to them a million times and in a million different ways," observes Peter Volkers in the last chapter of the novel.[9]

In *The Cradle Builder* (1940), the sequel to *In Praise of Life*, Schoenstedt documented his gradual disaffection with the socialist convictions of his youth, as well as his own growing alienation from German culture. Peter Volkers—the literary incarnation of Schoenstedt's own worldview—marries an American woman, and spends the entire novel anguishing over the conflicting desires of maintaining his German sense of identity, on the one hand, and adopting a new, uniquely American creed, on the other. Schoenstedt-Volkers's solution is to retreat in time, to seek the redeeming qualities of his German heritage in the past, while disavowing any affinity with contemporary German culture. By the end of the novel Volkers has abandoned much of his previous worldview and, together with his wife, moves to small-town America, where he begins a new life both spiritually and economically.[10]

Indeed, by 1940, Walter Schoenstedt had completed his spiritual conversion. He not only became an American citizen; he also joined the army. As a Morale Officer, Schoenstedt displayed a distinct animosity for contemporary German culture as well as all things socialist. Both personnel reports and Schoenstedt's army pamphlets revealed a sense of bitterness and disillusionment with Germans and Germany. This disenchantment was tempered by a persistent admiration for the "great German thinkers" of the nineteenth century and their heirs, the German intellectuals in exile who had discarded the blinkers of a narrow German nationalism.

Given the acute demand for German expertise in the armed forces, Davison's success in recruiting Schoenstedt was unusual. Presumably aware that another person with Schoenstedt's credentials would be hard to find, Davison turned toward the familiar terrain of academia. There he hoped to use personal ties for assembling an appropriate staff for the program. Curiously, a command of German was not a prerequisite for potential candidates. In fact, Davison appeared to rely on personal recommendations and acquaintances rather than some methodical search process. His first and most outstanding enlistees from academia were Howard Mumford Jones, the American Studies specialist of the program, and Henry Ehrmann, a European legal historian and political scientist who was transferred to the OPMG from the Office of War Information. Both these men served as civilian advisors. Both candidates were the only civilian members of the SPD staff.

Davison found his friend, Howard Mumford Jones, fulfilling the somewhat inappropriate role of assistant chief of the Harvard Auxiliary Police, a home guard unit comprised of the elderly and infirm. Jones leaped at the opportunity to abandon the ignoble task of parading his "soldiers" with broomsticks through the darkened streets of Cambridge. Trading the inglorious mission of chasing the young "brats," who attacked the rag-tag formations of the auxiliary police with showers of pebbles, for the intellectually challenging reeducation program was a more than welcome task.[11] Jones's designated role was that of the American intellectual booster, living proof that the United States was no modern-day Sparta, a warrior nation devoid of culture.

Davison and Jones had known each other for many years, and yet it is unclear why the commanding officer of the SPD chose this particular professor of English over many other available acquaintances. One may presume that Edward Davison, the poet, had found inklings of the qualities he was searching for in Jones's own modest stabs at poetry. In a collection of his works, *They Say the Forties* (1937), Jones presented a revealing personal autobiography, as well as a succinct summary of his understanding of American virtues and culture. Never one to be apologetic or too self-conscious about America's contributions to western civilization, Jones placed the United States within the context of classical empires, and then some:

> We have outsoared the soaring Roman arches,
> Building towers of steel with fronts of pearl and foam,
> We have made a Roman road from Tampa to Nome;
> And farther than Ceasar rode in all his marches,
> Our cars whirl up from the palms to the pines and larches;
> We have given the Vandal and the Goth a home;
> On higher Alps our aqueducts have clomb
> To descend where a vaster Barca shimmers and parches.[12]

According to Jones, the difference between the historical empires and the new American empire was the radically novel way that the United States chose to use its power:

> But though the republic touches mighty seas,
> But though our eagles, borne to distant regions,
> Have brought more ancient nations to their knees,
> While stands at Washington a Roman dome,
> We will not follow Europe's shirted legions,
> We will not take the Roman way to Rome.[13]

Howard Mumford Jones, Renaissance man and Harvard Dean, was responsible for many of the critical working assumptions of the SPD. To begin with, he held strong convictions about the positive and crucial role of the humanist in the modern world. Only the humanist, he stated some years later, had the ability to disavow "the zeal for limited knowledge and a tendency to minimize everything outside his field." Humanism, according to Jones, was ideally suited for the healing process of a fallen nation. The broad humanistic approach to culture represented the only avenue for uncovering and resurrecting a culture's "systems of value and patterns of organized perceptiveness."[14]

Having identified the appeal of totalitarianism with the ability to fabricate an attractive pantheon of heroes, Jones felt quite strongly about the professional historians' flirting with the social sciences. The social sciences were unable to conjure up the images that ignite people's minds, he argued. "The school of social historians has substituted movements for personalities, conflicts of economic interest for dramatic events, sociology for the romance of personal endeavor," thereby turning history into an uninspiring handmaiden of the social sciences. "It would be idle to deny the economic motive which sent adventurers to the New World, but it seems to me equal folly to omit for that reason the tale of the lonely and heroic exploits which they wrought," Jones wrote. Perhaps Washington "did not cross the Delaware in the fatuous manner of the celebrated painting; nevertheless he crossed it, and it was full of floating ice."[15]

In other words, Jones argued, a revival of an attractive format of history did not entail an emulation of the propagandist techniques of Fascism. Democracies could combat the attractive myths of Fascism through the romanticization of real heroic deeds rather than the distortion of facts, and by means of creative use of language instead of the drab language of the social sciences.

In addition to these very strong views on the mobilization of the humanities for the national cause, Jones was also a firm believer in redemption; he rejected the idea of the incorrigible nature of German society. "Even Satan in *Paradise Lost* knew justice and peace before he, ruining, fell, to experience the torments. . . . Phrases about lost Edens and lost innocence imply that there were innocence and Eden to lose."[16] His beliefs in German redemption were grounded in a very positive assessment of nineteenth-century German intellectual accomplishments. Such an understanding of the sublime cultural roots of the enemy dovetailed quite neatly with the views of the other civilian member of the SPD faculty, the resident expert on German history, Henry Ehrmann.

Ehrmann was by far the most energetic member of the cast. Under the somewhat vague title of educational advisor, Ehrmann was the principal reviewer of all German language books for the program. Subsequently, he devised the German history survey for the intensive crash courses in democracy that were held on the eve of repatriation.

Although he would eventually hang his hat in a number of political science departments, Ehrmann was also an intellectual historian, as well as a student of comparative political systems. Born in Berlin in 1908, Ehrmann had studied law in Berlin and Freiburg. He was arrested and subsequently sent to a concentration camp after the rise of Hitler. From there, and under mysterious circumstances, he had escaped to France, where he practiced free-lance journalism until the demise of the Third Republic. In 1940 he arrived in the United States, his first academic position being at the New School for Social Research.[17] This New York–based "University in Exile" provided a haven for many German academic exiles who espoused a liberal democratic political persuasion.[18]

Henry Ehrmann believed in a structural interpretation of German history, a format that he had developed during the course of writing his dissertation on the French labor movement. He attributed much of the malaise of those societies who had fallen victim to totalitarianism to a lack of a culture of cooperation and a false sense of class confrontation. Labor organizations often hastened political crises because of their rigid class consciousness as well as "an aloofness of labor from happenings outside the sphere of its immediate interests."[19] But, according to Ehrmann, the business classes in such societies were equally responsible for engendering class conflict; they were invariably vindictive, intransigent, and disinclined to address the legitimate demands of working people. Moreover, myopic governments usually proved unwilling to acknowledge the dangerous consequence of such social and political cleavages. "The strength of a state depends upon the organized representatives of employers and workers, and their collaboration with each other and with the institutions of government," he stated in what would become a guiding principle for organizing his course on German history in the final stages of the reeducation program.[20]

Because he believed in a structural rather than a cultural interpretation of recent history, Ehrmann rejected the ever-popular yet "utterly unhistorical" linear analysis of national character, which, in the German context, was often a predictable exercise in seeking a consistent violent streak in Germanic culture through the ages. After all, he observed, "the Mongols, universally feared under Genghis Khan, turned into peaceful lamaists; a century ago the Germans were thought a lovable and impractical people fit only for metaphysics, music and poetry."[21] His own point of departure for understanding German culture in general, and for developing his approach to the reeducation program in particular, was to assume a fundamental difference between the origins of nationalism in Western Europe and the Central European experience. Paraphrasing from conservative historian Hans Kohn's *The Idea of Nationalism* (1944), Ehrmann stated:

> In the Western World, where a new society was born in which the middle classes achieved a growing preponderance, the rise of nationalism was mainly a political occurrence, preceded by or coinciding with the formation of the national state. In Central and Eastern Europe the backward political and social development forced the rising nationalism to find its only expression in the cultural field.[22]

Cultural nationalism, he added in concurrence with Kohn, was later appropriated by conniving politicians and generals who selectively and deliberately misinterpreted the humanism of German intellectualism to suit their pernicious political objectives.

Given his structural explanation of German political culture, Ehrmann rejected ideas, such as the Morgenthau plan, that assumed pathological defects in German culture. Germany's problems were technical and not psychological, he argued persistently. If the country could rid itself of the military-industrial oligarchy—which should have been removed after the Great War—and if Germany would accept an American-style diffusion of political power, then Germany would no longer furnish a threat.[23]

Thus, Ehrmann brought to the reeducation program the ambitious objective of establishing within the minds of the students a benign interpretation of nineteenth-century German political philosophy, as well as an understanding as to how an insidious German military-industrial complex had distorted German culture to fulfill its own private agenda.[24] His objective, was to "depoliticize" nationalism, thereby removing from the German POWs the stigma of belonging to a pathological nation. "In the same way that religion was depoliticized," he summarized in his review of Hans Kohn's analysis of nationalism, "nationality might be transcended and, while remaining an 'intimate and moving sentiment,' lose its connection with political organization."[25]

Ehrmann's views were supported in large part by the SPD's third major recruit from academia, the philosopher T. V. Smith. A latecomer to the program, Smith's unusual credentials included academic, political, and even limited military experience in the field of education. Born in Texas, Smith had been an Illinois state senator and an Illinois congressman-at-large in addition to his position as professor of philosophy at the University of Chicago and editor of the *International Journal of Ethics* (later renamed *Ethics*). He had also been the creator and host of "Chicago Round Table," a popular radio show that presented intellectual issues in a middle-brow format.[26] T. V. Smith arrived at the program after serving as the educational program director for the military government in Italy. He was, then, the only member of the cast with any background in relaying abstract academic issues to a lay public, as well as the only one with any experience in re-educating an enemy nation.

T. V. Smith, a mainstream pragmatist and disciple of John Dewey, had gained modest fame through his so-called Doctrine of Compromise. The central facets of this doctrine were: Never presume that one's own values are the only authentic ones; in order to safeguard the sacred and uncompromisable, one must learn to compromise. Smith's doctrine stated that no principle warranted unquestioning acceptance; all ideals, however sacred, should be modified in order to avoid suicidal confrontations. In the context of the SPD, Smith's mission was to impress upon his "students" the dangerous role of unyielding beliefs in conflict management and international relations. In a successful democracy, "you must sometimes forego your principles to meet other people of other principles . . . half way." Smith argued that wars between nations resulted "from the deathly competition in principles." He described the faults of Germans as resulting from their "romantic, self-pitying, and fanatical, crucifying (of) reasonableness in the name of Reason." By contrast, the strength of the American system, one which he hoped to impart to his student-inmates, was its flexible approach to principles. The American tradition of negotiable convictions modified by experience had, according to Smith, fostered a "happy and efficient order" in the United States. By contrast, Germans and other Europeans had been sucked into debilitating and devastating conflicts by adapting uncompromising and unyielding ideological stances.[27]

Smith, much like the other principal members of the staff, never articulated his thoughts in narrow, parochial American terms. "Deeper than all our differences," he often observed, "there is a common touch of nature that makes all kin."[28] In fact, the fundamental common denominator among this eclectic crew of philosopher, novelist, literary critic, and historian was universalism, an attempt to analyze history without resorting to the concept of national uniqueness and exceptionalism, German or American. Howard Mumford Jones perceived the problem facing the educators of the SPD, as well as the larger looming problem facing the postwar world, in terms of "tribalism," a dangerous form of tunnel vision that arises when a nation, as "tribe thinks itself superior to the human family." Jones and others warned against the temptation to substitute for "Nazi tribalism a more genteel tribalism of our own."[29] They argued that "global warfare requires global thinking, and global thinking cannot be tribal." Somewhat paradoxically, these senior members of the SPD faculty urged using the American Studies curriculum to impart abstract universal concepts for a saner political future.

A host of other enlisted professors joined Schoenstedt, Jones, T. V. Smith, and Ehrmann as minor members of the cast. Brown University supplied numerous candidates, most notably the linguist, Major Henry Lee Smith. Aided by Captain William Moulton, then a young assistant professor from Cornell, Henry Lee Smith fulfilled the much-needed role of language program coordinator.

Not all of Davison's academic recruits were able to find their niche within the program. Captain Michael Ginsburg, a professor of Classics from the University of Nebraska was recruited for no other reason than the fact that he had studied at a German university sometime during the 1920s. His familiarity with the Nazi-German educational system was, however, nonexistent, an exasperated State Department official reported.

> He has no . . . knowledge of German schools, but has been designated the specialist on German education in Colonel Davison's group. Davison asked me to find out through conversation how much he actually knew about German schools and I had to report to him that his knowledge was practically nil. However, he still lectures on German education to the officers in the training course.[30]

The author of *Hunting Scenes on Roman Glass in the Rhine* (1941), Ginsburg was a typical example of a recruit whose only apparent qualification was an academic background in the humanities; he had no visible talents for the task at hand. The insistence on an intellectual approach to reeducation, manifested quite clearly by the indiscriminate recruitment of humanities professors, was all the more conspicuous given Davison's attitude toward the rival Social Sciences. Indeed, there were no behaviorists among the faculty of the Special Projects Division. The only senior staff member with no background in liberal arts was Lt. Colonel Alpheus Smith, a physics professor, who in the final stage of the program served as base commander for the crash-course democracy programs. As an administrator Alpheus Smith had little say in devising the intellectual content of the program.

Recruitment policy and the humanist didactic methods of Davison and his senior staff demonstrated little tolerance for alternative strategies. The

SPD faculty argued that they could enlighten the enemy based on experience derived from the dramatically different context of college classrooms. Such declarations were derived, in part, from a general sense of alarm concerning the diminishing prestige of the humanities in the eyes of both students and faculty from rival fields. University departments of literature and philosophy had been flooded by what Howard Mumford Jones called "hordes of young barbarians at play" who "if they had entered one of the professional schools, these same students would not dream of avoiding their responsibilities as they do in the college of arts." No less demeaning than the irreverence of students was the condescending manner of colleagues from more prestigious fields who reprimanded their students "by reminding them that they can no longer get by with the sort of thing . . . tolerated" by the less important humanities disciplines.[31]

The reeducation program represented an attempt to counteract the notion that humanities were "archaic" and "trivial" by proving that hardened Nazis could be transformed when exposed to college-type Western Civilization courses and reading material. The SPD's major figures devised a curriculum based on their own academic experience with few adjustments for their entirely different audience. Intellectual history, literary criticism, and the teaching of complex ideas and intellectual abstractions furnished the backbone for reeducation. These educators displayed a very human tendency to do what they knew best, namely, to re-create the intellectual climate of the liberal arts college behind barbed wire.

SPD architects were of course acutely aware of the suspicion and resistance that their program would arouse among POW camp commanders. Many camp commanders dismissed their wards as hopeless fanatics for whom reeducation was a waste of time; others feared that reeducation might erode discipline or foster strife among the inmates. The SPD sought to allay such fears and protect its investment by placing reeducation coordinators at all POW camps. These officers, known officially as Assistant Executive Officers (AEOs), were charged with administering the program of reeducation at the local camp level, monitoring the response of prisoners to reeducation material, as well as attempting to diffuse tensions between the mostly military concerns of individual camp commanders and the far-reaching intellectual objectives of the SPD.

This fundamentally sound plan for field representatives ran into immediate problems. According to the official monograph of the SPD, the effective functioning of AEOs was marred by an acute lack of suitable candidates.[32] There is little doubt that the SPD was hampered by a shortage of suitable persons for this complex assignment. Nevertheless, the personnel issue was only one of the factors affecting poor coordination between the architects of reeducation and their AEO field representatives. The wide rift between the intellectual approach of the American staff, on the one hand, and the POWs' lack of interest in such material, on the other, did little to contribute to a favorable working climate between headquarters and field representatives. AEOs confronted a bristling self-defensiveness among SPD staff officers whenever they raised the issue of the limited suitability of the SPD's academic-oriented curriculum.

Despite a very rigid screening process aimed at recruiting kindred spirits for the job of AEO, what little dissent that there was to the academization of reeducation came from these field officers. The most vocal dissenter was Major Paul A. Neuland, the supervising officer of the AEOs. Prior to joining the SPD, this multilingual former FBI agent had been involved in intelligence surveillance on German and Italian consulates in the United States. As the lone representative of the AEOs' sentiments at SPD headquarters, Neuland routinely protested the lack of contact between the program's hierarchy and the men in the field. He periodically passed on the critical comments of his liaison officers, in particular their disapproval of the program's elitist format, but he succeeded only in engendering the distrust of his fellow officers at SPD headquarters. Neuland felt that the persistent rejection of the AEOs' critical observations "by a man in the New York Office . . . doesn't make sense." However, as far as the other SPD officers were concerned, any form of criticism by field officers amounted to "sniping" and even a lack of "loyalty" to the division. When Major Neuland complained that this very defensive attitude on the part of the SPD would lead his men to "feel that their criticism as it is brought back from the field is not desired," SPD director Davison snapped back that "some of our officers were taking the viewpoint of the field instead of the division" and "were washing our dirty linen in public."[33]

Neuland was not the only officer who felt out of place at SPD headquarters. Another important dissenter within the midst of the reeducation hierarchy was Major John Dvorovy, the chaplain in charge of the religious affairs of the SPD. Like Neuland, Dvorovy had no academic background; he had been recruited at POW Camp McCain, Mississippi. The chaplain was not only the perennial outsider; he was also unsuited for the job. Dvorovy's major asset was his fluent German. He was however, an unlikely candidate for religious advisor. "With all due respect for the Chaplain," John Brown Mason of the State Department wrote, "there is some question in my mind as to the desirability of picking a Lutheran minister of the Missouri synnod [sic] for this particular job as that church is characterized by a strict orthodoxy which is foreign to the religious feeling of most German Protestants (the Evangelical Church in this country is the type of church the Germans are used to)."[34]

Whatever plans Dvorovy might have had to use religion for the benefit of the program were hampered by the attitude of his associates. According to the records of the SPD faculty, the place of religion in their plans ranged from nonexistent to marginal. Dvorovy was apparently embittered and estranged by the basically negative stance of his colleagues; he was also alienated by the intellectual aura of the program. In the latter part of the course, his pent-up sentiments translated into fateful action. During the course of a loyalty crisis that shook the SPD, Chaplain Dvorovy turned informer and betrayed the trust of his colleagues.

Aside from Dvorovy, Neuland, and the distant AEOs, there was no other meaningful dissent in the program, because its architects brought with them the urge to surround themselves with familiar faces as well as familiar ideas. Most of the SPD staff were previously acquainted and had been recruited to the program by mutual endorsement rather than a painstaking search for the right personnel. Perhaps nothing was more indicative of the mentality of the faculty club than the manifest aversion toward the presence of women colleagues in their midst. Irrespective of the vast pool of talent available at universities at the time, the program director made no attempt to recruit women for senior positions. Howard Mumford Jones could recall the presence of one woman only, "a very competent black typist, universally known as Maggie."[35] The State Department did, however, manage to foist upon a reluctant Davison two talented professionals. Dr. Marie Louise Actin, who held a Ph.D. from the University of Munich, had served on a variety of research projects at the University of Chicago and at Stanford; she was designated for stenography, and other secretarial tasks only. Ida Marie Owens, an American who had been schooled in Germany prior to the war, spent her tenure at the SPD doing clerical work and sifting through film reels in the New York office of the program.

These, then, were the faults and virtues of the primary movers and shakers of the SPD. They were the managers and foremen of a large and complex operation carried out by a production staff of carefully chosen German prisoners. The selection of this support crew proved to be as fateful as the decision to re-create the intellectual milieu of a liberal arts program. These German aides, designated to assist in writing the POW newspaper and translating the German material for a faculty mostly untutored in German, mirrored the worldview of the supervising faculty. They represented an alienated intelligentsia, who never bothered to hide their contempt for the rank and file within the camps.

Perhaps nothing sums up the single-minded dimensions of reeducation more than the nickname given to the camp where the handpicked POWs did their work. It was called the Idea Factory. Here, then, was a streamlined operation for the production of standardized ideas using familiar material hewed in the Groves of Academe. However, this intellectual factory did not adopt the rule of thumb of a mass-producing enterprise, namely the need to manufacture products catering to a broad common denominator. The Idea Factory assembled articles of faith that ultimately would be consumed only by a narrow section of the target population. As such, the Factory's products were more a reflection of the predisposition of its managers than any meaningful gauging of consumer tastes.

CHAPTER FOUR

The Idea Factory and Its Intellectual Laborers

IN HIS history of the Allied Forces Psychological Warfare Division in Europe, Daniel Lerner recalled that "characters" was the disparaging term reserved for the so-called misfits: the members of the many wartime intellectual enterprises implanted within the inhospitable setting of the military establishment. Lerner argued that this distrust over the intrusion of academia into military affairs was part of a more general "suspicion common among Americans of sustained intellectual activity"; it also reflected the particularly negative attitude of the military toward those who had never fully accomplished the transition from civilians to soldiers. "Largely exempt from the petty but continuous annoyances imposed by military status," Lerner observed, the civilian-minded members of the "special programs" were quick to arouse resentment among regular military personnel.[1]

Such image problems affected The Provost Marshal General's (PMG) reeducation program from the very beginning. Hoping to avoid the inevitable locking of horns with the professional military establishment, the PMG allowed the Special Project Division (SPD) to set up its headquarters in New York rather than in Washington, D.C. Proximity to New York's large libraries was the official reason for this unwieldy distance between PMG headquarters and the SPD. In reality the SPD simply strove to detach its unorthodox operation from the confines of a particularly inflexible military body. Safely tucked away on Broadway in Manhattan, the headquarters operations of the SPD did indeed avoid the scrutiny of officious military overseers.

However, SPD officials were unable to protect the main production center of their enterprise, the Idea Factory. In this special POW camp the numerous German assistants who did most of the daily work of the SPD—from editing the POW newspaper to reviewing books for prison libraries—discovered that their daily routine, unencumbered by trappings of military discipline or even prison life, aroused resentment. In Camp Van Etten, in upstate New York, where the Idea Factory had begun its operations before moving to its permanent base at Fort Kearney, Rhode Island, SPD officials confronted a typical military-minded base commander who treated the prisoner-Factory workers "as criminals."

Despite "the fact that the group of prisoners at Van Etten is a special group" engaged in a "highly intellectual" operation, SPD officials complained that the commander's treatment of these "selected men" was "comparable to that of prisoners in a strictly Nazi [POW] camp."[2]

The Factory workers, handpicked by Captain Walter Schoenstedt to produce material for the running of the program, did indeed enjoy an unusual routine. Upon joining the workforce of the Idea Factory, all inmates discarded their military ranks and, within the enclosure of Fort Kearney, managed their daily lives and settled internal disputes by means of their own "committee of governors." The Factory employed at its peak eighty-five prisoners of war who were for the most part engaged in translating program aids and reading material, monitoring the sentiments of their peers, and, of course, editing the POW newspaper, Der Ruf—"The Call."

Abandoning the trappings of military life and engaging in the intellectual activities of the Factory came easily to the inmates at Kearney. Walter Schoenstedt had apparently sought to fill all Factory work stations with kindred souls: alienated German intellectuals, disillusioned Communists, writers, and journalists like himself. These Kearney inmates espoused many of the cultural prejudices of their supervisors. They aided and abetted the construction of an intellectual enterprise with little acknowledgment of the cultural standards and preferences of rank-and-file POWs.[3]

The Factory was separated into a number of subdivisions: a film section, which reviewed movies and translated synopses; a review section, which made recommendations on the suitability of material passed on by other governmental agencies; a translation bureau which translated the curriculum designed in the New York headquarters; a camp newspaper section which monitored the tone of some seventy camp newspapers, and Der Ruf's editorial staff. Factory workers wrote, as well, position papers on various aspects of German society on which they claimed some expertise. The mass media and their reception in German society was perhaps the most prevalent topic for such position papers. Even though the Factory workers, by and large, found most aspects of mass culture quite distasteful, their many position papers signaled a cautious awareness of the ability of such cultural tools to sway the rank and file. Their writings on mass culture revealed a distinct contradiction between the Factory workers' espousal of democracy and free choice, on the one hand, and their negative assessment of the cultural maturity of their fellow countrymen.

Perhaps the most sophisticated of these analyses of mass culture emanating from Fort Kearney was written by Factory worker Oskar Wintergerst. His critical evaluation of Frank Capra's film series, "Why We Fight," was based upon an insightful understanding of film reception. Different cultures, he argued, "read" film differently because of the culture-specific process of "association of ideas." As an example he cited scenes of pompous S.A. parades, which aroused a mixture of amusement and fear among Americans because they "cannot understand this devotedness to an idea," or the blind "fanaticism" of a cultured European nation. However, as far as Germans were concerned, such scenes of hero-worshiping, rallies, and large parades did not serve the cause of reeducation. "The Nazi is fascinated by that picture and becomes ecstatic," he explained. Wintergerst therefore advised his American supervisors to produce their own film, using many of the scenes from the "Why We Fight" series, but placing them in a different sequence in order to achieve the ultimate objective of discrediting Nazi disinformation. Random shots of destruction, as used by Capra, were of little use, he wrote, because as soldiers and as "Nazis" many prisoners would justify destruction and death as an inevitable by-product, or a "necessary inconvenience" of war. Depictions of devastation by war would have to focus on the annihilation of German cities in order to clarify the self-destructive component of National Socialism and the entrapment of German society in a now "hopeless situation." Capra's series, he concluded, "cannot fill this demand because those films are cut for the orientation of the American soldier only." They were intended to arouse fear of the Nazi demon, rather than illuminate the inevitable hopelessness of the Nazi pipe dream.[4]

The vast majority of these Factory reports were not, however, as well-argued as Wintergerst's analysis of film. For the most part they were simplistic inquiries written by men who, due to their war service, had lost touch with their fields of expertise. Their reports offered vague solutions that were more an indicator of the Factory workers' own inability to fathom the deviant course of their country's political and social development rather than anything else. Thus, Eginhard von Lieberman's analysis of broadcasting policy for the postwar period never moved much beyond such gratuitous suggestions as to "keep military (march) music from the air" so as not "to remind the Germans too much of past 'glorious times.'" As alternatives, he suggested only a "School of the Air" as well as "typical American" programs because most Germans had formed basically negative impressions of American culture based on flippant "movies, stories about millionaires," and other misinformed sources.[5]

Even as he advocated strict censorship and rehabilitative programming, von Lieberman acknowledged the existence of ingrained prejudices which, as far as he was concerned, were best left untouched. "It is not advisable to use announcers or speakers with Jewish accent(s)," von Lieberman urged. "United with the hate of Jews in Germany is the dislike of Jewish accentuated voices, which are therefore not favorable" for "propaganda" purposes.

Indeed, the position papers indicated that even among the Factory workers, certain myths and prejudices of German society were hard to dispel. Factory Worker Gustav Weber's position paper on "immigration" accepted at face value many of the underpinnings of *Lebensraum*, the mythic lack of adequate living space for a "dynamic" German people. Weber explained that it was irrelevant whether Germany suffered from an objective fate of overpopulation—which he defined in terms of density per square mile—or whether the problem was one of an inadequate economic foundation for Germany's expanding population. Whatever the reason, Weber argued that a debilitated postwar Germany would suffer from the same "problem of density of population" that had afflicted her before the war. Peaceful immigration, rather than conquest, he stated, could provide a solution to insufficient *Lebensraum* and economic depression. The world, he noted, was full of sparsely populated regions. "This time the problem of over-population should be solved by the 'politics of room' "—a euphemism for the now insidious *Lebensraum*.

Perhaps the most salient feature of these position papers was the writers' underlying tone of alienation from, and distrust of, the German masses. Many of these papers stated in one way or another that the Germans were immature and erratic, and for the immediate future, they could not be trusted. Factory worker Karl Kuntze argued that even seemingly innocent material could undermine the rehabilitation of a nation as fickle and as impressionable as the Germans. He therefore strongly urged the removal of an innocuous filmstrip entitled "Boy and Girl Scouts" because, he claimed, it could be "used for the support of militarism or Nazism." He contended that a whole range of scenes in this film—signaling, cub induction, girl scouts with airplanes, and the gathering of scrap rubber, to name but a few—would lead "the average German PW, who was organized in the Hitler youth" to "compare the pictures shown in the filmstrip with just that and . . . say that education in the Hitler youth was right because they have done the same in democracies." The average POW, he added, would not grasp the theme of the "creation of global thinking of youth" which permeated the film. The German POWs would be unable to differentiate between "a youth organization helping in the war effort as a national duty, and a youth organization which even in peacetime had only one goal—to prepare for war."[6]

SPD officials reacted with puzzlement to Kuntze's report. The scout filmstrip had been chosen because it illustrated in simple terms the idea of global cooperation by stressing "the international aspects of scouting with shots of Chinese, Arabian, and Indian scouts." In rejecting Kuntze's paper, Captain Meyer of the SPD education branch stated that "the argument . . . that the Nazi still sees the world through Nazi eyes, could also be applied to any movies or articles on America's ability to wage war, because the prisoners would misinterpret that, too."[7] Meyer apparently did not understand that the Factory evaluation of the scouting film was not merely an expression of overzealousness or distrust of the tools of mass media. Such reports hinted at what the German aides could not say out loud: they did not fully believe in the mission of rehabilitation.

Nowhere were the Factory workers' misgivings on German maturity and suspicion of mass media more evident than among the POW editorial staff of *Der Ruf*—the German-language newspaper written by Factory workers. A lengthy report on guidelines for a postwar German press, written by *Der Ruf*'s editor, Gustav René Hocke, illustrated the gap between Factory workers and the rank and file by consistently using the term "the Germans" or "they" rather than "we" when referring to his countrymen. Hocke had little to say about the actual content and format of a successful postwar press aside from his advice to ban all partisan newspapers and to control the politics of new newspapers during their initial period of occupation. "They," the Germans, were not mature enough yet to appreciate the dynamics of constructive political differences.[8]

Hocke and his editorial staff were the most prized recruits of the Factory. Their uncommon life stories were quite illustrative of the irreconcilable differences between their own political views and that of their potential audience. Dr. Gustave René Hocke, a well-known author and antiquarianist, had been the Rome correspondent for the Catholic-oriented *Koelnische Zeitung*, where, apparently under duress, he had been inducted into the service of the occupying Wehrmacht as a civilian interpreter. This Catholic intellectual was the epitome of the alienated German, more at home abroad than in Germany, and an Anglophile to boot. In fact he bore the distinction of being the only prisoner of war to be repatriated to an Allied country, England, where his English wife and son were residing.

Two aspiring and subsequently well-known writers serving on the editorial staff of *Der Ruf* have documented the worldview of Factory workers in some of their postwar novels. In *Die Geschlagenen/ Beyond Defeat* (1949), Hans Werner Richter produced a well-crafted portrait of himself as representative of the spirit of *Der Ruf*. The novel presents the main character, Gühler, as a German version of David Riesman's inner-directed man. Gühler is a loyal soldier and patriotic German, yet, at the same time, an ardent socialist and anti-Nazi. After his captivity and subsequent arrival at an American POW camp, Gühler and a small group of associates find themselves at loggerheads with the vast majority of outer-directed prisoners, who continue to acquiesce in, and collaborate with, a Nazi hierarchy. Due to the naiveté and ignorance of the American captors in this novel, the Nazis run the daily life of the camp, crushing with brutal force all manifestations of dissent among their fellow POWs. Gühler-

Richter professes deep loyalty for German culture and heritage proven by his stubborn unwillingness to turn informer when interrogated by American intelligence officers. And yet, as the novel progresses, Gühler and his comrades find themselves estranged quite dangerously from the mainstream of fellow Germans interned in the camp. Throughout the novel, the hero is haunted by innuendos that he is a "traitor," an accusation which he vehemently denies, but with no great degree of success. In one of the book's most chilling scenes, Richter describes the "reception committee" of fellow inmates upon his arrival in an American POW camp.

> Prisoners from the camp, packed shoulder to shoulder, lined the side of the road. They all wore the same blue coats and blue caps. . . . They stood in silence, like a wall. Not a word of welcome, not a sign of greeting, not a shout escaped their ranks. "Deserters!" Gühler heard someone whisper beside him. He looked at the hostile faces in astonishment but said nothing. He sensed the threat that emanated from the silent wall. They marched faster and faster down the long road. "Traitors!" came the whisper from the dark ranks all around them. "Deserters! Cowards."[9]

These insinuations, ostensibly uttered by fellow prisoners but more likely the expressions of inner voices of self-doubt, figured prominently in the tone of *Der Ruf* and other Factory publications. The impossible task of cooperating with the enemy and, at the same time, professing loyalty to the German national cause would later be brought up as an explanation for the ineffectiveness of *Der Ruf* as an instrument of propaganda.

Richter was not the only Factory worker to record his wartime experiences. Alfred Andersch, another prominent novelist who served on the editorial board of *Der Ruf*, published a number of retrospective novels and short stories based on his war experiences. The central themes of all his war recollections, presumably a re-creation of his own youthful experiences and ideological inclinations, were escape and transformation. Born into a conservative and affluent family in 1914, Andersch expressed his discontent with the culture and politics of his background by joining the Communist party, an action that cost him a brief yet traumatic three-month prison term at the Dachau Concentration Camp. Upon his release, he broke ranks with the Communist party, which, in his mind, had not waged a resolute war on behalf of its objectives.

As this point and later, Andersch expressed his estrangement from his German origins as well as his disillusionment with the politics of the German left by renouncing revolution and withdrawing from all involvement in contemporary affairs. He ignored the rising storm of Nazism and, prior to joining the army, indulged in solitary nature hikes and pored over monographs of art history.

Like most German youth of his age, Andersch was inducted into the armed forces, where he served under Kesselring in Italy. In great contrast to his colleague Richter, Andersch never struggled with restraining bonds of loyalty to the German nation. Andersch pounced upon the first opportunity to desert and surrender to advancing American troops. He documented this decision in his autobiographical tale, "Die Kirschen der Freiheit/The Cherries of Freedom" (1952).[10] The act of desertion, Andersch explained, aroused little self-contempt because he had no sympathy for the foolhardy young men who unthinkingly supported an immoral cause.

> Was I to refrain from deserting on their account? Was I to stand by my outfit out of comradeship? Ridiculous. They had made it easy for me to leave. . . . I couldn't love my army comrades because I loved my party comrades who had been killed by those for whom my fellow soldiers were fighting. . . . By destroying the party, they deprived my youthful struggle of its meaning and drove me to introversion. For years I lived on the island of my soul. . . . Take up arms for them? Fire on the soldiers who might be able—a glimmer of hope—to change my whole life? The very thought was absurd. . . . Of course, I had still another reason for deserting: I had no desire to "push up daisies," as they say in the Army. . . . I wanted to give myself up because I was afraid of being shot and dying a meaningless or meaningful death.[11]

Once behind the barbed wire of his temporary American home, Andersch was, however, forced to reassess his decision to withdraw from worldly affairs. His postwar writings illuminate much of the emotional anguish that he experienced as he tried to decide between seclusion or involvement in the ideological struggles of his society. His important novels are all, in one form or another, stories of a defeated, bitter revolutionary and his inner conflict between continuing the fight or withdrawing, committing oneself to the common good as opposed to a flight into the comforting world of escapism. In his two important postwar novels, *Sansibar oder der letzte Grund/Flight to Afar* (1957), and *Die Rote/The Redhead* (1960), Andersch ends the convoluted plots by grudgingly acknowledging that in the vicious realities of modern times, escapism is not a viable option; people's lives as well as the fate of nations are intertwined and interdependent. It is the task of the intellectual and novelist to illuminate this, he implies, although it is unclear how far he had moved from disillusioned revolutionary to social democrat by the time he joined the Idea Factory.

Alienation from one's own culture was not the only issue to emerge from the writings of Factory workers. As another of Andersch's short stories illustrated, the Factory workers expressed as well an ambivalent attitude toward their American captors in general, and the quality of American intellectualism in particular. Andersch's "My Disappearance in Providence," relates the tale of T., "a middlingly well-known [West] German writer" and a former POW who returns to America seeking to clarify the essence of his experience as prisoner of war at Fort Getty, Rhode Island. Following a disappointing visit to the former prison site, where all tangible evidence of the camp has been eradicated, the prisoner does indeed relive his experience. He is lured into the house of an attractive couple in nearby Providence who imprison him in a small room. His only duty as prisoner is to write, but seeking guidelines from his host-guardians, he finds none. All they can tell him is that they want him to be creative. Even when the couple relaxes its guard, allowing the prisoner much freedom and ample opportunity to escape, he resists the temptation because of an erotic attraction to Eliza, his American captor. Sensually he is infatuated with the American woman; intellectually he finds nothing of value in the mind of her male counterpart who is presumably the representation of American intellectual achievements.[12]

Such indictments of American Philistinism were expressed openly by Factory workers in the immediate postwar years. Upon their release from the POW camps, Andersch, Richter, and others joined forces in establishing the important literary forum, *Gruppe* 47/Group 47, where they aired quite bluntly their ambivalence toward the American patron. This coalition of German writers, seeking to cull genuine forms of literature from the scorched earth of postwar Germany, edited a literary organ called, predictably, *Der Ruf*; the magazine clashed openly with the cultural guardians of the occupation forces. American authorities swiftly suspended publication because of the new *Der Ruf*'s very strong attacks on the American occupation administration in general, and the U.S. directed de-Nazification program in particular.

In part, at least, the anti-American tone of the new *Der Ruf* published in Germany was an attempt by both Richter and Andersch to absolve themselves of the taint of opportunistic cooperation with American POW authorities. One suspects that they themselves felt that in joining the Factory they had been drawn over, or dangerously close to, the fine line separating loyalty to one's culture from collaboration with the enemy. In the pages of the new postwar *Der Ruf* as well as in the many recollections of the POW experience, Richter, in particular, pleaded that the German Factory workers were anything but disloyal; they were, he argued, the epitome of the true German spirit. He complained incessantly of clashes with American supervisors over the ideological content of the POW newspaper and the whole concept of reeducation in POW camps. The record does not bear out these charges. In practice, the POW editorial staff of this Factory production enjoyed much freedom and wide discretion. Richter's accusations, it would appear, represented an attempt to amend the history of his Factory activities for posterity.

In fact, one of Richter's most revealing stories of his POW experience concedes that, despite many protestations to the contrary, the author had joined the Factory for basically selfish reasons. "Opportunism in Colorado," is a tale of three German POWs who have been rewarded for their good behavior by being allowed to work on a fruit farm in Colorado. With transparent symbolism, Richter relates how all three soldiers were swiftly enticed, perhaps even forced into sleeping with the farmer's three daughters. The farmer, symbol of the American public, "knew nothing of what was going on. He was completely wrapped up in his fruit-growing and money-making, in both of which he did very well." As for the three daughters, presumably representations of the American reeducation project, they were quite content to sleep with the enemy, and to use the three former SS soldiers for their own purposes without trying to induce any meaningful change in the worldview of their captive lovers. The Germans, for their part, displayed little admiration for their American bed-partners. The American woman who held the "whip hand" had a mouth "much too large and much too rouged," her "hair done in too boyish a style for his liking. . . . How fat she is and commonplace" the German soldier ruefully reflects as he unbuttons her pajama jacket. Despite the distaste and anger that she arouses, the soldier, who is hero of this episode, decides to collaborate. He sleeps with her, and avoids arousing her anger, even though he "was furious . . . and would have liked to hit her. He couldn't; she had the whip hand. He knew it wasn't only in Germany that punishment camps existed. They had them in America too. And he was afraid of punishment camps."[13]

Aside from the very tasteless comparison of German concentration camps with American "punishment camps," this vignette suggests that, contrary to Richter's insistent pleas that he never collaborated and that he never abandoned his principles, he was quite troubled by his wartime activities in the United States. He found it necessary to justify to himself and to others that his tenure in the Factory had not been an incident of mere opportunism; he had had no reasonable alternative.

Richter, Andersch, and most other German Factory workers were tormented intellectuals who had little in common with the POW rank and file and displayed, as well, a certain degree of contempt for their American guardians. They were not merely anti-Nazis. They were distinctly ambivalent about the fortunes of Germany's rehabilitation in particular, and the morality of their native culture in general. Their poor perception of American culture merely compounded the difficulties they had in campaigning for an American-oriented alternative to National Socialism. They were, therefore, problematic choices for key positions in this American program for German rehabilitation.

There is no better indicator of the irreconcilable differences between the intellectual elite at the Factory and their lesser peers in the camps than the journal, *Der Ruf*. As the prize product of the Factory ostensibly seeking the attention of the ordinary prisoner, *Der Ruf* was more a reflection of private intellectual controversies among the prisoner-aides than a meaningful attempt to proselytize among unrepentant POWs. The swift move from the original objective of providing monitored reading material for the average POW to the production of a journal for the privileged few was indicative of significant inconsistencies between the original objectives of reeducation and the actual agenda of its architects.

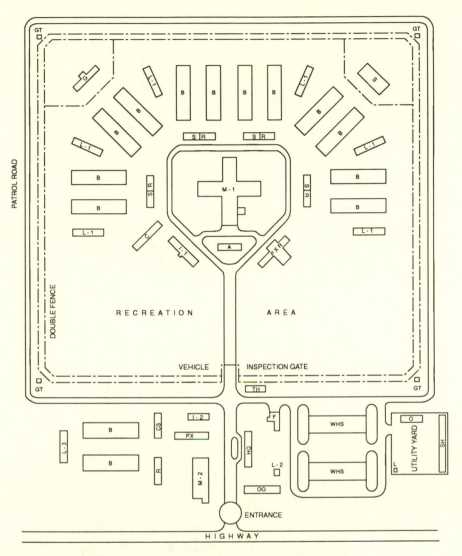

Fig. 1. Layout of typical POW camp in the United States.

SYMBOL	BUILDINGS	SYMBOL	BUILDINGS
A	ADMINISTRATION	Q	Q.M. OFFICE
HQ	HEADQ'TRS & CENTRAL GUARD	OQ	OFFICERS QUARTERS
B	BARRACKS	PX	POST EXCHANGE - DETACHMENT
C	CHAPEL	PXR	POST EXCHANGE - PRISONERS
F	FIRE HOUSE	R	DAY ROOMS - DETACHMENT
G	GUARD HOUSE - PRISONERS	CS	CO. STOREHOUSE & ADMIN.
I - 1	INFIRMARY - PRISONERS	S	WORK SHOP - PRISONERS
I - 2	INFIRMARY - DETACHMENT	TH	TOOL HOUSE & STOCKADE OFFICE
L	LATRINE	SH	UTILITY SHOPS
L - 1	LAVATORY	WHS	WAREHOUSE
L - 2	LAVATORY - OFFICERS	GT	GUARD TOWER
M - 1	MESS - PRISONERS	SR	STOREHOUSE & DAY ROOM
M - 2	MESS - E.M. & OFFICERS	L - 3	LAVATORY - DETACHMENT

Fig. 2. Distribution of POW Camps in the United States (1944).

Fig. 3. Major General Archer Lerch, Provost Marshal General (1944–1945).

Fig. 4. German POW student delivering valedictorian address at the graduation exercises, School for Democracy, Fort Eustis, Virginia, 1945. Seated to the right of the prisoner: Brig. General B. M. Bryan, Lt. Colonel Edward Davison, Henry Ehrmann, Captain Walter Schoenstedt. The remaining officers are unidentified.

Fig. 5. Brigadier General B. M. Bryan presenting the Legion of Merit Award to SPD director, Lt. Colonel Edward Davison. At the right is Mrs. Natalie E. Davison (1946).

Fig. 6. German POWs cramming for an exam on "The Principles of Democracy," at the School for Democracy, Fort Eustis, Virginia, 1946.

PART TWO

Reeducation and High Culture

CHAPTER FIVE

Der Ruf:
Inner Emigration, Collective Guilt,
and the POW

> The German Prisoners in the United States now have their OWN
> NEWSPAPER. . . . "Der Ruf" will be way above any party or
> small group quarrel. It will not serve the personal ambitions of
> the few. It will foster real German Culture. It will serve us all and
> through us, our country. It will denounce in the strongest terms
> any idle chatter and gossip. It will demonstrate clearly the seri-
> ousness of our position and will not hide the hard and cold facts
> of world events behind high sounding words. It is the reputation
> of the German people we have to serve, believing in a sense of
> goodness and decency. We must give it our full approval and
> cooperation. When "Der Ruf" reaches you, answer with a mili-
> tary "Present." Make sure that not one of us who still has a spark
> of feeling left for home and family is absent.
> —Editorial, *Der Ruf* (March 1, 1945), 1–2

CAPTAIN Walter Schoenstedt, chief of the programs branch in the Provost
Marshal General's Special Projects Division (SPD) and godfather of the
newspaper "written for and by prisoners of war in the United States,"
waited anxiously for the field reports following the distribution of the
first edition of *Der Ruf*. "You have hit the nail on the head" a regional
commander notified a relieved Schoenstedt and his commanding officer
Lt. Colonel Edward Davison, as he sifted through the reports from a
number of camps. The paper had sold extremely well. Major Kreze of the
First Service Command reported that a measure of the publication's success was the displeasure it aroused among both radical anti-Nazis and
die-hard National Socialists; "but the middle of the line . . . they are only
in accord with what you are doing." Schoenstedt was elated. He had
planned for a negative response from pro-Nazi elements. The bonus of an
unfavorable response from radical anti-Nazis—in particular those suspected of Communist leanings—would, according to Schoenstedt, raise
the paper's credibility in the eyes of middle-of-the-roaders.[1]

Edward Davison did not share this enthusiasm. Apart from a few laconic remarks he had nothing to say in this conversation. But a few days earlier Davison had advised Schoenstedt that the newspaper's text was dense to the point of being incomprehensible. Davison apparently felt that the negative comments from both extremes of the political spectrum were signs of confusion rather than actual dissent. The difficulties involved in deciphering the ideological content of this newspaper encouraged the politically active POWs of both the left and right to "discover" treasonable, cryptic messages embedded in the text.[2]

Typically, the lead article of the paper's very first edition, entitled "The Inner Powers," was shrouded in obscure analogies and an ambivalent tortured syntax. This centerpiece of the first edition of *Der Ruf* condemned the "'massification' of man," the tendency toward group behavior at the expense of an inner creative urge, which had been weakened by the "noisy slogans" of modern industrialized societies. The nebulous tone of the article could be interpreted as a critique of popular support for National Socialism, or, conversely, a vaguely worded disaffection with mass culture, American-style or, possibly, a combination of both sentiments.[3]

Not surprisingly, prisoners at the anti-Nazi Camp Devens discovered "hidden Nazi Propaganda" in this article because it failed to deliver any "aim or positive thought."[4] By contrast, inmates at the "strong Nazi" Aliceville camp complained that the "Inner Powers" was blatantly anti-Nazi because "it was diametrically opposed to the basic Nazi philosophy that the state, rather than the individual spirit, is all-important."[5] Lt. Colonel Davison interpreted these conflicting opinions as a fundamental weakness rather than a strength, observing that the article "seems to me rather ponderous, overworded, and even a little stilted."

> Don't you think a lighter touch is needed if "Der Ruf" is to be written on a level that will be read by the many instead of the few? Shorter words and as little of the abstract as possible—concrete all the way, pungency as well as pith. . . . Above all, we shouldn't let "Der Ruf" be too literary or philosophic, even though Germans may be more literary and philosophical than we are.[6]

Davison was not alone in his lack of enthusiasm. More critical reports filtered in, belying the optimism of the initial appraisal. The Assistant Executive Officer (AEO) at Camp Aliceville, Alabama, enumerated a long list of reasons why most prisoners refused even to believe that the paper was written by prisoners of war. The expensive chrome paper of *Der Ruf* contrasted dramatically with the spartan stenciled camp newspapers printed on poor quality, recycled paper; photographs and wide margins suggested that *Der Ruf* had no budgetary constraints. But perhaps the most obvious blunder was the newspaper's mailing address. "The use of a GPO box, rather than a POW camp address caused doubt as to whether the editors were in fact prisoners of war or, if they were, whether they really 'leben wie ihr' [living like you] as they state to the prisoners on page one."[7]

Der Ruf did indeed seem to be nothing more than a piece of misconceived propaganda written by outsiders. Its contents puzzled the majority of POWs. The articles addressed the concerns of typical inmates in passing only. *Der Ruf* disregarded the thirst for information on Germany and the POWs' craving for light entertainment to ease the oppressive routine of life behind barbed wire. Front pages were devoted to esoteric literary and philosophical debates. The inner pages on Germany were agonizingly short on substance. The so-called lighter parts of the paper—those items devoted to leisure—featured ponderous reports on theater and poetry readings. The soccer craze, perhaps the most riveting aspect of daily life in the camps, was virtually ignored. Instead, a typical edition of *Der Ruf* contained snippets—Flashes/*Zwischenrufe*—on a wide range of irrelevant issues such as a ten-year-plan for the improvement of highways in England, the establishment of the "first helicopter line in the world" between Caracas and other parts of Venezuela, as well as an item on the marriage ceremony of octogenarians in Racine, Wisconsin. The lack of humor, German human interest stories, or other forms of light reading only compounded the irrelevance of the paper for the vast majority of prisoners. In a typical complaint, the SPD's representative at Camp Carson protested that among the two thousand inmates at his camp "there are perhaps 5 or 6 who are intellectuals" able to understand the paper.[8]

Ironically, *Der Ruf* was indeed the creation of German POWs who enjoyed a great degree of autonomy in deciding upon the content of their paper. The convoluted articles that characterized *Der Ruf* were, curiously enough, the product of writers who espoused terse, expository prose. Editor-in-chief Gustav René Hocke dismissed the German tradition of elaborate and complex syntax as "calligraphy." He implied that such a florid style served a decadent role by beclouding the issues at hand. Hocke rejected the tangled and detached poetic approach to writing because it failed to address contemporary problems and was removed "from the basic contents of life."[9] Still, he chose to edit a newspaper in a style that contradicted these professional convictions.

Moreover, the densely written texts of *Der Ruf* clashed openly with the literary creed of its chief mentor, Captain Walter Schoenstedt, whose own novels were exercises in terse prose. In his original proposal for *Der Ruf* Schoenstedt had envisioned a newspaper of "sober journalism" aimed at "the broadest audience possible" based upon "exact news of all important military and political events," as well as "news from the homeland." None of these features characterized *Der Ruf*.[10] From its inception, then, the POW newspaper clashed with the professional intuition of its German writers as well as the professed objective of its American underwriters to produce a readable journal.

When called upon to defend such discrepancies, Walter Schoenstedt argued somewhat unconvincingly that the disposing of the original plan for a simple, popular journal of news and entertainment was merely a technical issue. The awkward tone of *Der Ruf*, he stated, was very much in the tradition of good German journalism. By avoiding comic strips, light humor, and an extensive sports section—the most conspicuous trappings of what Schoenstedt considered to be trivial American journalism— he claimed to have circumvented the prisoners' ingrained and self-defensive disparagement of American culture. In the eyes of many POWs all things American were lightweight, unimportant, fleeting. "If we had a full page of funnies," Walter Schoenstedt explained, "we would get the wrong type of reaction from the prisoners of war like: Ah, ha American culture!"[11]

Schoenstedt avoided mentioning that pre-Nazi Germany had enjoyed a thriving industry of what he considered to be American-style newspapers ranging from the urban mass circulation *Generalanzeiger* press to the Social democratic press of the late 1920s. Seeking to rivet as large an audience as possible, both the "politically colorless" *Generalanzeiger* as well as the ideologically motivated social-democratic newspapers featured large doses of human interest stories, serialized novels and womens' sections, in sum all those attributes that Schoenstedt claimed were foreign to the German newspaper.[12]

It would appear, then, that Schoenstedt's defense of *Der Ruf*'s format was more complex than a mere disparagement of American-style mass media. He was presumably expressing a commonly held opinion among the staff and supervisors of *Der Ruf* that the pervasiveness of mass culture had facilitated the demise of democracy in Germany. These intellectuals, who espoused a variety of political persuasions, ranging from conservative Catholicism to Socialism, all agreed that the rousing of emotions and anti-intellectualism had hastened Germany's fall from grace. By purging mass-culture from their journalistic enterprise and, conversely, by producing an intellectual newspaper, the protagonists of *Der Ruf* registered a symbolic break with the anti-intellectual tone of National Socialism.

"The ideological trend of *Der Ruf* springs from the traditions and convictions which the staff possesses in common with a large section of the German people at a time when the German spirit and the German conscience was not dictated by one faction in the homeland," declared an article in the June 7, 1945, edition of *Der Ruf*.[13] The dictatorship of National Socialism had been fundamentally anti-intellectual, this article noted. Therefore, *Der Ruf* promised to liberate its reading public from the "Rosenberg cultural morass" by providing liberal portions of native German intellectual antidotes for the numbing effects of mass culture, such as the works of Schiller, Goethe, and other apostles of rational thought.[14]

An intellectual counterattack on the supposedly symbiotic link between National Socialism and mass culture was not the only reason for the often ponderous tone of *Der Ruf*. Evasive prose had the obvious advantage of avoiding direct confrontation with any segment of the reading public, including those who still identified some redeeming qualities in the National Socialist cause. Schoenstedt advised his staff to employ "subtlety," as well as to avoid topics and debates "stirring up political emotions or injuring national pride." Indeed, the only significant restriction on the editors was to refrain at all costs from antagonizing the camps' inmates by belittling German nationalism.

> In view of the fact that certain German prisoners have become highly sensitive to attempts to "propagandize" them, every effort will be made to avoid antagonizing them at the outset. Although there can be no compromise with the Fascist ideology, the magazine should avoid a too obvious glorification of the democratic ideals. Criticism of Germany and Germans, as distinct from Hitler and the Nazi party, will have to be handled most delicately. . . . Military themes, when appropriate, should be treated in such a way as not to offend the prisoner's natural pride as soldiers. For example, the Stalingrad debacle should be treated not as an indictment of the *German* military strategy but of the High Command—with the implication that the Supreme Commander was responsible for this spectacular defeat.[15]

Driven by this requirement to abstain from direct attacks on contemporary German culture and society, the texts were collections of nuances and veiled, often hesitant criticism. Thus, in lauding the liberal thought of Gotthold Ephraim Lessing, in particular his endorsement of cultural tolerance and opposition to "exaggerated nationalism and the narrow-minded spirit of caste systems," *Der Ruf* lamented the sad fact that between 1933 and 1945 "the critical spirit of Lessing was suppressed." This use of the passive tense circumvented the need for finger-pointing or for a painful autopsy of the demise of German Enlightenment, an issue that might have irked some of the readers.[16] As part of *Der Ruf*'s effort to dodge such potential political landmines, the Germany presented in its pages was extremely abstract, curiously devoid of regional differences and ethnic loyalties, and deliberately silent on religious rifts between Catholics and Protestants.

References to the Holocaust and Jews were also quite few and far between. Of all the sensitive issues tackled by *Der Ruf*, the "Jewish question" was, of course, the most sensitive. It involved developing a strategy of ambiguous prose that would acknowledge the great tragedy of the Holocaust without challenging too strictly the latent anti-Semitism of the average POW. Indeed, the first article that actually recognized and even condemned German atrocities against Jews softened the blow with innuendos that Germany's Jews were partly responsible for their tragic predicament.

> The situation of the Jews in Germany was altogether more complex than in England because certain groups among them did not act discreetly in defending themselves, a defense which in itself is understandable. Important German Jews such as Rathenau and Wassermann had emphasized the care that they should exercise, but in many instances their exhortations went unheeded.[17]

In this paragraph, inserted in the middle of an article that laid the blame for the Holocaust on Hitler rather than on the German people, *Der Ruf* appeared to accept, albeit cautiously, the commonly held view that Jews in highly visible occupations, such as international banking, had not always placed German interests before their own personal and ethnic loyalties. As this article demonstrates, hazy prose and complicated syntax facilitated discussion of contentious problems; one could deflect attacks on the politics of sensitive articles by claiming miscomprehension on the part of readers.

Ambiguity as a procedure for veiling politically uncomfortable or intellectually precarious opinions was not invented by *Der Ruf*'s writers. Nuance had a long history of use in German political discourse; it was an especially favored form of expression in the contemporary and very riveting debate concerning the "real" attitude of the German people toward National Socialism. A central point of contention among German intellectuals in general, and the prisoner-writers of *Der Ruf* in particular, was the controversy over what, in retrospect, qualified as resistance to National Socialism. Key members of the editorial staff argued that not all Germans had acquiesced to the onslaught of the Nazi party. In addition to the few who actually belonged to underground resistance groups, Germans from all walks of life, so the argument went, had adopted a stance of passive resistance. Ordinary citizens had resisted the grip of Nazism through minor routine acts of defiance: by strengthening one's allegiance to the church, circulating antiestablishment jokes, or deliberately working in a shoddy manner. Some apologists even identified resistance in the act of joining the Nazi party for practical reasons while continuing to live a private life of decent human values. As men of letters the POW personnel of *Der Ruf* were particularly interested in the notion of passive, camouflaged resistance in the literary circles of Nazi Germany, the so-called genre of *Innere Emigration*/Inner Emigration.

The term Inner Emigration was coined by the novelist Frank Theiss, who had attempted to rationalize the position of those intellectuals who had remained in Nazi Germany after the rise of Hitler. Unable or unwilling to emigrate, these intellectuals allegedly sought to maintain their moral integrity by withdrawing from contemporary events into an introspective and purified fictional world of their own creation. Given the Third Reich's eagerness to project an image of an empire in which the arts flourished, Nazi Germany had tolerated literary works that did not conform to official dogma, provided that they were sufficiently removed in content and style from contemporary political and social affairs. Thus, an escapist literature based on distant historical themes as well as detached, aesthetic preoccupations survived, and even flourished under the Third Reich.

As the war drew to a close, the writers of this genre of Inner Emigration claimed that their deliberately nontopical writing qualified as resistance to the regime. Their works, the apologists contended, encouraged anti-Nazi sentiment through literary metaphors of opposition to National Socialism that were too subtle for the Nazi censors to perceive. Some members of the Inner Emigration even went so far as to claim that their contribution to the anti-Nazi cause far surpassed that of the literary exiles; the inner emigrants had stayed behind to fight the battle and confront the enemy under personally dangerous circumstances. Frank Theiss, the self-appointed spokesman for those who claimed resistance through detachment, accused Thomas Mann and other illustrious exiles of having deserted the German people, and therefore, of forfeiting the right to speak in their name.[18]

The articles in *Der Ruf* reflected sharp differences among its staff concerning the contribution of inner emigres. Those who rejected any glorification of Inner Emigration supported their views by quoting the prominent leaders of German intellectual opposition to Nazism. Thomas Mann's blunt rejection of the premise of Inner Emigration received ample coverage in *Der Ruf*. The ninth issue of the paper carried a report of Mann's speech at the Library of Congress, where he attacked the historic tendency of German intellectuals to avoid confrontation with reactionary political forces, preferring instead to withdraw within themselves. "Revolution did not occur in the intellectual realm of the Germans," Mann stated. Whenever confronted with the opportunity to take a moral stand against reaction, German intellectuals "shied away at the appearance of freedom and took refuge in the realms of music and metaphysics," which he identified as being "mystical, removed from reality, individual and anti-social."[19]

The opposing faction within *Der Ruf* quoted Friedrich Meinecke's answer to those who admonished the silent intellectuals of the Third Reich. These critics, Meinecke maintained in an article originally published in a Munich newspaper edited by American occupation forces, were unaware of the reign of "paralyzing terror" under which he and others had lived. He argued that despite extremely difficult circumstances, the intellectuals who remained behind had made a significant contribution to humanity by keeping the flame of Germany's "divine and eternal" intellectual contribution to western civilization, be it the music of Bach and Beethoven or the treatises of Kant and Goethe.[20]

In the tradition of the Inner Emigration many of the articles in support of introspective resistance were couched in subtle metaphors and vague illusions taken from nature. "Just as the . . . river always seeks the path of least resistance, making one compromise after another with the terrain and landscape through which it must wind its way to the sea," the paper quoted Stephan Jenard, "so we humans must adapt ourselves to life. . . . This doesn't mean renunciation," the article continued with obvious allusions to the Inner Emigration, "but involuntary adaptation without taking our eye from the goal."[21]

By late 1945, references to Inner Emigration suggest reconciliation among the staff members and a gradual acceptance of intellectual introspectiveness as a bona fide form of resistance. "The Spiritual Powers," published in mid-November 1945, informed the readers of *Der Ruf* that all intellectuals who had found a way to resist the onslaught of National Socialism—those who had chosen to oppose the Third Reich in exile as well as those who had retreated from reality into a detached intellectual world—were equally worthy of praise. In fact, the article singled out those citizens of Germany who remained at home "often in despair and isolation" but did not stop believing in the spiritual powers of their nation."[22]

The closing of the ranks over the issue of Inner Emigration resulted most probably from the need to resist a common threat. Gradually, as the true nature of Germany's horrors became public knowledge, the German POWs found themselves at loggerheads with some of their American overseers. The issue of contention was the idea of collective guilt, the culpability and ultimate punishment of the German people as a whole for the crimes against humanity carried out in their name. Some of the POW custodians were the children of Jews of German descent. Others were German-Jews who had read the writing on the wall, or intellectuals who had chosen to leave Germany rather than attempt to practice their individualistic craft under the mantel of harsh political censorship. Not surprisingly, some of these individuals charged with running the lives of German POWs were supporters of a policy of collective guilt. Naturally, even the most guilt-ridden POWs, including the inmate staff of *Der Ruf*, rejected the notion of communal culpability. Swiftly, the POW writers found their relations with their guardians quite strained by this significant difference of opinion. The German author and former *Der Ruf* staff member, Hans Werner Richter, recalled acrimonious arguments with unnamed American custodians over the issue of collective guilt, arguments that he claimed included threats of removal from the Factory and editorial staff of *Der Ruf*.[23] Elsewhere an anonymous staff member, presumably Alfred Andersch, stated that Captain Walter Schoenstedt was responsible for these threats. He insinuated that Schoenstedt's allegedly harsh censorship was not only anti-German, it was anti-American, too. Schoenstedt, he suggested, was a Communist sympathizer.

> Schoenstedt was a modestly well-known Communist writer during the Weimar period. . . . Anyway, during the *Ruf* period, he somewhat secretively, but strictly, espoused the Communist-Russian line. Regarding such issues as the collective guilt of the German people, or the benefits of the Potsdam Agreement, he adopted, at the very best, the American position. [His position] on cultural, literary, and other issues evoked strong differences of opinion as well as threats to deport both R [Hans Werner Richter] and myself to a penal camp. Anyway, Schoenstedt saw to it that *Der Ruf* would feature nothing that contradicted either the American or the Russian position.[24]

Nothing in the records of the SPD supports these grave contentions, which were made after the fact and as part of a campaign to remove the cloud of collaboration from *Der Ruf* staff members. In fact, quite the opposite seems to be the case. Whatever pressure might have been applied on the editorial staff of *Der Ruf*, it definitely did not affect their articles on the cardinal issue of collective guilt. The prisoner-writers rejected quite openly the idea of "guilt." They used *Der Ruf* to advocate, instead, the idea of "collective responsibility," by which they meant that Germany had an obligation to aid the surviving victims of Nazism. Such a commitment would be voluntary and not part of an Allied attempt to punish the entire German people. Collective responsibility was based on the assumption that most Germans had been seduced and deceived, and had not been active participants in or supporters of the Nazi state. *Der Ruf*'s editorial staff attempted to support such a presumption and soften the tenor of their American adversaries by citing venerable Americans who had opposed collective punishment. Abraham Lincoln appeared as a historical analogy to the German predicament. During the American Civil War, *Der Ruf* observed, "Lincoln was often accused of being too lenient toward the hostile South. A lady even advised him to annihilate his enemies. But Lincoln answered her, 'Madam, don't I annihilate them by making them my friends?' "[25]

"With good reason," the article added in an obvious reference to collective punishment, "this humane act toward one's enemies" was an example of why "Abraham Lincoln is considered one of the great statesmen of all time." In addition to historical analogies, *Der Ruf* also relied on the comments of contemporary Americans. A typical article, entitled "The Voice of Reason," cited University of Chicago President Robert M. Hutchins's rejection of the "pernicious doctrine of communal guilt." Hutchins argued that a doctrine that implied "that all Germans are murderers" conflicted with the insistence "that we are working for a world in which all men would be brothers." The editors of *Der Ruf* craftily linked Hutchins's opposition to collective guilt with his views on Communism. The contradiction between the humanism of the American body politic and the policy of collective guilt, according to Hutchins, was as ludicrous as the idea that "we are opposed to dictatorship, but the dictatorship of the proletariat is an exception."[26]

All these various challenges—the variety of political shadings among the POW staff, their desire to avoid antagonizing any segment within the enclosed world of POW camps, as well as the ideological clashes with American custodians—contributed in one way or another to the dissipation of clear prose from the pages of *Der Ruf*. However, in distinct contrast to those parts of the magazine devoted to German issues, some aspects of the publication were clear, uncomplicated, and comprehensible.

The America presented by *Der Ruf* at the behest of the supervising officers was a world without confusing ideologies, a country governed by common sense, personal restraint, and totally devoid of the great ideological cleavages of the Old World. This American society, lacking the cultural and political trappings of despotism, had produced a healthy society, quite immune to the pernicious hold of vested interest and entrenched elites. If any part of *Der Ruf* was dictated by American supervisors, it was this depiction of the United States. These portions of *Der Ruf* were distinctly different in style and content from the German-oriented segments, and were obviously fashioned or perhaps written by someone outside of the POW staff of the magazine.

The most distinctive facet of American society presented in the pages of *Der Ruf* was the conspicuous lack of ideological parties and class tensions in American political life. The articles explained that because of the local loyalties of candidates, both major political parties were equally lacking in abstract doctrines. "Their task is a merely practical one and does not include any ideological quarrels. . . . They do not pursue any confessional or class interests." Under these circumstances, the issues facing both the parties and the electorates were fleeting and transitory, never arousing the depths of passion associated with entrenched political beliefs. Germany, too, *Der Ruf* implied, could obtain a similar political system, where voters would be called upon to decide upon swiftly changing "momentary program[s]" rather than to vote according to enduring commitments.[27] These presumably American-dictated articles lauded German emulation of their democratic conquerors' creed, such as the Five-Point Program endorsed by the political parties of postwar Germany which renounced "all ideological and doctrinal platforms," focusing instead "on the necessities of daily life."[28] Much like their American masters, the anonymous authors of the pro-American texts believed that the harmonious, casteless American system could be reproduced anywhere, including in Germany, through artful social engineering.

This fervent belief in the universality of important aspects of the American political culture was an integral part of the SPD's endorsement of internationalism. This gospel of One World claimed ecumenical political values ranging from a sometimes elusive codex of human rights, to the more practical opening up of the marketplace of ideas. Early editions of *Der Ruf* cautiously presented this idea in the form of pan-Europeanism, the existence of a common European heritage forged in antiquity, and gaining substance from the Enlightenment. Later editions spoke of shared universal values. The omnipresent articles on the virtues of social engineering lauded a humane and rational "world architecture" sharing characteristics "beyond the sphere of any individual nation or even . . . continent."[29]

The newspaper relied heavily on architectural metaphors in its preaching of a new, democratic world order. Almost every issue of the periodical had long discussions on the merits of democratic, antidespotic architecture. In the spirit of the Bauhaus, one of the primary symbols of the Weimar Republic discussed on the pages of *Der Ruf*, the periodical advocated "rational" city planning, based upon economic imperatives and fostering individual freedom through a deliberate planning process of decentralization. The old imperial cities had been reduced to "rubble," thereby providing a unique opportunity to renounce the intimidating trappings of an elitist "historical decorative and ornamental art."[30] This enthusiastic endorsement of internationalism, and the belief that even the most abysmal political system could be salvaged through expert tinkering, appears to have been dictated by American overseers. The prose was lucid, and the positive prognosis for German redemption contrasted sharply with opinions of the POW writers of *Der Ruf*.

Indeed, the staff's articles on Germany's future, in general, and the POW camps, in particular, projected a significantly more pessimistic forecast. In the issues of late 1945 and early 1946, the prisoner-writers wrote in no uncertain terms that the changes that American officials had discerned among their fellow POWs were superficial, smacking suspiciously of opportunism rather than true conversion.

An angry article, scheduled for publication in the November 15, 1945, edition of *Der Ruf*, but subsequently deleted at the last moment, lashed out at the charade of democratic politics in various POW camps. Overnight, and triggered by rumors that cooperative prisoners would be the first to be repatriated, both irredentists and the noncommitted prudently feigned conversion to democracy. "So Camp Butner, North Carolina voted ninety-five percent in favor of democracy, thereby obediently falling into the ranks of a new ideology," the offending article commented in disbelief. "Ninety-five percent—it sounds like an old well-known fairy tale. As you know, Goebbels never allowed lower figures," the article added in obvious allusion to what appeared to be a disingenuous demonstration of mass conversion. On the formation of democratic parties in the camps, all of which instantaneously endorsed a strong anti-Fascist stance, *Der Ruf* proposed adding a "Party of the Knights of Opportunism" and a "Party of the United Former National-Socialistic Santa Clauses."[31]

In open defiance of American supervising authorities, the Staff of *Der Ruf* refused to publish favorable accounts of these elections. The staff's spokesman, Karl Kuntze, informed the PMG that the Factory workers believed that the whole idea of political elections in the POW camps "was entirely wrong and will do more harm than good." He added that the staff of *Der Ruf* refused to pay tribute to the election experiment.

> We believe that the practice of creating parties in prisoner of war camps is the best way to split the whole camp and give Nazis still existing there the best opportunity to hide. . . . As in the case of camp McKall, only 10% of the inmates have ever voted in a true democratic election. Therefore we believe that, at the beginning of a true democratization of our fellow men, an education for democracy should take place and not the foundation of parties with slogans. . . . The German has, during the time of the national socialistic government, never had a democratic election. He could give his vote for a plebiscite. He voted for "Adolf Hitler as Fuehrer"; "For the annexation of the Saarland"; "For the war." And these elections always came out with 99%. If today a camp votes 95.9% "For Democracy," we believe that the majority has understood very little the idea of what democracy really means.[32]

Der Ruf staff members argued that the reactionary politics of the youthful inmates in the camps proved that POW endorsements of democracy were superficial, if not disingenuous. "Most of the youngsters in the prisoner of war camps are still the same swaggering braggarts who want to talk big and set the policy in our barracks," an inmate from Camp Dexter complained in an unusually frank letter to the editor. "Megalomania, and the idea of being supermen are still to be found in most of these youngsters," he added.[33]

The inmate-editors of *Der Ruf* found additional evidence of the powerful pull of National Socialism in the persistent tendency of inmates to wear "Nazi emblems," by which they meant any form of military regalia other than the insignia of rank.

> Don't be proud of medals and tinkling,
> Don't be proud of scars and our glorious time,
> For, those who sent you to the trenches,
> Were Junkers, frantic politicians, and devious bosses.[34]

In quoting the words of dissident poet Kurt Tucholsky, written between the two world wars, *Der Ruf*'s editors lashed out at the nagging presence of "that dead bird"—the swastika eagle—on the uniforms and caps of inmates. The intellectual staff of *Der Ruf* never understood the function of defiance in maintaining one's self-respect in captivity. "I am not a Nazi, despite my sticking to the eagle; but at least I have character." Such a statement made no sense to the staff of *Der Ruf*; these Factory workers were, after all, the marginal men of the military subculture.

There is little doubt that *Der Ruf* made little impression on the politics and worldview of the average POW. Frederick Joseph Doyle's oral history of German prisoners of war in the southwest United States shows quite clearly that most prisoners did not even remember the existence of such a magazine. Those who recalled the paper stated that they did not bother to read what was basically an irrelevant publication.[35] Helmut Hörner's diary of his life as a POW in the United States records disbelief that the paper reflected the views of his peers. "Do you seriously believe that this newspaper was written by German prisoners of war?" a friend asks rhetorically, describing *Der Ruf* somewhat cryptically as "manure in a cheesebox."[36]

The POWs' poor assessment of *Der Ruf* had little to do with Nazi intimidation and/or the hopeless political passivism of the German people. In actual fact, *Der Ruf* failed to accomplish its goals because its editors and mentors maintained their studious detachment from the concerns of ordinary POWs. As such, *Der Ruf* introduced nothing new into the lives of the cross section of the German nation incarcerated in the camps.

In a particularly personal exposition of the worldview he brought to *Der Ruf*, Alfred Andersch explained why *Der Ruf* seemed so detached and aloof. "I hope I shall always refrain from any attempt to convince people," Andersch wrote in "The Cherries of Freedom," his tale of his own war experiences.

> One can only try to show them the possibilities they have to choose from. Even that is presumptuous enough, for who knows another man's possibilities? Another man is not only a fellow man, he is also *other,* someone we can never know. Unless we love him. I didn't love my comrades. That is why I never tried to convince them of anything.[37]

The detached tone of *Der Ruf* resulted mainly from the predominant presence of intellectual staff writers who harbored contempt for the ordinary soldiers in POW camps. Instead of producing a journal for public consumption, the inmate staff of *Der Ruf* treated their operation as a private forum. The concerns of the potential audience of POWs were superfluous. "It seems strange," an American captor informs Alfred Andersch in another of his semiautobiographical stories, "that living as a prisoner under conditions of the most perfect artistic freedom, conditions that ought to enable you to carry out your most ambitious plans, you confine yourself to a direct treatment of your most immediate preoccupations. You insist on being subjective; it's a pity."[38]

Such aloofness did not go unchallenged. *Der Ruf*'s attitude toward popular culture, in particular, produced intense demands for change. Most outside analyses of *Der Ruf* focused mainly on the "highbrow" content and language. "The average German of military age is intensely interested in sports, particularly in soccer, swimming and skiing," a report from the Department of War observed. Therefore, the report advised, "articles and photographs dealing with such activities in the U.S., together with more non-political cartoons, including one or two comic strips, would develop a much larger body of readers and help to engender a friendlier attitude towards this country."[39] In a somewhat half-hearted gesture of compromise, the supervising SPD official, Walter Schoenstedt, suggested using German cartoons from 1848 so as "to remind them that there was a time in Germany when they were willing to fight and die for democracy."[40] However, he adamantly refused any fundamental popularization of the paper.

An equally significant criticism of the paper, written by the exiled political scientist Kurt Hesse, focused on the anomaly of a German newspaper with little or no news from Germany, and the studious avoidance of the most central concerns of the inmate-audience. "Commonplace human issues," such as "is the currency stable? What is being done to care for the small investors who have lost their savings, widows and orphans? Is anything being done for the women and children of the war prisoners?" were conspicuously absent from *Der Ruf*. Rather than "opening up problems in the editorial articles" Hesse urged the insertion of "extensive news reporting from Germany."[41]

Critics of *Der Ruf* complained that, in their zeal to avoid antagonizing potential readers, the editors had failed to impress upon their audience the unprecedented scourge of National Socialism and the irreparable destruction of cherished human values that Germany had inflicted on the entire world. A Pentagon report noted that some articles in *Der Ruf* deliberately distorted the horrific dimensions of Nazi Germany's war against humanity. The report singled out as an example the lead article of the April 15, 1945, edition of *Der Ruf*. Entitled "The Productive Powers," this anonymous article compared the Second World War to the Napoleonic Wars. Postwar Germany, the article noted, could take comfort from Germany's swift recovery in the post-Napoleonic period. "Century after century Germany, devastated and despoiled by war, has been able to recover because it was able to preserve its productive powers." The implication that World War II was merely another war and that Germany was the perennial victim did not serve the purpose of "dispelling Nazi ideology," the Pentagon report observed.[42]

The report went on to note that the paper appeared at times to perpetuate dangerous myths, most particularly the "stab-in-the-back" explanation for Germany's military defeats. The April 15, 1945, edition contained a critical article on Japan, but one that condemned Japan for all the wrong reasons. The article rebuked Japan for her "selfish" decision to not "join the war against Russia in the Autumn of 1941 notwithstanding her military alliance with Germany and Italy."[43]

As early as July 1945, and in response to such criticism, the embattled staff of *Der Ruf* offered its collective resignation citing, among other things, an unwillingness to lower standards and popularize the newspaper. Moreover, the staff complained of demoralization, "since they have seen other less cooperative prisoners of war repatriated to Germany."[44] Indeed, toward the end of July 1945, the SPD began planning for a new editorial staff who could write on "a low enough level to be readily understood by the vast majority of the prisoner of war population . . . a combination of the quality of the *New York Times* and the simplicity of the N.Y. *Daily News*." Major General Archer Lerch, the PMG, concurred, although he cautioned not "to bring it too low. Mix in a little (not less than 25%) 8th grade stuff with the high level."[45]

Der Ruf's staff, was, however, left intact, with no discernible change in style and content. By autumn 1945, the SPD had begun planning new and direct forms of reeducation through crash courses on democracy. Therefore, reform measures for *Der Ruf* no longer seemed as urgent as they had before. Moreover, the American supervisors at the Factory were never entirely convinced of the validity of the criticism leveled against *Der Ruf*.

They shared the POW staff's misgivings about popularizing the paper. In fact, the entire tone of the program, of which *Der Ruf* was merely one element, suggests that the American staff members were as responsible as the Germans for the elitist nature of the paper.

As intellectuals, the Americans accepted the assumption that the target audience should be primarily intellectuals—the men they regarded as the potential leaders of a new, postwar Germany. American officials sympathized with their German compatriots and endorsed their suspicion of low common cultural denominators. The officers of the SPD never seriously attempted to bridge the intellectual chasm between the content of *Der Ruf* and the interests of the rank and file. Instead, they urged increased production of a similar product. By offering a series of Great Books, translations of exemplary fiction and non-fiction, the managers of the Idea Factory showed no inclination to retool their production line to meet the demands of a wider marketplace of ideas.

CHAPTER SIX

Literature: The Battle of the Books

IN A WORLD dominated by contests of technology and brute force, the officers of the Special Programs Division (SPD) remained convinced that the rational exposition of ideas could solve the scourge of global conflict. They argued consistently that controlling intellectual expression by such means as the regulation of reading material represented the key to ultimate and enduring victory. Technology might decide the battle, but winning the war hinged upon the triumph of ideas.

In their war of words, the SPD's commanding officers did not limit their concerns to the curtailing of enemy propaganda, or, conversely, the saturating of the enemy with bombardments of ideologically correct thoughts. They were equally preoccupied with ostensibly innocuous material, including popular escapist literature. Such material was considered highly prejudicial to the war effort because of the demands it made upon the reader's time and interest. Major Maxwell McKnight, the assistant director of the SPD, charged that the "distribution of books which serve no other purpose than to entertain" severely undermined the command and control of POW camps by providing distractions and avenues of avoidance.[1]

McKnight and his fellow officers in the reeducation program maintained that it was possible to engineer consent and acquiescence to American control, both in the camps and beyond, through the minds of their prisoners. The management of POW literature was based on the assumption that controlling the prisoners' intellectual diet would diminish the need for a harsh penitentiary regime. The literary program strove to pierce the mass deception of National Socialism by replacing the false consciousness of Nazism with an alternative, and thoroughly American cultural agenda. Acceptance of the aesthetic and social standards of the rulers would lead to the authentic cultural reorientation of a defeated enemy. Most SPD officers agreed that the point of departure for such an exercise was the regulation of the prisoners' reading material as the primary conveyor of ideas. However, devising the actual inventory of politically correct literature proved to be somewhat more difficult than agreement on the strategy itself.

The SPD launched this campaign for a methodic regulation of reading material only after V-E Day. Previously, local camp commanders had enjoyed considerable discretion in defining the content of camp libraries as well as approving lists of magazines and newspapers, foreign and domestic, that passed their censorship. The Office of the Provost Marshal General (OPMG) and the SPD had limited their role to issuing periodic lists of acceptable and inappropriate German books as an aid to camp commanders who lacked the necessary language or cultural background to review German reading material.

Guidelines issued to Assistant Executive Officers (AEOs) offered rules of thumb for the banning of books. "All books which misinterpret . . . the significance of the contributions of all races" to American civilization must be rejected, the instructions stated, presumably referring to the anti-Semitic undertones inherent in many German appraisals of America's strengths and weaknesses. In addition, the SPD banned books laced with "contempt for America as a country without its own 'culture,' without a 'soul,' a country which is only interested in making money." The guidelines also urged removing "books which represent the Allied Nations," including the Soviet Union, in an unsympathetic light.[2]

As far as books on Germany were concerned, AEOs were ordered to ban all references to the "Shameful Peace" of Versailles or the "stab-in-the-back myth." In addition to the banning of obvious works of propaganda written under the auspices of the Third Reich, AEOs were forewarned to censor literature that covertly supported National Socialism. Hence, the SPD systematically barred historical studies and novels that sang the praises of powerful German political figures or anything that smacked of pan-Germanism.[3] AEOs received little guidance as to what books they should actively seek other than some vague advice to adopt books "which show the contribution to civilization of countries which have none of the Nazi complexes such as 'living space' or 'Volk ohne Raum,'" as well as "books which stress the contributions of German culture in the early part of the 19th century."[4]

Eventually, as the program progressed, the SPD became dissatisfied with the merely weeding out of questionable books. Instead of censorship, the reeducation staff sought control. In a May 1945 memorandum to the Provost Marshal General (PMG), SPD director Lt. Colonel Edward Davison proposed for the first time to "discourage the distribution of technical books" because "they are of no value to this program." The underlying premise behind the control of literary material, he argued, was that

German prisoners of war are intellectually and ideologically adolescent. They will need intellectual protection and guidance before they will be qualified to form judgments actually representative of their native intelligence. This protection and guidance must carefully establish a sound balance of emphasis. Nazi propaganda has emphasized and distorted such subjects as Anglo-American imperialism, capitalistic decadence, race supremacy, and the glory of military conquest. To establish a balance in the minds of prisoners of war, they must be shielded from any emphasis of these subjects which in any way parallels Nazi propaganda.[5]

By June 1945, the SPD initiated the move beyond an advisory role and the drawing up of lists toward a more exacting procedure. The new policy entailed a thorough sweep of camp libraries, as well as a prohibition of "the further entry into prisoner of war camps of any book or other literature which does not directly serve the interests of the program."[6] In deciding to ban material "which in any way parallels Nazi propaganda," the SPD established an elaborate mechanism for sifting through books, both English language and German. Each suggestion for camp libraries received an evaluation from two monitors from among the POW Idea Factory workers. The standard reader form required a short synopsis of the content, a "suitability" recommendation for distribution among all POWs or only certain "safe" segments of the population, as well as suggestions for distribution: sale in camp canteens, or library use only.

The POW readers routinely provided suggestions for changes in the text, such as subtle shifts in the translation of key terms, or the actual removal of questionable passages. In a typical evaluation of a popular sociological study, *Children of the USA*, the reader, Karl Kuntze, suggested "to use the word 'Democracy' only very seldom" in order to remove the suspicion of propaganda from the minds of potential readers.[7] These prisoner recommendations were then passed on to a supervising staff official for final evaluation. Henry Ehrmann, the scholar of constitutional history who had joined the program as a civilian advisor, filled this role along with a small group of junior officers.

Ehrmann's personal recommendations reveal standardized guidelines for final decisions, presumably rules passed down by his superiors. He routinely banned material that doubted the ideological cohesion of Allied forces and questioned the motives of the Soviet Union, obviously the most problematic of allies. The prisoner "reviewers at the Factory recommend . . . the volume by N. Micklem, *National Socialism and Christianity*," Ehrmann noted in a typical report to his superiors. "However, I advise once more strongly against distribution, because the volume, written in 1939, constantly puts Russian Bolshevism and Nazism on the same level."[8] Factory censorship maintained, of course, the previous policy of banning books that rationalized German aggressiveness, or blamed outside forces for precipitating the war, such as "fickle" American resolve at Versailles. But the new policy did not stop at censoring criticism of the Allies; comments detrimental to German culture and the culpability of ordinary Germans were also banned. In order to avoid antagonizing the

POWs, Ehrmann and his assistants censored references to the notion of collective guilt.

The most important aspect of the new policy was not, however, its deletion of reading material, but its guidelines for appropriate literature. The approved reading material effectively rewrote the history of Germany by emphasizing disproportionately the presence of consistent humanistic and democratic trends in Germany's recent political past. The readers' reports demonstrated a determined effort to explain away National Socialism as an aberration and a conspiracy of the powerful few, rather than a natural, pathological consequence of German culture. The general tone of the readers' reports implied that the ultimate concern of the SPD's literary program was to highlight the existence of democratic elements in German politics, even in its darkest moments. A typical report on a controversial study by Emil Ludwig, *The Moral Conquest of Germany* (1945)—written by the prisoner-monitor Karl Kuntze and endorsed by Henry Ehrmann—illustrates the type of historical interpretation sought by the SPD.

> He [Ludwig] writes in one of the next chapters: "The Germans in 1932, in their last free elections, having choices among eight principal parties, cast 12,000,000 votes for the Nazis, against 7,000,000 for the Socialists." In saying so he is entirely right as far as only these two parties are concerned. But Mr. Ludwig probably forgot to mention that the Socialists were not the only ones opposing Nazism. In this election the Nazis cast 33.1% of all votes against 54% of [*sic*] Democrats, Socialists, and Communists. By not mentioning this fact the uninformed reader gains the impression that there was no real opposition at all.[9]

Driven by this effort to reinterpret German society and culture in a favorable light, prisoner-readers as well as their supervisors sought literary counterpoises to some of the cultural stereotypes of German culture. Ehrmann expressed great satisfaction with a pamphlet on the history of political thought published by the YMCA because of its treatment of both Fichte and Hegel "as protagonists of liberal thought" rather than as ideologues of "reaction or even totalitarianism."[10]

In addition to offering revisionist interpretations of German history, the reading program sought to eliminate detrimental depictions of the United States as the land of under-culture, materialism, deep racial cleavages, and isolationism. The United States, as represented in the approved library selections of the SPD, was a country without substantial class differences, united in its support of universal humanistic values, and devoid of profound ethnic tensions.

The political contours of the United States that the SPD hoped to convey to the prisoners were outlined in a report on the decision to ban Charles and Mary Beard's *Basic History of the United States* (1944). The program's monitors and the staff supervisors expressed concern with the "latent isolationism" inherent in the Beards' economic interpretation of America's involvement in international power politics, as well as the book's consistent portrayal of idealism and principles as nothing more than a rationalization of economic and political considerations. The Beards' "attitude becomes particularly clear in their treatment of the origins and consequences of the Spanish-American War," the monitors noted. They cited the authors' analysis of turn-of-the-century American politicians' "burning desire" to partake in the colonial adventures of western powers in order to "divert the people's thoughts from domestic discontent over plutocracy and poverty . . . to world politics" and to dampen "if not extinguish radicalism at home."[11] The Beards' detrimental interpretation of the efficacy of democracy, and their contention that public opinion rarely affected the concerns of American politicians, was in itself grounds for banning the book:

> On page 464, the authors speak first about the American resolve to stay out of the next war and add immediately afterwards that President Roosevelt at Chicago 1937, "to the amazement of the country," indicated a change in his previous position of abstention from any foreign quarrels. . . . On page 465, commenting on the destroyer deal of September 1940, the authors say that "objectors" charged the president with arbitrary actions, and accused him of having committed an act of war as defined by International Law. This method of stating the President's foreign policy by quotations from the speeches and writings of isolationists is then adhered to by the authors continuously.[12]

To a large degree, the policies of the reading program prefigured a dominant strain in postwar American historiography that portrayed America as country unafflicted by the social cleavages of the Old World. The reports, as passed on to the SPD's commanding officers, conveyed a quest for a consensual interpretation of American society. The officers in charge of literature devised a reading list that focused on the unifying dimensions of American society rather than on its divisions. Their choice of suitable reading material trivialized the ideological, social, and economic schisms in American society. Hence, the very few German-language textbooks on American history—even the explicitly favorable texts—raised doubts in the minds of the program's reviewers due to the inordinate attention paid to ethnic and other forms of multiple loyalties in the United States. A fairly positive textbook on American history, the 1932 edition of Schoenemann's *Geschichte der Vereinigten Staaten* received unfavorable reviews at the Idea Factory because it "repeatedly regretted that the Americanization of the German-Americans has caused the loss of valuable elements to the Deutschtum."[13]

The SPD attempted to support this elaborate mechanism for monitoring the flow of books to the camps by publishing its own versions of approved literature. The *Buecherreihe Neue Welt*/New World Bookshelf was a series of ideologically correct books published by the OPMG and sold exclusively at local camp canteens. The premise behind this New World series was, of course, the endorsement of the "Great Books" tradition that the drafted professors brought with them from their college campuses. It was mainly for the purpose of planning such a literary endeavor that SPD director Edward Davison had recruited Howard Mumford Jones, the esteemed Harvard scholar. However, instead of simply prescribing a list of great books representative of a universal tradition of humanism, Jones began his mission by criticizing the underlying principles of such an exercise.

While never actually challenging the fundamental assumption that the control of minds was of greater importance than the mere coercive control of behavior, Jones argued that literature offered poor material for such an enterprise. Shortly after joining the program, and in a thinly veiled attack on the SPD's literary program that he chose to publish in the *New York Times*, Jones challenged the supposition that there was anything universally redeeming in literature. He contended that any comparison between the "German tradition of art and literature" and the commercial nature of contemporary American literature—"determined by values in a land of billboards, headlines, commercial broadcasting, skywriting, and the comic strip"—was quite self-defeating.

It is . . . unfortunate that Germans cannot be confidently referred to a body of contemporary writing admired and respected by the Americans themselves, writing which is not involved in violence or in abnormal psychology or in the tensions on which the modern novel has been stretched as on a rack. . . . If one refers the German reader to Jefferson, Emerson, Thoreau and the American classics, he is likely to ask: "Very good, indeed. Now who follows them?" If one answers that the many notable literary names are not representative of American values, the German answer is: "Why not? Do your critics admire what is essentially unrepresentative or are you whistling against the wind? If the flood tide of your literature is one picturing an America that is violent, restless, unhappy and ill at ease, how do we know, how shall we be assured these quieter and perhaps lesser books you want us to read are not the propaganda from your OWI [Office of War Information]?"[14]

The problem of the literary approach to indoctrination, Jones summarized in an article written after the dismantling of the reeducation program, was the erroneous endorsement of literature as "an aid to intercultural understanding." In a scholarly analysis, which presumably served both as an autopsy of the POW literary program as well as a critique of "our teachings in the schools, the colleges, and the universities of the United States," Jones exposed two substantial caveats in the literature-as-cultural-bridge approach. To begin with, he dismissed the idea that literature provided understanding and "insight into an alien way of life." Intercultural understanding among nations through the medium of literature had indeed occurred in the past, Jones conceded, but only among well-defined intellectual sectors of society:

> For example, in the eighteenth century the Western World (including the future United States) nourished a truly cosmopolitan, a truly international culture operative among a small literate minority in some nations. Horace Walpole, Frederick the Great, Catherine the Great, Benjamin Franklin and Voltaire could in a sense participate in this culture because they were products of the same literary and philosophical system. But what quality of intercultural understanding this fact exhibits is not clear. These persons and others like them were, to the extent that they participated in this cosmopolitanism, products of a single culture and not of the several national cultures to which they geographically were born.[15]

Jones went on to deny the presence of a class-transcending and universal force of humanism in great literary works. Instead he stressed the divisive currents of most national literatures, currents originating in the "emotional desire to keep the national language (and literature) unique and unbeholden to other nationalities." Moreover, and in direct challenge to the underlying propositions of the SPD, Jones stated that even if some "kind of intercultural understanding" could be gained from literature, the so-called great books would never yield the ever-elusive universal "emotional allegiance" sought by their champions. Jones illustrated his point by recalling the ambitious objectives of a class-conscious socialist literature in Europe prior to World War I, in particular its failure to evoke international condemnation of war among the ideologically faithful. Such fervent belief in the power of ideas expressed through words proved naive, he maintained.

> The German Socialists behaved like Germans; the French Socialists behaved like Frenchmen; and, by the by, to the great grief of American isolationists, American Socialists behaved like Americans. It was clear that the German Junkers understood German Socialists as Germans better than American Socialists understood them as Socialists.[16]

But perhaps the most severe limitation on the great books approach for either "cultural understanding" or indoctrination was the tyranny of the reader. Jones argued that great works of literature produced multiple interpretations, which were more a product of an individual reader's frame of mind than of some abstract cultural common denominator. One could not rely on any standard evocative message in great works, Jones stated quite categorically.

> Take as an instance the case of Homer. Consider the image of Homer in the mind of Virgil, in the mind of Chaucer, in the mind of George Chapman, in the mind of Madame Dacier, in the mind of Alexander Pope and in the mind of Lawrence of Arabia! In the course of this wonderful transformation we do not so much use Homer as a means of understanding Latin, medieval, Elizabethan, neo-classic and modern cultures as use these cultures to understand the minds of those who understood or misunderstood Homer![17]

Presumably affected by the misgivings of Jones as well as by the limited availability of politically reliable German translations, the OPMG included only a small number of American literary works in the New World series. Out of the original list of twenty-four books, only five were the works of American authors. None appeared to belong to the category of American classics; all were non-fiction, or semiautobiographical. Stephen Vincent Benét, modern American storyteller and creator of such seminal folk tales as *The Devil and Daniel Webster*, led the list. From all of Benét's wonderful tales and exciting panoramas of Americana, the SPD chose *America* (1944), an unfinished work, published posthumously by the Office of War Information (OWI). "Explicitly written with the aim of making the foreigner familiar with the main features of American history and American life," *America* was retranslated, presumably purged of any ambiguous prose "to fit the needs of the prisoners of war."[18] Of course, Benét's work revealed none of America's blemishes.

The second American choice was Wendell Willkie's *One World* (1943). Translated as *Unteilbare Welt*—"an indivisible world"—the book "demonstrated to the German prisoners of war that American isolationism is definitely dead and therefore there is no hope for a renewed German aggression." Undoubtedly, the former Republican presidential candidate's positive assessment of the Soviet Union as a workable "effective society" and "our ally in war" affected the decision to include this remarkable book in the series. The directive to seek books praising the United States' troublesome ally, also led to the inclusion of John Scott's, *Behind the Urals/Jenseits des Ural* (1942), the chronicles of a young American worker in the Soviet Union, "because of the need to counterattack Dr. Goebbels's propaganda on Soviet Russia" and "provide a healthy respect for the Russian achievements in this war."[19] In retrospect, such unqualified praise of the Soviet Union would come back to haunt the program in its final phases.

The great works of contemporary American fiction were represented by William Saroyan's *Human Comedy* (1943), "a fine picture of wartime America by an American author of foreign stock," and Ernest Hemingway's *For Whom the Bell Tolls* (1940), which the SPD described laconically as "a representative novel of an American writer."

Conspicuously absent from this short list of American literature for POWs was Jack London, by far the most popular American novelist in Germany between the two wars. London appealed to many Germans, according to literary critic Wayne Kvam, because his works catered to a wide variety of tastes. Socialists were attracted by London's leftist leanings, and the "youth of all ages" found his adventure stories appealing.[20] Moreover, National Socialists were fascinated by his many negative portrayals of "lesser" races, as well as London's infatuation with the Anglo-Saxon superman. Indeed, despite London's socialist creed, the cultural monitors of the Third Reich chose not to ban his books, thereby assuring his removal from the SPD's list of approved American literature.

Much like London, Hemingway was a highly popular American author in prewar Germany; he held a similar appeal for many different sectors in German society. His saving grace, and one of the reasons for his inclusion in the New World series, was his prominent critical attitude toward Fascism and National Socialism. He was one of the most widely translated American authors until the banning of his books in 1933. Writing on the eve of Hemingway's disappearance from German bookshelves, the literary critic Max Dietrich praised the American author for the elevation of his characters' own personal feelings above the ideological struggle portrayed in his books. The hero's individuality was the central theme of Hemingway's novels. His plots avoided overriding subservience to a greater cause or any sign of the tiresome metaphysical trappings that one would find in German historical novels, Dietrich added.[21]

American critics agreed. *Time* magazine noted in its review of *For Whom the Bell Tolls* that "however he may fancy himself as a leftist sympathizer, . . . Hemingway is well over the red sash. The bell in the book tolls for all mankind."[22] Writing for the *Saturday Review of Literature*, Howard Mumford Jones called the book "one of the finest and richest documents of the last decade." Jones noted that the novel's most redeeming quality was its ability to rise "out of partisanship into imaginative comprehensiveness."[23] Jones was particularly intrigued by the fact that Hemingway's hero, Robert Jordan, never displayed unquestioning ideological commitment, even though he fought for the Communist cause. Quite the contrary; Jordan—Hemingway's alter ego—acknowledged quite openly a variety of other motives for fighting other than political allegiance.

Hemingway's representation of his main characters as free spirits rather than embodiments of political ideas was the basis for the novel's suitability for reeducation. The book served a central facet of the SPD's reeducation program: the linking of all political evils to an uncritical acceptance of rigid ideological dogma of either left or right. *For Whom the Bell Tolls* reiterated a recurrent message in the SPD's curriculum that unbending "moral principles," rather than the acceptance of compromise and "constructive" ad-hoc assessments of crises, were the causes of war and human tragedy.[24] The American system had succeeded because it was based on an ideology of improvisation, individualism, and ad-hoc solutions to crises, rather than subservience to principle. Hemingway's *For Whom the Bell Tolls* illustrated this point neatly and with great literary skill.

The inclusion of Saroyan alongside Hemingway had little to do with literary merit or notoriety in Germany. Saroyan was unknown outside of the United States; *The Human Comedy* was Saroyan's first venture in writing a full-scale novel. Moreover, this tale of wartime in small-town California received scathing criticism when first published in the United States. Wallace Stegner described the novel's moral that "good always drives out sickness and evil, and that love conquers all," as naive and trite.[25] William Philips, who wrote a highly unfavorable review for the *Nation*, characterized Saroyan's world as an affected, overstocked and "enormous Five-and-Ten seen through the eyes of a child." In the course of his uncharitable review, Philips did, however grudgingly, acknowledge the wide appeal of the novel, and, presumably, the underlying reasons for its inclusion in the New World series for German POWs.

> He [Saroyan] has a touch—as the doctors used to say—of everything, a little of Eddie Guest, Billy Sunday, Ring Lardner, Henry Miller, even Hemingway. Hence he has been able to appeal to so many different kinds of readers and keep alive a sense of uncertainty as to whether he is a genuine *enfant terrible*, or merely an engaging raconteur.[26]

Such wide appeal, as well as Saroyan's studious avoidance of branding any one person, nation, or ethnic group as "bad" or incorrigible, made *The Human Comedy* a particularly appealing choice for reeducation. The novel was all the more attractive for these purposes because Saroyan portrayed ethnic and class divisions in the United States as nonissues. The America sought by the SPD was represented vividly in the ancient history classroom of old Miss Hicks, where the poor rub shoulders with the rich, and Catholic immigrants sit side by side with old Protestant stock. When, during the course of her lessons, tempers flare between the rich and the poor, the newcomer and the native-born, Miss Hicks swiftly places these altercations in their correct proportions.

Whether one of my children is rich or poor, Catholic or Protestant or Jew, white or black or yellow, brilliant or slow, genius or simple-minded, is of no matter to me, if there is humanity in him—if he has a heart—if he loves truth and honor—if he respects his inferiors, and loves his superiors. . . . (E)ach of you will begin to be truly human when, in spite of your natural dislike of one another, you will still respect one another. That is what it means to be civilized.[27]

Saroyan and Hemingway had been chosen as contemporary representatives of American literature mainly due to a favorable political evaluation of their respective texts; their personal history was important but, as the choice of the politically radical Hemingway suggests, obviously secondary. By contrast, choosing German authors was a more complex undertaking. The political credentials of the authors were at least as important as the ideological implications of the books. The only contemporary figures who made the list were the most outspoken critics of National Socialism. All German authors included in the series were exiles; the list did not include works of inner emigrants, perhaps a signal of the skeptical attitude of SPD staff officers toward the idea of resistance through introspection.

Thomas Mann led the field with three books. Mann's *Lotte in Weimar/ The Beloved Returns* (1939), a revival of "humanistic traditions of the Goethe period," and the collected speeches of the author in *Achtung Europa/Europe Beware* (1938) were included in the series alongside *Der Zauberberg/ The Magic Mountain* (1924), his magistral saga of a tuberculosis sanatorium as symbol of an ailing world. This challenging political allegory of disease was chosen, according to SPD records, because of the Socratic dialogue "between a defendant and a critic of western civilization."[28] The SPD apparently hoped that at least some of the POWs would see the analogy between Hans Castrop's confinement in the mountainous sanatorium, and their own state of imprisonment. Cut off from the wrenching experiences of reality, the prisoners, like Castrop, would undergo a "hermetic pedagogy" [*hermetische Pädagogik*]; they would learn to appreciate the redeeming qualities of Western humanism without having to deal with the distortive affects of contemporary events. Imprisonment, like confinement in the sanatorium, represented paradoxically, freedom; it liberated the inmate from preoccupation with the overpowering events of the real world beyond the barbed wire, or below the Magic Mountain.[29]

Guided by the adage of "divide and conquer" the New World series included numerous works aimed at reviving a uniquely Austrian sense of identity. For these purposes, the SPD chose Joseph Roth's *Radetzky-*

marsch (1932), "a historical novel with an Austrian background with special appeal to Austrian prisoners of war." Roth suited the program's needs given his eloquent yearnings for a cosmopolitan world unhindered by national enmities, which he portrayed through his romantic yearnings for the halcyon days of the multinational Austro-Hungarian empire. Roth's distaste for all forms of modern nationalism, including democracies, and his strong endorsement of monarchy were politely swept under the SPD carpet.

The Austrian section of the New World series featured as well two of Franz Werfel's books: *Die Vierzig Tage des Musa Dagh/The Forty Days of Musa Dagh* (1933), and *Das Lied von Bernadette/The Song of Bernadette* (1941). The SPD described *The Forty Days of Musa Dagh*, the story of the 1915 Turkish siege and ultimate annihilation of Armenians, as a "particularly appropriate" historical novel of "resistance of a suppressed people against the brutal methods of their conqueror." Quite fortuitously, the novel featured a German as its most positive character. Dr Johannes Lepsius, a German protestant missionary, pleads incessantly, although futilely, with the Turkish authorities to cease their policy of genocide. In perhaps the most intriguing section of book, Lepsius does not identify this instance of genocide as resulting from some inherent evil quality of Turkish culture; the Turks were merely overcome by a lethal combination of the two distinctly European poisons of nationalism and progress. As for Werfel's other selection, *The Song of Bernadette*, the SPD obviously hoped that this strong appeal to the latent national-Catholicism of many Austrian prisoners would serve as a tool for undermining residuals of pan-Germanism.

In addition to this fostering of national differences through literature, the series attempted as well to slaughter the sacred cow of German militarism. Karl Zuckmayer's *Der Hauptmann von Köpenick/The Captain of Köpenick* (1930), "a very amusing satire on the stupidity of the German adoration of uniforms and officialdom," was complemented by Arnold Zweig's *Der Streit um den Sergeanten Grischa/ The Case of Sergeant Grischa* (1932), "a novel which makes an impressive case against the war policies of the central powers of this last war." Somewhat surprisingly, this subsection of antimilitarist literature included Erich Maria Remarque's great pacifist novel *Im Westen Nichts Neues/All Quiet on the Western Front* (1929), "because of its objective account of the horrors of war" and the fact that it was "extremely popular in Germany but was viciously attacked by the Nazis ever since its publication." Indeed, as early as December 1930, and in response to massive pressure from and demonstrations by the budding National Socialists, the film version of Remarque's book was banned throughout Germany. In 1933, after hastily abandoning Germany, Remarque was stripped of his German citizenship, and his books were burned. Remarque's redeeming qualities and, most probably, the factor that clinched his inclusion in the series, was the fact that he never became a spokesman for pacifist causes; first and foremost he was a casualty of the general anti-intellectualism of Nazi Germany.

The German authors selected for inclusion in the series shared other important denominators aside from their impeccable anti-Nazism. All were exiles. In addition they had all demonstrated exemplary positive assessments of the United States. Thomas Mann and Franz Werfel, both with multiple selections in the New World series, spent the greater portion of the war years in California. Werfel, who died in the Californian diaspora, had made the transition from an outspoken critic of American materialism to one of its warmest advocates. The admiration was reciprocal. Millions of Americans read *The Song of Bernadette* after its acceptance by the Book-of-the-Month Club and Werfel reached the height of his popular success when a screen version of the book was filmed in 1943.[30]

Karl Zuckmayer and Erich Maria Remarque also had a Californian period. After arriving in the United States in 1934, Remarque spent his first eight years of exile in Los Angeles. In 1942 he moved to New York and, in 1947, he acquired U.S. citizenship. Zuckmayer's first job in the United States was as a scriptwriter in Hollywood; he then became a drama teacher in New York, before finally purchasing a farm in Vermont. Zuckmayer's major claim to fame, and presumably an important reason for his inclusion in the New World series, was his leadership as spokesman for the anti-Nazi literary movement.[31]

The inclusion of Zuckmayer in the New World series was equally compelling because of his ambiguous assessment of his own cultural identity. Much like the German-born staff officers of the SPD, who lived in an intellectual limbo between the culture of their birth and that of their adopted homeland, Zuckmayer expressed constant doubts about his identity, doubts that he had expressed in a poem written in 1939, a year after his arrival in the United States:

> I know that I shall return hesitantly,
> at a pace that is not urged on by desire.
> The heart's longing for its home has lost its spark,
> and what we sought ardently is now dead.[32]

Karl Zuckmayer, the tormented exile, saw himself as neither German nor American. Upon returning to Germany in 1946 as the representative of the U.S. government charged with supervising the reestablishment of German theaters, he was pained by a feeling of homelessness as well as by mixed emotions toward both the conquerors and the vanquished. Like his illustrious colleagues, Thomas Mann and Erich Maria Remarque,

Zuckmayer compromised by settling in Switzerland, where a diluted version of German culture had been spared the contamination of National Socialism.[33]

The authors of the New World series reflected in many ways the ideological inclinations of the SPD's faculty. Walter Schoenstedt and Henry Ehrmann, the two German faculty members, were repentant Socialists who had undergone a political transformation after arriving in the United States. Quite predictably, then, the New World series included authors who had converted from leftist sympathies to a variety of right and right-of-center views. Joseph Roth, for example, had undergone a dramatic transformation from a left-wing revolutionary to conservative Austrian monarchist.[34] Similarly, the works of Thomas Mann included in the series reflected the SPD's official outlook on the power of ideas and, conversely, the deliberate disregard of class or other economic factors as historical forces. Mann's representation of Germany was that of the educated middle class, the *Bildungsbürger*. The thoughts of Hans Castrop, the symbol of Germany in *The Magic Mountain*, are deliberately abstract and socially confined. Common people in Mann's work, the literary critic Herbert Lehnert has observed, serve as mere background, or reflections of the values of a relatively small, highly educated middle class.[35] The POWs who belonged to this subculture of the intelligentsia were also presumably the only inmates who were able to decipher Mann's metaphysical ponderings.

Another noteworthy feature of the New World's German section was the disproportionate number of Jews included in the series. Among the nine contemporary German-language authors chosen by the SPD, three were Jews: Franz Werfel, Leonhard Frank, and Arnold Zweig. The Jewish selections studiously avoided introspective Jewish subjects, and were chosen, apparently for their more ecumenical qualities. Werfel's compassion for and understanding of Catholicism as displayed in *The Song of Bernadette* were particularly in line with the didactic objectives of the SPD. Here was a member of National Socialism's most despised minority displaying empathy for and comprehension of a faith which had bound together many of its persecutors. Werfel's other selection, *The Forty Days of Musa Dagh*, was a particularly attractive novel due to its subtle interplay of Jewish and Christian elements and motifs drawn from the New and Old Testament all focusing on the ecumenical message of deliverance from oppression and communal responsibility.

Not all the Jewish writers included in the series displayed a background so conveniently appropriate for the cause of reeducation, American style. The choice of Arnold Zweig, was, to say the least, problematic. Zweig was a prominent and vocal Communist, who spent the war years in Palestine, apparently attracted there by the presence of a thriving enclave of Jewish socialism. His work, for the most part espoused the socialist cause. But in contrast to the general tone of his writings, Zweig's story of a Russian prisoner of war during the Great War was less concerned with advocating a particular dogma than with a human story of the anguish of a prisoner of war. Grischa's story does indeed take place immediately following the abdication of the Tsar; it is the eve of the Russian Revolution. However, behind Grischa's flight from his POW camp lies a burning desire to see his wife and child, not a determination to join the revolution. Grischa, as literary historian Ronald Taylor notes, is the ultimate ordinary man, "the scapegoat caught up in a whirlpool of uncontrollable events."[36] An additional redeeming quality of the book is the fact that most of the characters who both sympathize with Grischa and attempt to help him are Jews.

It is, of course, quite unclear if the POW reading public unraveled the rationale behind the choice of reading material or even noticed such issues as the authors' backgrounds, the hidden messages in the texts, or the overarching American designs behind the selections. In fact, the SPD never attempted any systematic monitoring of its literary program. Sales volumes served as the only consistent measurement of the success of the New World series.

Sales figures were impressive. Camp after camp reported brisk business. "The response to the *Buecherreihe Neue Welt* at our two Branch Camps of Grady and Altheimer, Arkansas, was beyond our fondest expectations," Camp Monticello, Arkansas, reported. "Grady expressed a desire for almost 600 more and Altheimer for about 400 more. They are being read widely and passed around. . . . These books have certainly filled one of our greatest needs, since the German book market is so limited."[37] These reports by the SPD passed on to the OPMG were accompanied by a small selection of made-to-order comments from cooperative inmates. An unidentified German officer from Camp Concordia, Kansas, stated in typical fulsome fashion that the appearance of the series "was the cause here of general rejoicing and gratitude." In lavishly worded prose, the anonymous reader ordained the series as "a ray of light," which would bring "comfort and strength to all who do not close their hearts and minds to the signs of the coming new world (Neue Welt)."[38]

And yet, brisk sales and selective comments did not necessarily reveal the entire picture. The utter boredom and isolation of the POWs led many to snatch up all publications in the German language. Moreover, the New World series reached camp canteens after V-E Day, at a time when growing numbers of prisoners had begun to absorb the significance of defeat, and had begun mental preparations for their imminent repatriation. The attractively priced books—about 20 cents each—promised to be wonderful souvenirs of their American incarceration.

It appears, too, that in the few remaining obdurate camps, the swift disappearance of New World books from canteens was part of the ongoing effort by radical German loyalists and POW leaders to eliminate the infiltration of what they considered to be subversive literature. Ample evidence suggests that in many camps there was a concerted campaign to undermine the reading program. In some camps the library fell under the control of the German prisoners' internal military chain of command. Books that questioned any aspect of German nationalism or the integrity of the armed forces never reached the prisoners. An investigation at Camp Forrest, Tennessee, revealed that the POW-librarians routinely blacklisted books according to the directives of their own officers. "If books are not allowed to be read in Germany, they should not be read here," a prisoner-librarian stated during the course of the investigation. "After all, they are Germans even if they are prisoners of war, and they are still held responsible for their actions as prisoners of war. They swore allegiance to their fatherland."[39]

This strenuous countercensorship on the part of zealous POWs was to a large degree superfluous given the inherently elitist slant of the reading program. Much of the approved material soared way above the comprehension capabilities of the average inmate. The multiple selections from the works of Thomas Mann, for example, illustrated the program's bias toward a distinct intellectual minority. In this sense the reading program duplicated the intellectual parameters of *Der Ruf*.

At the same time, some of the works did signal a shift in SPD policies. Selections such as *The Human Comedy* and *The Song of Bernadette* were indicative of the growing realization that in order to reach the prisoners, readable texts and popular tastes had a place in the program, too. Whether motivated by an awareness of the limitations of its intellectual outreach or otherwise, the SPD finally and quite belatedly reached out in a diametrically opposite direction.

In the final months of 1945, and as an indicator of the program's gradual evolution, the SPD initiated its first and only foray into the field of popular culture by including alongside its large selection of reading material a limited exposure to popular motion pictures. This acknowledgment of the tastes and preferences of ordinary prisoners was, however, quite limited, and never quite accepted by the SPD's professors in uniform.

CHAPTER SEVEN

Film: Mass Culture and Reeducation

"THE PRISONER OF WAR activities most naturally susceptible to the influence of the program are those recreational diversions that move more or less entertainingly in the realms of social ideas," the Provost Marshal General (PMG), Archer L. Lerch, wrote in his initial proposal for what he called the "re-orientation" of German POWs.[1] The "most effective media" for indoctrination "in probable order of popularity among prisoners are *a*) motion picture programs; *b*) recreational readings; *c*) radio programs; and *d*) theatrical performances." Films, Lerch noted, represented a particularly sensitive issue because of the prisoners' insatiable appetite for this medium. He apparently feared that counterproductive thoughts might infiltrate the prisoners' minds and impede reeducation through "casual and haphazard" handling of the movie diet in the camps. Motion pictures demanded, therefore, special attention.

These recommendations did not fare well once plans for reeducation began to materialize. Upon the establishment of the Special Projects Division (SPD), movies received marginal attention only. The architects of reeducation either ignored the use of motion pictures or damned the medium with faint praise.

Several factors had combined to produce this unfavorable attitude toward movies. Lt. Colonel Edward Davison, Lerch's choice for director of the SPD, alluded to the primary reason by describing his program as "intellectual diversion" instead of the vague, open-ended "reorientation" or the more insidious sounding "indoctrination" employed in other descriptions. Here Davison hinted at a deep mistrust of popular culture and, conversely, a commitment to education by rational persuasion that he shared with most of the senior SPD officers. Reeducation planners would admit in passing that from "time to time good non-political Hollywood productions" could provide some positive input. However, they envisioned the fundamental purpose of the film branch as a repository of government filmstrips on science and education, all of "which could furnish excellent indoctrination material."[2] Having committed themselves to a program of scholarly enlightenment, these officials approached the medium of film as an auxiliary tool for intellectual persuasion and ignored its popularity among the prisoners.

At least as important as these staff presumptions on the efficacy of film was the attitude of the auxiliary German prisoner staff employed in the Idea Factory. As intellectuals removed from the typical concerns of the cross section of the German population represented in the camps, they too espoused a traditional pedagogical approach to reeducation. The German assistants persistently decried what they feared would be a pandering to counterproductive popular tastes. Factory worker Dr. Wilhelm Doerr, who wrote a position paper on American movies and the German public, stated quite clearly that as far as postwar German society was concerned, "American box-office hits . . . might prove to be politically detrimental." He called for "no gangsters, no horse thieves, no play-boys, no vamps, not too many millionaires. Not too much 'Society,' as it inevitably provokes feelings of envy and hatred in people who were forced to give all that up." Doerr also frowned upon slapstick and Westerns. "Everybody in the motion-picture business knows how strongly art, entertainment, and life in general is dominated by the so-called escape mechanism," Doerr noted. For Germans who "want to be taken to a fairy land" via movies, "let it be one of innocent minds like that of Grimms' and Anderson's tales," he urged. American movies most likely to fit this litmus test of innocence were musicals, "especially in technicolor," and cartoons. Both genres demonstrated technical skill and were innocent in content.[3]

Doerr was willing, albeit grudgingly, to accept American movies as a necessary evil, providing that the selection would be purged of its most popular and fascinating features. Other prisoners in the Idea Factory expressed even less charitable views about movies and reeducation. Hans Werner Richter, the German author-inmate and Idea Factory worker recalled his aversion to motion pictures and their supposedly mesmerizing effect on the masses by relating an incident that occurred in the final phase of his status as a POW. Richter was a passenger on a Liberty Ship carrying a group of certified anti-Nazis back to Germany instead of to the labor camps in France, where the rank and file were destined to endure an additional period of incarceration before returning home. "We were all anti-Nazis, who had been freed due to our [political] views," Richter recalled.

> One evening I went to the movie theater on board the ship. They were showing a movie with Jane Russell, an actress well-known for her impressive breasts. The American guards were whistling, hooting and throwing whatever they could find at the screen. As for the Germans, they followed suit, throwing things just like they [the Americans] did. The whole spectacle was beastly; it was behavior that I deeply detested. It reminded me of the anti-Semitic manifestations [in Nazi Germany]. It was revolting; but I remained silent.[4]

Through this equation of the boisterous behavior of young men deprived of female companionship with popular manifestations of anti-Semitism, Richter registered a deeply imbedded fear of mass culture as the opium of the masses. Among all forms of mass culture, film was the most mesmerizing. Movies left little room for reflection; they induced preordained, mindless, responses from audiences. Richter believed that the sensuous stimuli typical of American movies stifled the intellect and encouraged bursts of brutal, animal-like emotions such as the frenzied behavior triggered by Jane Russell's anatomy. Movies cretinized the masses. Driven by these concerns for the beast within, Richter and his colleagues constantly protested against attempts to "lower" the intellectual tone of the reeducation program by introducing trappings of mass culture, such as movies.

Such detrimental attitudes on the part of the staff and workers in the Idea Factory slowed down, but could not eliminate, the unfolding of a movie program for reeducation. The prisoners' fascination with motion pictures undermined all attempts to marginalize the medium of film. The SPD was obliged to adopt a more methodical approach to movies by the rank and file who poured into screening of German and American B movies in the camps. As part of a reciprocal agreement mediated by the Red Cross, the Allies sent a small selection of preapproved movies to their prisoners in Germany. In exchange, German prisoners in Allied POW camps viewed a limited number of German film productions. All these German movies had been meticulously censored for any overt or covert Nazi propaganda. Nevertheless, they did not serve the purpose of entertainment as a tool of reeducation, as they had no relevance to the overriding objectives of the SPD.

In addition to this meager diet of German movies, and without prior consultation with the SPD, the local Service Commands routinely permitted the screening of a variety of thriller and gangster movies at the request of the prisoner-spokesmen in most POW camps. This unregulated infusion of made-in-America movies, according to the final report of the film branch, alarmed the staff of the SPD.

> Nazi-indoctrinated camp spokesmen made excellent use of the opportunity to prove to their camp fellow-inmates that Nazi propaganda which had emphasized the senility of the American people, rampant gangsterism in the United States, the corruption of the U.S. government and the debilitating effects of democracy and the American way of life, was true. A preliminary investigation of motion pictures shown in prisoner of war camps disclosed that among others, the following films were exhibited: *Lady Scarface, Millionaire Play Boy, Play Girl, Reno, Seven Miles From Alcatraz, Petticoat Larceny, Parole, Dead End, Little Tough Guy, Boy Slaves, Legions of the Lawless, Wolf Man, Too Many Blondes, Swing It Soldier, Highways by Night*; all motion pictures detrimental to efforts of engendering respect for the American way of life.[5]

SPD officers feared that these mostly B movies would subvert the projection of a positive American image, although they were not distressed, apparently, by the films' usual dose of violence, nor by the portrayal of lawlessness as a normative feature of daily life in the United States. In fact, once the SPD began its own systematic selection of movies, the film branch routinely ordered films that glorified violence. The apparent issue was that most of the movies mentioned in this assessment of the role of movies in reeducation had an unusual twist. Instead of focusing on the stereotypical criminal element, a hardened yet mature male, movies like *Lady Scarface* (RKO, 1941) and *Play Girl* (RKO, 1941) had women gangsters as their central characters, while *Dead End* (Samuel Goldwyn, 1937), *Little Tough Guy* (Universal, 1938), and *Boy Slaves* (RKO, 1938) depicted the exploitation of children and their swift transformation into implacable criminals. By portraying the most vulnerable elements in society—women and children—as victims of pathological aspects of American society, these movies suggested a basic perversion of American society. Women and children, according to the cultural conventions of the day, represented purity and innocence. The male character was an individual; women and children, as their mostly passive representations suggest, were symbols of their societies. Men resorted to crime and deviance for a variety of personal and social reasons. By contrast, the fallen women or the warped innocence of a child represented decadent societies rather than individual degradation.

Given this obviously unfavorable projection of American society, the SPD's film branch proposed an ambitious series of countermeasures and a more methodical approach to the movie medium. The first and primary task of the newly formed film branch was the development of a movie circuit of constructive feature films, as well as documentary films featuring Allied perspectives of the war and official American interpretations of the impending new world order. These movie bills mixed documentaries and light entertainment.

This central assignment of the film branch, which entailed the compilation of a list of ideologically positive feature films and their circulation, hit a series of technical and political snags at its inception. Service rivalries over responsibility for distribution, the lack of suitable equipment, as well as unequal distribution of theater facilities in the various camps conspired to slow down the initiation of the process.

These birth pangs were not the only reason for impeding the use of motion pictures for reeducation. In fact, the entire program almost died a premature death due to the fierce opposition of prominent studio executives. Many of the industry's leaders were Jews, who quite predictably expressed outrage at the very idea of "entertaining" German POWs in their midst. The most vocal critic in the industry was Harry Warner of

Warner Brothers. Warner and many of his colleagues faulted the premise behind the request for movies. In an irate letter to Lt. General W. D. Styer, Chief of Staff of the Army Service Forces and mediator between civilian bodies and the still-secret SPD, Warner expressed "strong disagreement" with the concept of reeducation in general and the use of commercial entertainment movies in particular.

> I say this not out of a lack of humanity, but because of a strong conviction that our good intentions will almost certainly be misunderstood by these Nazis. The character of their tradition and indoctrination is well known and has brought them so far from the ordinary mental processes of civilized human beings, that they can interpret kindness only as weakness. They cannot appreciate it,—they can only despise it. . . . These men have been trained to believe that we are soft, muddleheaded idiots. They have been taught to believe that their cruelty and brutality is a virtue, and that our humanity is a fault. . . . I just received a letter from one of my family who was liberated, and this is what he says: "This little unreadable note is just to let you know I have been at last liberated. The true story of what the Nazis did to us is simply unbelievable. All I shall say is that I weighed about 84 pounds when set free." AND WE WANT TO ENTERTAIN THEM![6]

Warner's opposition could not be brushed aside; he was highly respected in government circles for actively supporting the administration's policies through his movies. As early as 1941 his studio had been the main target of an investigation by the isolationist Senate Interstate Commerce Committee which had accused the movie industry of a widespread monopolistic campaign to "vilify" Hitler in order to soften up public opinion for eventual American participation in the war.[7] Warner Brothers was the first studio to endorse a strong anti-Nazi stance with the release of *Confessions of a Nazi Spy* (1939), the semidocumentary story of the FBI's smashing of a Nazi spy ring in New York in 1939. This vivid portrayal of the Nazi threat to the American system by both German agents and the German-American Bund led to the banning of the film in over twenty countries. Despite such setbacks, the film was a tremendous hit at the box office. More important, as far as the SPD was concerned, Warner's actions endowed him with special status in government circles. Consequently, his displeasure with the film program for reeducation posed a distinct problem.[8]

Unwilling to have Warner as an enemy, the SPD decided to reveal the exact nature of the reeducation program. This step did not elicit any significant change in the movie mogul's attitude. In a meeting with SPD director Edward Davison, Warner hinted darkly at his personal ties with President Truman and his intention to voice his opposition in the highest quarters. He did, however, shift his opposition from criticizing reeducation in general, to what he considered to be an unprofessional, dilettante selection of movies. In an angry letter to Secretary of War Henry L. Stimson, Warner expressed particular irritation with the choice of movies for the program, citing *The Oklahoma Kid* (Warner, 1939) and *The Frisco Kid* (Warner, 1935) as examples. Both these Warner Brother productions were specifically requested by the SPD for its movie program; both films, by Warner's own account, glorified gratuitous violence.

Of course, Warner was feigning ignorance of the moral code of large studios in this analysis of violence in wild-west movies. In the cautious, self-regulated movie industry, violence was never gratuitous. Gangster movies and their wild-west counterparts were, for the most part, carefully crafted variations of the Horatio Alger myth. In typical rags-to-riches fashion, gangsters and outlaws also rose to success through enterprise and self-reliance; their eminence and power was, as Lawrence Levine and Robert Middlekauff suggest, invariably fleeting, because they denied pivotal moral values that the true Alger characters espoused. Their punishment for the rejection of traditional ethics was violent destruction and imminent demise.[9] Maxwell McKnight, Assistant Director of the SPD, attempted to explain the importance of this recurring moral of violent movies in his justification for the SPD's choice of these contested Warner Brothers movies.

> *Frisco Kid* . . . doesn't white-wash conditions in parts of the country opened up by our expansion to the West. But it does stress that lawlessness was overcome by the efforts of the people themselves and that justice finally prevails. In the end the "Kid" says, when he is taken away by the strong arm of the law, "Some day I'll return and then I'll help to *build* instead of *destroy*," an attitude we should very much like the Germans to develop.[10]

Movies such as *Frisco Kid* served as parables of world politics. The outlaw's demise in the gangster and Western movies of the 1930s and 1940s was, as the film critic Robert Warshow wrote, an inevitable consequence of an individual setting himself apart from and above "the people" and conventional moral codes. The visual cliche signifying the moment of demise for the outlaw was his sudden isolation from others. Maxwell Mcknight explained that *Oklahoma Kid*, another of the movie selections criticized by Warner, was chosen precisely for its disapproval of radical individualism and, conversely, its emphasis on the triumph of collective struggle.[11]

What McKnight did not mention was that the use of Westerns for purveying American values was particularly valuable because popular German culture often employed the Western as a metaphor for illustrating both the faults and virtues of American society. The novels of the German writer, Karl May, describing the adventures of frontiersman "Old Shatterhand, and Winnetou, the Apache warrior," held a wide audience well into the years of the Third Reich. According to historian Ray Allen Billington, Karl May wrote over thirty books, which sold over thirty million copies; among his fans were such disparate characters as Adolf Hitler and Albert Einstein.[12]

Predictably, the Nazi propaganda machine used the Western in its attempts to vilify American society. Concerned about lingering sympathy for the United States, Joseph Goebbels's Reich Ministry for Popular Enlightenment and Propaganda had enthusiastically supported the production of Luis Trenker's dramatic Western, *Der Kaiser von Kalifornien/The Kaiser of California*, in which the hardy German pioneer, John Sutter, finds his idyllic life in the far west shattered by greedy Anglo-American gold seekers.[13] Under these circumstances, it made sense to employ "positive" Westerns to win the hearts and minds of German POWs.

Regardless of the intrinsic value of good American Westerns as antidotes to the negative metaphors of the Nazi film industry, the SPD readily removed the offending Warner Westerns from its planned circuit. Hoping to mollify the powerful Warner Brothers, Lt. Colonel Edward Davison pledged, as well, to produce documentary accounts of real German atrocities rather than the make-believe brutality of feature films.

The SPD did not suffer irreparable damage from the removal of *Oklahoma Kid*, *Frisco Kid*, or any other offending movie; the program was not overly dependent on any one genre or any particular studio. Moreover, the objectives of the SPD's film branch were, of course, far more complex than mere depiction of the triumph of law, or the struggle of the American people against a hostile wilderness and the forces of lawlessness. The wide variety of pictures chosen by the staff—musicals, situation comedies, melodramas, and war films—suggests more intricate objectives. The film branch was efficient, professional, and quite successful in compiling a well-honed and visually attractive interpretation of contemporary American culture through film.

Movie selections, the only element of mass culture used in the reeducation program, also represented the most significant crack in the intellectually restricted veneer of the SPD. Quite clearly, the most salient feature of movies contradicted the underlying intellectual tone of reeducation. The film branch used visual material rather than written tomes, and sought to instill educational messages through the medium of entertainment instead of rational persuasion. In the early stages of the movie program, a typical evening of visual entertainment began with a number of "shorts"—travel documentaries, educational films, and cartoons, and even an occasional German film production; these were followed by a main feature film, carefully chosen for its covert educational value. By V-E Day, the shorts were almost exclusively OWI newsreels or other documentary material depicting the grim consequences of National Socialism.

In part, the film branch's ability to develop this radically different, non-intellectual form of reeducation material was the result of benign neglect. Such pivotal figures as Walter Schoenstedt, Henry Ehrmann, Howard Mumford Jones, and other intellectuals on the staff of the SPD ignored the existence of the film circuit, or did not see fit to meddle in the content of what they presumably thought was a basically irrelevant footnote to their academic project. Given this marginal prominence in the eyes of the key figures of the SPD, the film branch was free to develop an independent approach to reeducation.

The ideological dimensions of the film branch and the degree to which its didactic approach differed from the official dogma of the SPD does not appear in any of the final reports of the program. The historical monograph of the program, written by film branch chief Captain Otto Englander, described the branch's philosophy in a deliberately consensual manner. The objective, he stated, was "painless" indoctrination. "Here was entertainment in its purest form," which covertly and subtly bore "the message of the free American way of life." Written toward the end of the war, and with an eye on posterity, Englander's report piously stated that the approved list contained an exclusive selection of wholesome family pictures "based on common human experience," dramas, and comedies "of a universal character; good musical films; adaptations of fine stage plays (classical or modern); realistic 'action' pictures with Western or Northwestern contemporary or historical background" and, of course, the obligatory biographies of great men and women, historical films, and travelogues.[14] These films, according to the historical monograph of film branch activities, were charged with impressing the German prisoner of war with American might in the various theaters of war, engendering respect for American statesmen, inventors and their technological achievements, lauding the pioneer spirit and the dedication of the American home front, and highlighting the character of American men and women in situations that required ingenuity and courage.[15]

Written toward the end of 1945, the historical monograph of the film branch stated somewhat disingenuously that in order to achieve this goal, films "glorifying gangsterism or dealing with prison life and prison escapes; ridiculing any member of the United Nations; misrepresenting the American scene by stress on plutocratic or other distorted aspects; the so-called "hot" musicals; depression and slum pictures; films containing racial slurs; depictions of strife between capital and labor; the so-called 'blood and thunder' cowboy pictures; and films on the unrealistic Holly-wood scene were disapproved."[16]

This synopsis of film branch activities was only partially accurate. The final selection of movies did indeed avoid blatant slandering of Allied countries and, aside from the stereotyped depiction of Native Americans and Japanese, the movies contained no overt racial slurs. Sexually explicit movies, presumably what was meant by "hot" musicals, were also absent. But the actual archival records of the film branch reveal the inclusion of many ambiguous feature films, with heavy doses of street violence, thinly veiled criticism of plutocracy in America, as well as much chauvinistic material that, by implication at least, denigrated the traditions and values of other nations. The historical monograph of the film branch did not reflect such a selection of movie material.

Written shortly before the dismantling of the SPD, the film branch monograph was quite selective in its listing of themes and genres, reticent on its ideological objectives, and deliberately technical in detail. Perhaps unwilling to reveal internal disagreements within the SPD, the author intentionally conveyed an image of prudence, conservative decisions, and consensus among the reeducation staff. For posterity's sake, he preferred to gloss the problems generated by the creative use of mass culture in a program that advocated traditional intellectual persuasion.

A more revealing record of film branch objectives appeared in the German-language film synopses prepared by the branch. All movies approved by the film branch were accompanied by page-long outlines of their content and educational significance. The ostensible purpose of these documents was to solve the problem of using an English-language soundtrack for an audience with limited knowledge of foreign languages. However, by the time the film circuit was activated, a majority of POWs had acquired a basic knowledge of English. It would appear, then, that the synopsis policy had another didactic objective.

Unlike their superior officers, Captain Englander and his associates argued that even such formulaic material as the modern Amercian movie left much room for creative interpretations. As far as they were concerned, the POWs were not a passive audience; the movie experience left ample room for amateur hermeneutics and subversive interpretations to fit the worldview of the prisoners. As such, film branch personnel were anxious to convey their own orthodox interpretation of the movies, and emphasize those particular aspects of the film to which the POWs should pay attention. The page-long documents distributed to the inmate audiences before each performance highlighted what the film branch thought were the most redeeming features of the film. These plot descriptions demonstrate that, despite the wide variety of genres employed in the movie circuit, the film branch only utilized movies with certain recurring social and political motifs. Pragmatism, not unyielding principles, common sense, rather than blind loyalty, were the most important recurring themes in the carefully crafted descriptions of these movies.

War movies, in particular, provided attractive vehicles for portraying the way Americans resolved the inherent clash between ideology and pragmatism, unwavering obedience and common sense, altruism and individualism. Given the amount of sacrifice, blind loyalty, and unyielding acceptance of orders associated with the German approach to war, the American films demonstrated vivid visual examples of an alternative form of patriotism in wartime. A typical emphasis on the pragmatic and flexible approach to the issues of war, the individual, and the national cause appeared in the synopsis of *The Story of G.I. Joe* (United Artists, 1945), the film biography of war correspondent Ernie Pyle. The plot description contained a detailed analysis of the "special section of the film" describing the Allied attack on the Abbey of Monte Cassino. "The American troops had orders not to open fire on this Abbey" because of its religious significance. These strict orders to respect the sanctity of a religious shrine, even to the point of hampering an important military mission, were abruptly overturned when the loss of American lives became too great. In marked contradiction to his previous orders, the commanding officer of the campaign ordered an unyielding and decimating "bombardment of the Abbey till its surrender." The SPD synopsis implied that symbols and principles, even of the highest order, should never elicit blind, unyielding loyalty. Once events proved them to be inoperable, they ceased to function as guidelines for human behavior.[17]

Of course American war movies screened before the POWs never completely rejected the concept of sacrifice in battle. Risking one's life, and facing certain death in battle were acceptable norms when the results were tangible and immediate, and motivated by personal loyalties rather than abstract principles. Moreover, such altruistic actions often involved disobeying illogical or erroneous orders. The synopsis of *The Sullivans* (Twentieth Century–Fox, 1944) described in glowing terms the self-sacrifice of the five Sullivan brothers who lost their lives on the cruiser Juneau in the battle of Guadalcanal. Four of the brothers "disobeyed their superior officer's orders" to abandon ship in order to attempt a hopeless rescue of their sibling trapped in the sick bay. "The boys died as they had lived—the five of them together," the film branch's summary concluded, obviously approving of their sacrifice as well as their capability for independent thinking.[18]

The descriptions of the Sullivans's bravery and the battle of Monte Cassino contrasted quite markedly with central motifs of Nazi cinematography, in particular the glamorization of death in battle and an overall pattern of submissive behavior. The blind, unquestioning "Die For Germany" motif was a cardinal theme of Third Reich films. In contrast to the Abbey scene in *G.I. Joe*, Karl Ritter's popular film of a Great War battle on the western front, *Unternehmen Michael/Operation Michael* (1937) glorified the capture of an insignificant pile of ruins of no notable strategic value at the cost of thousands of lives. The battle and ensuing sacrifice were displayed as a triumph of will and obedience rather than an important military achievement. "You know as well as I do that posterity will measure us not by the greatness of our victory but by the dimension of our sacrifice," the commanding officer informs his troops on the eve of the battle.[19] As for the conflict between unquestioning discipline and other values such as comradeship or family loyalties, the hero-pilot of Roger von Norman's *Himmelhunde/Skydogs* (1942) stated quite categorically that "we have no use for scabs who always think of themselves first and question the reason for an order instead of simply carrying it out."[20]

The Sullivans's sacrifice, by contrast, was of a personal nature, and was glorified despite, and probably because of, the fact that it displayed the primacy of individual loyalty and familial piety over unwavering obedience to some larger national issue. The synopsis of *Gung-Ho* (Universal, 1943) reiterated this message in its central battle scene. When two of the movie's characters, Larry and Kurt, find themselves side by side in an offensive against Japanese troops, "Larry confides that he never was in love with Kathleen," the girl they both have been courting, "and that she loves Kurt. When Kurt is ordered forward, Larry goes instead and is killed."[21] Larry sacrificed his life, for a very personal reason. By contrast, a central figure in one of the most significant war movies of the Third Reich, Karl Ritter's *Stukas* (1941), illustrates the fatal attraction of death in German culture by quoting Hölderlin:

> O Take me, take me into your ranks,
> That I will not die a common death!
> To die in vain, I crave not that, but
> Only to fall on the hill of sacrifice
> For the Fatherland, to bleed the heart's blood.[22]

The film branch presented the American approach to death in battle in distinctly different terms. Both the film selection, as well as the wording of the synopses, described war deaths as an event with tragic, rather than heroic, consequences, an event which invariably scarred the living. The program produced numerous movie synopses portraying the emotional sufferings of survivors. One of the central characters in *So Proudly We Hail* (Paramount, 1943), the dramatic story of army nurses at Bataan in 1942, is "Lt. Olivia D'Arcy [Veronica Lake], a sullen, cynical nurse" who has lost her faith in life after the death of her fiancé in the Pearl Harbor attack.[23] *Happy Land* (Twentieth Century–Fox, 1943) tells the story of a village drugstore owner who has lost his son "in a distant ocean battlefield." The father becomes "inconsolable as a result of this tragic loss. Where formerly he had been a friendly, neighborly sort of man, he now becomes an introvert, a brooding, taciturn, morose man, who withdraws into his shell whenever he is accosted by his friends." The father finds partial consolation in the discovery of the indelible mark that his boy has left on the community. The "final healing of the wound, however, is left to the real flesh and blood influence of the dead boy's homeless shipmate, who pays a visit to the community of his friend," and, the movie synopsis implies, fulfills the role of the deceased son.[24] A similar scene appears in the screen adaptation of William Saroyan's *The Human Comedy* (MGM, 1943). The despair of the Macauley family over the death of their son is mitigated only by the appearance of an unknown, yet familiar-looking, soldier, who decides to remain in their household as a "new brother."[25]

Beyond the sphere of world wars, the movies dealing with personal, social, and political conflict, in which ordinary people were motivated to take uncharacteristically extreme action, were remarkably free of ideological undertones and the preeminence of principles. The film section of the SPD deliberately ignored the role of ideological tenets and dogma in shaping human behavior. In its synopsis of *Going My Way* (Paramount, 1944), the popular depiction of a clash between two priests in a New York parish, the film branch painstakingly pointed out that the clash was "not predicated on clerical lines and that fundamental religious questions are not involved because they are never involved" in the generational clash represented in the movie.[26]

Indeed, political and social dilemmas in the film branch's choice of movies were presented as trivialized personal conflicts. The only depiction of the Civil War—the most fundamental of conflicts in American history—appeared in *Wells Fargo* (Paramount, 1937), the story of Ramsey Macrea, a Wells Fargo manager in Northern California, and his wife, a "gentile [*sic*] Southern belle" who married the Yankee against her mother's wishes. The central conflict of the plot centers on Ramsey's attempts to transport a shipment of gold to Washington, D.C., for the Union effort. His mother-in-law, who never approved of the marriage, informs a Confederate officer and disgruntled suitor of her daughter of the impending convoy. In the ensuing battle the confederates are routed by Union troops led by Ramsey. The entire clash between North and South is depicted as a very personal dispute, involving love and jealousy. The principles and politics behind the Civil War never enter the plot.[27]

By the same token, the struggle of wits between Abraham Lincoln and Stephen A. Douglas in *Young Mr. Lincoln* (Twentieth Century–Fox,

1939) appeared in the film branch's synopsis as an opportunity for Mary Todd "to decide which of the two men she will accept as husband, as an instrument through which she could work her overpowering ambition." The tumultuous events of the period and the impending struggle between North and South supply mere scenery for this popular vilification of Mary Todd Lincoln.[28]

War was not, of course, the only form of conflict trivialized in the selection of movies. Economic disputes, and by implication the ideal form of American capitalism were depicted by damning all sides who chose drastic measure over compromise, principle over empirical solutions. In *Valley of Decision* (MGM, 1945), the story of the industrialization of Pittsburgh, starring, among others, Greer Garson, Gregory Peck, and Lionel Barrymore, "the natural growth of America as an industrial power" is depicted through the lives and loves of workers and capitalists. Most of the film's synopsis deals with an unwarranted steel strike "fanned" by a devious union leader and an embittered mill worker crippled in a freak accident. These radical workers are not the only villains. "Old Mr. Scott," the owner of the mill, who represents the unfeeling capitalist of the pre–New Deal period, "stubbornly insists on breaking it [the strike] by means of hired hoodlums." The synopsis of *Valley of Decision* associated conflict with age and European origins. The two unyielding figures in the drama are "old Mr. Scott" and the crippled mill worker, an immigrant from Ireland. Through the eventual marriage of Paul Scott, son of the mill owner, and Mary Rafferty, American-born daughter of the embittered strike leader, the film synopsis celebrated the victory of progress over class conflict in modern American society.[29]

The attractive fluidity offered by the American brand of democracy was represented by a long list of movies of mistaken identity. *It Started with Eve* (Universal, 1941) depicts the story of a "pretty hatcheck girl" who successfully poses as the rich fiancée of a chance acquaintance, while another Universal production, *His Butler's Sister* (Universal, 1943), is a typical comedy of errors of a butler posing as a wealthy businessman, a girdle salesman being mistaken for a noted composer, and a talented actress who has no qualms about masquerading as a maid in order to expedite her professional ambitions. In *Tom, Dick, and Harry* (RKO, 1940), "Janie, a pretty small-town telephone operator" who has ambitions about "marrying a man with means" mistakes a young automobile mechanic for a wealthy suitor and eventually marries him too. In *The Cowboy and the Lady* (Samuel Goldwyn, 1938), a "delicate, high-bred product of the social set" (Merle Oberon) successfully masquerades as a working girl in order to ensnare a rugged, honest, and impressive cowboy (Gary Cooper).[30]

Women appeared quite frequently in the films involving mistaken identity. In fact the role of women in general, and in particular the traditional function of marriage and family in these SPD selections contrasted sharply with contemporary German representations. The typical heroine of the entertainment films of the Third Reich espoused the subordination of women. The German musical in particular, observes literary critic Eva-Maria Warth, "with its postulation of marriage as a happy ending, as a space in which all conflicts are transcended, contrasted with the American musical and its fantasies of social climbing." As opposed to the implicit approval of "kids and kitchen" in German musicals of the Third Reich, the American films screened before the POWs did not present marriage as submission, nor did the newly wed female protagonists routinely and naturally withdraw from economic or cultural activities outside the home.

Hence, *Roughly Speaking* (Warner, 1945) "is a story of a career woman who defies the fashion of the time and enters the business world" where she proves that "ambition and marriage do not contradict each other in a relationship based on true love and mutual respect."[31] *What a Woman* (Columbia, 1943) centers around the clash between an outstanding female publicity agent and a male magazine editor who "has nothing but derision for career women." The agent and editor eventually recognize their mutual love; the ultimate moral, according to the film branch's summary, was that a successful career and true love do not necessarily clash.[32]

As these portrayals of American women suggest, the ultimate goal of the film branch was the presentation of a social system uninhibited by custom and outmoded tradition. In distinct departure from the other branches of the SPD, with their emphasis on intellectual spheres of American culture, the movie branch presented to its public a very different window into American society. These visual expressions of American values addressed the intellectual level of the average POW and avoided placing artists, writers, and philosophers on a pedestal.

The film branch's espousal of popular culture as an efficient medium of reeducation was not the only point of departure from official SPD dogma. Captain Otto Englander, the commanding officer of the film branch, proposed confronting POWs with the consequences of their wartime activities, and abandoning the SPD's official policy of reeducation without confrontation. The film branch proposed screening explicitly anti-Nazi movies, including *Confessions of a Nazi Spy* (Warner, 1939), *The Moon is Down* (Twentieth Century–Fox, 1943), *Tomorrow the World* (Lester Cowan, 1943), *Watch on the Rhine* (Warner, 1943), *The Hitler Gang* (Paramount, 1943), and *Hitler's Children* (RKO, 1943) as well as Frank Capra's "Why We Fight" series.

Englander wanted the SPD to convey the motif of collective guilt. In explaining his deviation from SPD policy, Englander informed his superior officers that, in addition to explaining American ways of life to the inmates, he saw no reason to protect the POWs from facing the consequences of their deeds.

> The Film Branch foresaw the possible unpopularity of war themes among men who seek complete escape from ideas and thoughts dealing with war, and possible morals that could be drawn therefrom. It is exactly for this reason that good war pictures were chosen. It is deemed undesirable that war prisoners, who have participated in the rape of the Sudetenland, Poland, France, the Netherlands, Denmark, etc., be shielded from themes dealing with the horrors of war just because they are physically removed from them.[33]

Englander argued that the shock and shame that realistic anti-German movies would engender in some of the POWs would be significantly more useful than mere "ideological" persuasion. Englander, one of two Jewish officers among the senior staff of the SPD, was unusually frank in his criticism of the SPD's guidelines to avoid antagonizing the POWs. After all, V-E Day had passed, Germany's moral, military, and economic collapse was irrefutable, and there were no compelling reasons for shielding individual German soldiers from the results of their "instigation of and participation in the war." Unless otherwise ordered, Englander informed his superiors, "the Film Branch will therefore persist in selecting good American war features and shorts, based on either fact or fiction, which tend to bring home to the average prisoner of war the effects of the terrible catastrophe which has come upon the world as a result of the policies and actions of the former German government."[34]

Englander's superiors balked, and in fact rejected his request. However, it would appear that at this stage, late August 1945, such a decision was motivated more by suspicion and distaste for feature films rather than by any lingering doubts concerning the benefits of confronting POWs with the consequences of their deeds. Indeed, the refusal to use anti-German feature films came at a time when the PMG began to screen atrocity footage before POWs. Moreover, the film branch was in the midst of producing its own tailor-made documentary series of "deglamorization films" focusing on German atrocities and the devastation of Germany. The film branch's Hollywood liaison officer—Lieutenant James E. Stewart—had managed to persuade Darryl Zanuck, executive director of Twentieth Century–Fox, and Ernst Lubitsch, the great German director and a fugitive from the Nazis, to produce such a film. Stewart reported that

> Ernst Lubitsch recommended that instead of showing several types of footage with no story line . . . film which depicts the "glory" of the Third Reich should be contrasted with the best footage from newsreels

and combat films which shows the demoralization and ruin of Germany . . . the total impression of the picture is to make the prisoners aware of their misconceptions and to abolish any idea that they might still retain about the "glory" of the Nazi government or the ultimate accomplishments of its "culture." The Provost Marshal General would be responsible for the ideology and philosophy expressed.[35]

In theory then, this combination of documentary film with carefully chosen feature films had the makings of a powerful weapon for undermining the worldview of POWs. In practice, however, neither the documentary material nor the feature films achieved their projected objectives. Army rivalries slowed down the SPD documentary project to a veritable snail's pace. Despite SPD protestations that the proposed film for POWs was quite unique, the Signal Corps was less than enthusiastic about approving a documentary that would rival its own productions, in particular Frank Capra's "Why We Fight" series, which had also utilized the services of Lubitsch. The Signal Corps argued that, given the release of powerful documentary footage on concentration camps after the fall of Germany, the SPD's documentary project would appear redundant. SHAEF's Psychological Warfare Division, together with the American Council for the Prosecution of Axis Criminality had released *Nazi Concentration Camps*, a one-hour film containing graphic footage of Nazi atrocities. Moreover, the Anglo-American newsreel released on June 15, 1945, was dedicated entirely to terrifying concentration camp footage, and other atrocity films were already in the pipeline.[36] The SPD eventually concluded its project by mid-September 1945, by which time it had become a ghoulish version of yesterday's news. All POWs had already been force-fed a large dose of atrocity footage, and had made up their minds whether to accept such film as truth or, conversely, as propaganda.

Similar delays affected the feature film project. To be sure, over two hundred feature films from the major studios, all of which served the film branch's didactic purpose, were included in the circuit. However, by the SPD's own admission, "it was not until the middle of June 1945 that circuits had begun operation in all service commands, and not until the middle of September 1945 that all base and branch camps were receiving film."[37] In this sense, the depiction of American culture and the consequence of Nazi warfare by means of a popular and unpretentious form of reeducation never fulfilled its potential.

In the final analysis, however, the film branch did record one significant success. The sheer numbers of prisoners who poured into the impromptu movie theaters were too overwhelming to ignore. Even though the SPD charged a 15-cent admission fee—most POWs earned an average of 40 cents a day—prisoners voted with their feet. By the end of September 1945, about four months after the inception of the program, the SPD reported over three million admissions, an average of about ten films per prisoner.[38] Thus, as the SPD moved toward the restructuring of the reeducation program in preparation for the POWs' pending repatriation, the medium of film became an integral part of a revised strategy. Even though the architects of reeducation would never fully overcome their aversion for mass culture, movies supplied an inroad into the POW mentality that could no longer be ignored.

PART THREE

The Prison Academy

CHAPTER EIGHT

Politics and Scholarship:
The Reeducation College

ON JUNE 15, 1945, about a month after V-E Day, the Office of the Provost Marshal General (OPMG) declassified the reeducation program for prisoners of war. The general public officially learned of the covert American program to rehabilitate German soldiers in the some two hundred POW camps throughout the United States. In a series of press releases the PMG informed a hitherto critical American press that the government had not, as many feared, shirked its duty. Enemy POWs would return home well prepared for the new world order, having received the necessary exposure to American values.

The prisoners, of course, were not caught off-guard by the announcement. The existence of the program was common knowledge within the camps. The efforts to disguise its presence had been awkward, perhaps purposefully so. As for the staff of the Special Projects Division (SPD) who ran the program, they were quite relieved. The clumsy veil of secrecy had evoked a mixture of confusion and derision among the prisoners. Few inmates had accepted the argument that such central projects as *Der Ruf* operated without an American guiding hand. Moreover, the SPD's cautious policy of avoiding any head-on confrontation with National Socialism merely beclouded the clarity of the American creed as relayed to the prisoners. Now that Germany had finally fallen, the SPD was absolved of the need to navigate a circuitous path to the hearts and minds of the prisoners. The reeducation staff began plotting a new and bolder course for the program.

A sense of urgency characterized the restructuring of reeducation. War Department policy called for the departure of all POWs by March 31, 1946. All military personnel involved in the program were anxious to demonstrate tangible and positive results prior to repatriation. Accordingly, the SPD set about revising its syllabus, timetable, and objectives.

As a point of departure, the SPD abandoned its effort to influence every facet of prison life. Instead, the program officers sought to identify the noncommitted and "moderate" anti-Nazis, expose them to a crash course in American democracy, inform them of American objectives in occupied Germany, and send the graduates of this program back to Germany before the remaining POWs.

The format for these crash courses leaned on the university model in more than one sense. The pedagogical and political tensions of American academia during this period permeated the university behind barbed wire. Aside from the predictable pattern of a college framework for this stage of reeducation, the POW schools reflected the political controversies of contemporary American academia, in particular the battle over academic freedom and the right to monitor the educator's private political convictions.

The SPD began tinkering with its program as early as May 7, 1945, one day before V-E Day, when it established the "Experimental Administrative School for Selected German Prisoners of War," at Fort Kearney, Rhode Island. This hastily organized affair laid the groundwork for the new phase in the SPD program, the preparation for repatriation through crash courses and the selection of cooperative prisoners for future collaboration.

Howard Mumford Jones, the senior civilian on the SPD staff, was appointed director of the Experimental School. In addition to his administrative duties, he also designed and taught a survey course in American institutions and government. Jones's chief associate and major collaborator in devising the intellectual content of the program was Henry Ehrmann, the other civilian advisor of the SPD. He took upon himself the delicate task of presenting a survey course in German History.[1] Major Henry Lee Smith, the Brown University linguistics expert headed the English language department, together with Captain William Moulton, a newcomer to the program from the linguistics department at Cornell. Another newcomer, Major Burnham N. Dell, the only member of the senior faculty not associated with a major university, taught Military Government.

Given the experimental nature of the school, and lacking any precedent, the faculty had much leeway in designing the curriculum and defining its objectives. The original mandate called for the training of administrative personnel to support American occupation forces in Germany. In addition to this primary and mostly technical goal, a supplementary and somewhat hazy directive suggested the instilling of "principles of democracy," on the one hand, and glorifying "American developments," on the other.

The faculty of the Experimental School quickly turned this mandate on its head. The administrative course in military government became the secondary focus of a syllabus centered upon a series of German and American history courses. Jones and his associates envisioned a college model for their program. The school offered a sixty-day semester, with all the trappings of an academic environment. In addition to a daily dose of extensive lectures on Military Government and "Democracy"—the equivalent of the liberal arts American Civilization and Western Civilization courses—the experimental school offered morning discussion groups modeled after the undergraduate seminar. The faculty implemented a variety of familiar tools for monitoring progress, including "hour examinations at least as severe as college examinations" as well as term and midterm papers. A battery of teaching assistants, composed of promising prisoner-students and Idea Factory workers, graded papers and exams, presided over review sessions, and assumed "other burdens of the small faculty." In addition, the school offered a series of colloquia. These guest lecturers were mostly middle-of-the-road experts on German culture from Ivy League schools. The most illustrious guests were Arnold Wolfers, the Swiss-born Yale professor of German political history; Harvard professor Robert Ulich, who lectured on plans for the reform of the German educational system; and Karl Vietor, also from Harvard, who discussed "Goethe and the cosmopolitanism of Germany in Goethe's time."[2]

Howard Mumford Jones and his colleagues had implemented the American college archetype because it was comfortable and familiar; but they also pleaded a pedagogical reason. This exposure of Germans to an American educational model represented a positive alternative to the rigid divisions of the German educational system. Given the early separation of German youth into mutually exclusive vocational and academic streams, there was no German equivalent of the American public university where a socially and academically diverse student body could receive a broad liberal arts education prior to some form of specialization. The German educational system produced a rigid, socially stratified student body with no interdisciplinary exposure and very little social rapport among its graduates. Thus, in addition to its immediate academic goals, the SPD Experimental School at Fort Kearney sought to demonstrate the social benefits of the American alternative. Howard Mumford Jones explained the virtues of his approach as follows:

> The directives governing the school announced the desirability of training both technicians and administrators; and the students selected represented both humanistic and technological education. After some discussion of the possibility, the faculty refused to separate the two kinds. If the technicians were usually less well prepared in English and less able to grapple with ideas, they benefitted from sharing the talk of those more capable of discussing the political philosophy of democracy; on the other hand, the technicians often deflated the balloons of ideologists more interested in *Weltanschauungen* than practicality.[3]

Of course, the unusual didactic mission of the SPD demanded some modification of the American college model. The prospective students approached the program with the hardened attitude of the inmate. They did not expect to receive an education—the imparting of objective knowledge. Instead, they braced themselves for an exercise in indoctrination, the completion of which would hasten their return back home. Well aware of these circumstances, the faculty developed a strategy for lowering the guard of the prisoners.

> To make a direct assault upon German preconceptions in the name of democracy seemed injudicious, especially as the prisoners were naturally looking for propaganda. The same end was sought by indirection. In view of Nazi perversions of German history and of the history of Western Europe, it was decided to teach German history . . . with a view to examining its democratic tendencies . . . for the thesis cannot be defended that Germany alone is incapable [of] democratic growth.[4]

By the same token, rather than presenting a hagiography of great men and great ideas, the parallel course in American history focused mainly on technical and mundane reasons for the rise of democratic institutions in the United States. The common thrust of both courses was to demonstrate that the gap between Germany, an archetype of modern despotism, and the United States, home of an international brand of democracy, was not unfathomable. The American "units" emphasized the success of democracy in the United States despite "many and grievous faults," while the German course focused on positive political developments in Germany, which, for mainly technical reasons, had never reached fruition. Henry Ehrmann noted that his German history courses sought "the destruction of yet another myth: that democracy has to be imported to Germany and is basically 'undeutsch.' . . . [T]he ignorance about democratic traditions in Germany was so great that it actually was possible to besmirch the first German republic with this stigma of being an alien product."[5] Of course, in order to accomplish this goal, Ehrmann's lectures made no mention of the preponderance of Jews, the perennial foreigners, among the framers and upholders of Weimar's constitution.

Aside from the Jewish question, Ehrmann encountered many other obstacles in his revisionist presentation of German history. Routinely, he confronted a fundamentally adversarial historical orthodoxy. Most students, irrespective of academic background, shared an "enormously widespread conception that there is a historical Destiny, which cannot be changed by individuals, fate and the law of history playing the role of convenient scapegoats." Such notions, Ehrmann recalled, were responsible for the "general lack of guilt feelings among Germans," and undermined the purpose of the reeducation program.[6] Moreover, most of his students were young men of limited education who had been exposed exclusively to narrow nationalistic interpretations of German history.

Ehrmann decided to avoid the typical presentation of history as "the chronicles of wars and dynasties" and to focus, instead, on "politico-economic and social developments." He speculated that the presentation of selective events from Germany's past by means of an unfamiliar format had a greater chance of "destroying . . . historical myths" and "debunking . . . those concepts which had served in the past to fill the youth with arrogant and chauvinistic attitudes."[7]

Not all of Ehrmann's students had been captivated by a narrow nationalistic interpretation of Germany's past. The school naturally had its fair share of intellectuals who had privately dissociated themselves from strident German nationalism but without ever translating their personal misgivings into any form of active dissent. These students resented "the stress laid on the authoritarian tendencies in German history" because "they regarded themselves as convinced anti-Nazis and therefore so far removed from the reactionary forces that they need not be subjected to a discussion of the weaknesses of German democracy."[8] Ehrmann hoped to use his presentation of German history to unsettle and destroy the self-righteousness of this group. He was no partisan of Inner Emigration; he rejected the notion that intellectual introversion had served a constructive purpose in the battle against Nazism. He gave "only secondary" and mostly negative consideration to intellectual history "in order to combat escapist tendencies in which German liberal elements especially like to indulge."[9] To this group of prisoner-students he sought to demonstrate that there had been real democratic tendencies in German thought, and, if anything, they had petered out due to the lack of encouragement from intellectual circles.

The American civilization and institution course complemented much of Ehrmann's didactic approach. "In the spirit of 'look now upon this picture, then on this,'" the parallel course in American institutions sought to explain how and why "the United States, with many and grievous faults" had succeeded where Germany had failed. Instead of merely supplying a historical survey of American history, Howard Mumford Jones focused on the technical reasons for the endurance of democratic institutions in the United States.

Jones argued that the strength of American democracy was not the work of great men and great ideas. Geographical expanse was mainly responsible for the success of democratic institutions in the United States because it had limited the ability of a central government to rein in the entire country. Jones placed a large wall map of the United States before the class in every one of the lectures and commenced his course with a discussion of the geography of the United States. The "vastness and resources of the country made an impressive opening," he noted.[10] Just as Ehrmann had tried to suggest that there was nothing inherently evil in the makeup of German society, Jones argued that decentralization, rather than unique personal traits of the people or their leaders, had endowed the United States with a different political fate. Geographical circumstances had produced a deconsolidated government in the United States, a prerequisite for a healthy popular democracy. Jones's course suggested quite explicitly that if the Germans would make dispersal of government a central tenet of their reconstruction efforts, they might duplicate the American political experience.

Seventy-three out of the original 101 students eventually graduated from the Experimental School; the concluding "commencement" ceremony was held on July 6, 1945. In his final report, school director Howard Mumford Jones appeared quite satisfied with the intellectual content and the didactic approach of the school, but when called upon to assess the entire experiment, his appraisal was severely critical. The administration of student recruitment, he stated, had been so poor as to undermine the entire course. The criteria employed for this delicate task had been haphazard at best. Recruiters never applied a standardized policy regarding such crucial features as educational background and the political credentials of the candidates. Perhaps forgetting that his experimental administrative school was not originally conceived as an intellectual enterprise, Jones complained of an unduly high number of students with only a *Volksschule* education; they were unable to cope with the academically rigorous requirements of the school. To make matters worse, those in charge of student recruitment had not bothered to investigate the prerequisites for recruitment to civilian government in Germany. Somewhat belatedly, the faculty had discovered that most army groups in occupied Germany refused employment to anyone with even nominal ties to Nazi-affiliated organizations, including trade unions and professional guilds.[11] Such stringent criteria had not been used by the SPD's liaison officers at the various camps; they had recommended candidates on the basis of personal assessments.

Jones also complained that the uncoordinated arrival of new students as well as confusion over the exact date for repatriation left large numbers of "graduates" wandering aimlessly through the camp between completion of requirements, commencement ceremonies, and actual repatriation. He feared that POW-students would interpret such bureaucratic snags as examples of "the inability of the American government to follow a clear plan," or, even worse, that "democracy is inefficient." The final report also noted that an uneven knowledge of English among the students undermined much of the intentions of the American institutions and military government courses. Both courses, at times, were "crippled" by different degrees of competence in English. The military government course, originally meant to be the most crucial facet of the entire program, suffered from poor liaison with the occupation forces in Europe.

Major Dell continuously discovered that he was teaching obsolete material as American military authorities in Germany frequently adjusted and refined their policies without informing the school of policy changes.

Perhaps the most serious problem affecting the school was the inability to re-create the conducive social environment of an American campus. The faculty had attempted to gain the students' confidence and reduce their reserve by minimizing the trappings of military discipline and camouflaging the restrictive ambience of the POW camp. Upon entering this camp-turned-campus, the students relinquished the crucial hierarchical aspects of military life. Officers "had to forgo their privileges and to remove all distinguishing insignia, and the groups into which the students were divided were, except for the language instruction, composed in a purely mechanical" and random manner.[12] By eliminating the symbols of military life, the faculty had hoped to encourage individuality and intellectual inquisitiveness among the students.

The students remained, however, reticent, obedient, and maddeningly docile. Fostering a sense of "independence, dignity, and responsibility," the important by-products of American campus life, suffered from "the persistence of an attitude of reserve" among the students. The faculty attributed the tenacious formality of their students to deeply rooted German cultural traditions. The culprits, the final report speculated, were two: the "uncertainty of the prisoner of war as to his status" as well as "the traditional gulf between the professor and the student in German educational practice."[13]

In actual fact, the reserve and caution of the students were due to the mixed cues they received from the faculty. While ostensibly a demonstration of American educational objectives, numerous aspects of the program signaled otherwise. The German-language material at the Experimental School informed the students that their program was part of an American "reeducation" program. "The German word for 'reeducation' is 'Umschulung,' the word used by the Nazis for forcible 'reeducation,'" Jones noted belatedly in his summary of the activities of the school. Such an unfortunate association had "the wrong connotation for the purposes of the school," he added in a rare understatement. Furthermore, the school had blundered in its decision to allow instructors to teach in uniform. The original idea was to demonstrate American democracy by placing all faculty members, irrespective of rank, on an equal footing. In practice, however, such a policy caused tension among the students. The prisoners who had sergeants and other enlisted personal as instructors suspected that they were considered less promising than those students with officer-instructors.

Jones's candid assessments of the strengths and weaknesses of the Fort

Kearney Experimental School provided the basis for the move beyond an experimental project toward a larger, more ambitious effort to teach democracy to a broader selection of prisoners who would furnish a cadre of politically acceptable potential civil servants. Upon receiving official permission for its school projects in mid-March 1945, the SPD established a new branch, the Prisoner of War School Center. Unlike Jones's Experimental School, the new School Center developed two separate programs which took into account the divergent educational levels of the POWs. The SPD chose two adjacent camps in Rhode Island, Fort Getty and Fort Wetherill, for its school sites. Lt. Colonel Alpheus Smith, a physics professor–turned-soldier, was appointed as director of the School Center.

Fort Getty housed Project II, the ambitious administrative school for the cream of the POW population. Here the SPD painstakingly chose the most academically promising and educated among the prisoners of war. Project II predictably placed a greater emphasis on political indoctrination than it did on the instilling of administrative skills. The focal points of the syllabus were revised, amplified, and streamlined versions of the courses in German history and American institutions which had been developed in Jones's Experimental School. Fort Wetherill, also known as Project III, served as the police school. The primary focus of this program was the training of a collaborative civilian police squad for occupation forces in Germany. The two-month course at Wetherill focused primarily on such issues as crowd control, self-defense, first aid, and basic legal issues. The history courses as developed at the Experimental School played second fiddle to what was mostly a vocational program.

Both projects applied significantly more cautious political qualifications for recruiting potential students than had the Experimental School. The SPD devised a detailed policy for screening applicants. Unwilling to waste energy on the young, who had received all their education and formulated their historical consciousness within the hermetically sealed world of the Third Reich, American officials restricted nominations to candidates aged 25 years or older, preferably, "but not mandatory . . . between 30 and 40 years of age." The new guidelines called for the selection of "anti-Nazis in the broad interpretation of the word," including "not only those who are actively opposed to Nazism, but also those who are merely non-Nazis. However, career or regular army officers above the grade of captain" were automatically disqualified. A total of 17,883 were screened for Projects II and III: 14,172 were rejected, 816 were classified as possible candidates for the administrative school, and 2,895 qualified for police training. Further screening, including lie detector tests for problematic cases, as well as logistical and time constraints reduced the actual number of students at the administrative school and police school to 455 and 488, respectively.

The final screening process of candidates introduced a new and crucially important political approach to reeducation. The guidelines introduced, for the very first time, a new political qualification that disqualified "prisoners of war with definite communistic backgrounds or tendencies." In distinct contrast to the rest of the carefully worded criteria for screening, the deliberately vague "communistic" rather than "Communist" endowed the screening officers with the discretion to reject a large number of possible candidates aside from bona-fide Communists. Suspicion of leftist leanings was enough to eliminate a candidate.[14]

One possible explanation for the SPD's heavy-handed attitude toward ideologies of the left was what Henry Ehrmann described as an attempt to control the destabilizing "moral and psychological vacuum" caused by the demise of National Socialism. In an article published in *Social Research*, about a year after the dismantling of the SPD, he recalled contemporary fears that "the material collapse of Germany would be followed by a spiritual breakdown resulting occasionally in a nihilistic attitude even toward the survival of Germany as a national entity."[15] When translated into the political reality of the time, Ehrmann's explanation suggests that the real issue was the fear that the failure of virulent nationalism in Germany would enhance the attraction of transnational movements of the left. "Nihilism" served as a buzzword for all antinational political theories. Under these circumstances, the presence of Communist advocates, sympathizers of leftist causes, or fellow travelers was something to be avoided.

There was another compelling reason for the anti-"communistic" policy for Projects II and III. Following in the footsteps of the Experimental School, the historical programs in the projects devised an interpretation of history which blamed strong ideological movements—be they of the left or right—for all major political catastrophes. To avoid undue questioning of this central tenet, the SPD invoked the anti-communistic clause in order to ban the ideologically motivated from a program which preached the unimportance of ideas and ideology. All convinced Nazis were already disqualified; the new clause purged the true believers from the left, as well.

The person most responsible for the historical indictment of ideological stances was Colonel T. V. Smith, the University of Chicago philosopher, Illinois congressman, and radio personality. Smith, the former director of reeducation for American Occupation Forces in Italy, had joined the staff of the SPD toward the final phases of the Experimental School, where he served as an educational advisor. Shortly after the establishment of Projects II and III, he replaced Howard Mumford Jones as director and principal instructor of the American history program.

Smith informed his students that poets, religious leaders, and advocates of spiritual issues, not politicians, had been responsible for most modern political calamities. He taught the POW students that one should divide the world into "high-tensional" persons—advocates of principle, high-minded, but dangerously detached from reality—and low-tensional counterparts—pragmatic, practical people who, through a process of give-and-take, were able to find a silver lining of compromise even in the worst of confrontations. The United States, Smith taught his students, had managed for the most part to avoid catastrophic conflict because this country enjoyed a low-tensional political culture.

> We Americans who in general have succeeded in making our worst conflicts constructive through low-tensional give-and-take have nevertheless had our democratic failures and the greatest failure in our history was the Civil War. Through the democratic folly of trying to solve our worst moral problem of minorities by means of force we not only impoverished the South and corrupted the North with fictitious hope . . . but we also rendered the minority problem itself hardly less insoluble after slavery than it was during slavery. . . . This failure of our own proceeded, too, from consciences so impetuous as to snatch the problem of slavery from the low-tensional men, the politicians, who had arranged one compromise after another until finally the preachers and poets and pietists got so stiff-necked with righteousness that politicians found grounds of peace no longer tenable. . . . The spiritual tragedy of it all was . . . that it was not the bad men of either section who turned a repressible into an irrepressible conflict; it was the good people, the most sensitive of both sides who abolished all the middle ground upon which both Lincoln and Douglas could stand.[16]

Smith hoped that his German students would reach the inevitable conclusion that their own political catastrophes and failures in democracy had occurred because, like those unyielding men of principle who had forced the United States into a civil war, German politicians and philosophers had never been willing to modify their principles to suit reality. "Their ideals are so high and their devotion to duty so tensional that they take the quick-course to coercion to achieve what only the slow-course of persuasion and toleration can yield. . . . Conflicts between men, I explained to them, do not usually become lethal until it is 'the principle of the thing' that gets into dispute."[17]

The course in German history, once again devised and taught by Henry Ehrmann, conveyed, in part, an analogous message. Ehrmann focused most of his lectures on the Weimar Republic. He argued that this had been a period of notable democratic achievements in the area of local government and industrial relations. His approach attributed the demise of the German republic to the breakdown of the art of compromise on which German democracy, like any other, had to rely for the solution of conflict.[18]

By Ehrmann's own account, these expositions on democracy and compromise delivered in both the German and American courses had no immediate results. Ehrmann concluded that these historical warnings against unyielding stances did not affect the everyday behavior and attitudes of his students. Very few of his students, he noted, "discovered the methods and techniques of tolerance," or, "were able to listen to divergent opinions without undue agitation."

> The students showed, for example, a general inability to conduct an orderly debate. This trait was caused primarily by a complete ignorance of the most elementary rules of parliamentary procedure—and those prisoners who had lived through fourteen years of the republic were usually no better in this respect than "Hitler's Children." But it arose also from a lack of self-restraint and from a disinclination even to attempt to grasp the significance of an opponents' opinion.[19]

Ehrmann neglected to mention that the ideological intolerance of his students was not a uniquely German problem. As early as the final phases of the Experimental School, SPD officials found themselves in the uncomfortable position of defending their own political credentials. The SPD's discrediting of ideologies in general, and the disqualification of German leftists from participation in Projects II and III, in particular, opened the door for an uncomfortable scrutinizing of the program's own instructors. By sanctioning a very harsh attitude toward political trends from the left, the movers and shakers of the educational school had unleashed a demon. Encouraged by the rhetoric of the SPD educational staff, the OPMG moved beyond the screening of prisoners and began to investigate the reeducation tutors as well.

The PMG had initiated a process of ideological purification among reeducation officials as early as June 1945. Loyalty investigations coincided with the planned absence of the SPD's two most important officers, the director Edward Davison and his right-hand man, Walter Schoenstedt. Both were assigned on temporary duty to Europe in order to establish a similar reeducation program for the European theater PMG in Querqueville, France.

In mid-June, a few weeks after the departure of Davison and Schoenstedt, Major General Lerch abruptly ordered the SPD to transfer its headquarters from New York to Washington. Lerch explained that the move was partly in compliance with State Department pressure. The State Department had complained bitterly about the new crash-course phase of the SPD which ostensibly contradicted the original mandate of abiding by the Geneva Convention. The department's liaison officials wanted the program's headquarters nearby in order to monitor SPD policy more closely.

In complying with this State Department request, the PMG made it clear that he had his own personal score to settle with the SPD. He raised suspicions of a grave political nature. He claimed that the patriotism and loyalty of many staff members were in question. Lerch used the Washington move to dismiss much of the New York office staff and induce a major shakeup in personnel. In addition, OPMG intelligence officers began to routinely deny the SPD's own personnel requests, claiming vague, yet ominously sounding loyalty issues.

Howard Mumford Jones was the first member of the faculty to understand the implications of the new political climate. In a curt letter addressed to Major General Lerch, Jones announced his forthcoming resignation.

> Lt. Col. A[lpheus] W. Smith [the Director, Prisoner of War School Center], in whom I have complete confidence, seems to meet unparallel difficulties in having his requests for personnel filled; and I understand this difficulty arises out of doubts concerning the patriotism, loyalty or adherence to democratic principles of those officers and others asked for. I do not understand why men already cleared by American officials from all taint of suspicion need at this late hour to be reinvestigated, nor, since Col. Smith does me the honor to consult me about all teaching appointments, do I like the inference that I am recommending suspected characters.[20]

Given the climate of suspicion and the questioning of loyalties and goals, Jones concluded, "I must ask to be relieved of my responsibilities . . . in order that I may return to my normal occupations, which I gave up for the good of the service." On the following day, July 19, another key figure resigned his post. Major Maxwell McKnight, the acting director of the SPD in Davison's absence, tendered his resignation. McKnight was particularly upset over the reassignment of his acting executive officer, Lt. Handschy, a move that fell upon McKnight without prior consultation.[21] Handschy had been reassigned because he posed an unspecified security risk. "Probably . . . he subscribed to the *New Republic*," McKnight noted bitterly in a letter sent to Edward Davison in Europe.[22]

McKnight could have saved himself the trouble of resigning. Major General Lerch, the PMG, had already decided upon his removal. McKnight's successor was a Colonel Ben Powell, a trusted member of Lerch's executive staff. The deposed McKnight stayed on briefly as Powell's assistant director, but was soon transferred, at his own request, to the School Center, where he briefly taught American institutions before leaving the SPD completely. It should be noted that while many of the faculty members complained among themselves, the actions of Jones and McKnight were exceptional. No other member of the academic staff resigned or protested officially in writing.

As for Howard Mumford Jones, he departed from the program in good humor, and with little rancor. On the evening of August 6, 1945, his colleagues held a farewell dinner for him at the Idea Factory. The PMG, Archer Lerch, sent his personal secretary, Major Gemmill, to the dinner in order to gauge the staff's mood. The affair was attended by most of the senior faculty, including Davison and Schoenstedt who had returned hurriedly from Europe in order to somehow contain the situation. Gemmill reported that "considerable 'kidding' was heard about all of them being Communists, but at no time during the evening was there any serious discussion concerning either Communism or loyalty investigations." As far as the staff and faculty of the SPD were concerned, Gemmill added:

> Though I am not an expert, my personal opinion is that there are no Communists among them. . . . I feel certain there is not a single officer in any of the projects who considers himself or his personal beliefs of more importance than his loyalty to or general self-respect for the Provost Marshal General. It is also my personal opinion that, though the departure of Dr. Jones may be considered a loss, his leaving is really a blessing in disguise. Colonel Davison will have more complete control of the situation with Dr. Jones away, and I am sure that Colonel Davison's foremost desire is to carry out your policies without equivocation.[23]

In all fairness, one should note that Lerch explained that his political purging of the SPD had not been some personal crusade. Both the fate of the program as well as his own future would be jeopardized, he claimed, "if personnel were not snow-white." He was merely adhering to the "adamant views of the highest people on top-side in the War Department" and exercising caution given "the fact that Burton was on the rampage again."[24]

Lerch was referring to H. Ralph Burton, chief counsel of a congressional military affairs committee, who had released a list of sixteen commissioned and noncommissioned officers with backgrounds "which reflect Communism." The list, which included three highly decorated OSS officers as well as Sergeant Dashiel Hammett, cited offenses such as contributions to the *Negro Quarterly* and participation in the Spanish Civil War on the Republican side as evidence of the army's lenient attitude toward those who espoused Communist views directly or indirectly. Even though Secretary of War Stimson rejected these charges and personally defended the sixteen soldiers, the events within the SPD suggest that his Department may have been placed on the defensive.[25] Ironically, the SPD loyalty crisis occurred even though in January 1945 the War Department had issued a new directive banning discrimination against members of the armed forces "that is predicated on membership in or adherence to the doctrines of the Communist party unless there is a specific finding that the individual has a loyalty to the Communist Party . . . which overrides his loyalty to the United States."[26]

Lerch's protestations of innocence were, nevertheless, somewhat suspect. The entire affair, including its timing and tone, bore a distinct personal stamp. To begin with, the loyalty issue reached breaking-point only after the two key figures, Davison and Schoenstedt, had departed for Europe. Davison had no apparent knowledge of the intention to replace his trusted assistant, Maxwell McKnight. The swift dissipation of the crisis, following the hasty return of Davison and Schoenstedt, appeared to have halted plans to purge the SPD staff entirely. Moreover, as soon as Lerch had departed from the OPMG in late October 1945, reeducation officials swiftly reinstated a very liberal curriculum.

It appears that Lerch tolerated, perhaps encouraged, if not actually initiated, the loyalty purges. Such a stance was due, in part, to his reading of the geopolitical situation. Like so many other Americans in the final phases of World War II, he believed that the Soviet Union, imbued with the creed of revolution without borders, was a significantly greater threat to the American way than the rapidly fading Nazi specter. Lerch's last act as PMG had been to order a toning down of anti-Nazi propaganda emanating from the SPD. Much to the chagrin of the film branch of the SPD he held back the release of the SPD atrocity film in order to edit out what he considered to be "objectional features," those harsh graphic displays of German atrocities which might have offended and alienated some of the prisoners.[27] In the early phases of the POW program in the United States Lerch had been responsible for the curious policy of isolating the most strident anti-Nazis and placing them, rather than the fanatic Nazis, in separate camps. Like so many other staff members of the PMG, he considered many of the vocal anti-Nazis to be crypto-Communists who would be best isolated from the rank and file.[28] The dismissal of suspected leftists from the faculty of the SPD was a natural continuation of such policies.

Lerch's support for the loyalty purge did not derive solely from ideological convictions. His zeal was probably part of an effort to improve his job resume. In his reading of the impending postwar map, Lerch had presumably understood the importance of strong anti-Communist credentials, and had acted accordingly. His actions paid off handsomely. In the fall of 1945, Lerch was appointed to the high-profile position of

American military governor in Korea. He died shortly thereafter of a heart attack, apparently brought on by the stress of the new job.[29]

Prior to his death, he made a statement that was quite revealing of his attitude toward the type of person he had hounded among the staff members of the SPD. In one of his periodic and basically futile attempts to quell the civil unrest and unsettling political agitation in Korea, Lerch singled out intellectuals as scapegoats. He threatened arrest and jail terms for "speakers, writers, publishers, editors, and pamphlet distributors" who, in his opinion, had disturbed "peace and order" in the "unrestricted license they attributed to freedom of the press and freedom of speech."[30]

Of course, to place blame for the loyalty purges on Lerch alone would be incorrect. Those who remained silent were equally guilty. The faculty's acquiescence in, if not the acceptance of, ideological cleansing in the name of phantom loyalty transgressions, demonstrated one of the most fascinating paradoxes of the American academic milieu at mid-century. These instructors, mostly professors from esteemed universities who espoused academic freedom and the free exchange of ideas, accepted with little debate and only token protest the curtailing of the very values that they taught.[31]

Presumably some of the faculty chose silence because, after all, they were soldiers; orders, no matter how distasteful, had to be obeyed. Others probably feared for their own skin. Henry Ehrmann often expressed a very positive assessment of Germany's working class, and his background prior to arriving in the United States was irrefutably left-wing. Any overt support for the discredited members of the SPD might have evoked a past he would rather forget.

There were some faculty members who simply agreed with the policy. In a special issue of *American Scholar* on academic freedom and Communism, published in 1949, T. V. Smith stated quite frankly his long-held position that those suspected of communistic leanings had no right to teach in institutions and programs "whose ends they disavow and whose means they subvert as best as possible." As an advocate of expediency over principle, Smith added that he saw no point in the martyr complex of his colleagues who were prepared to defend left-leaning professors against the tide of public opinion.

> We need not be afraid of a hand-full of Communists in colleges, but we might well be afraid of a land-full of citizens, who will never understand how our academic freedom requires them to stomach Communist teachers. . . . Once we have made up our mind to sacrifice the Communists, we will begin to lose the disbelief in our fellow citizens, which in no small part we have borrowed from the Communists themselves.[32]

As for the fear that in the process of a loyalty purge in academia some innocent souls might be wrongfully indicted, the Chicago philosopher professed belief in the where-there-is-smoke-there-is-fire school of thought. "People get persecuted—as they get bitten by dogs—who show themselves afraid."[33]

As historian Ellen Schrecker observes in her study of the Red Hunt in American academia, many members of the academic profession chose silence or even condoned loyalty purges "because they sincerely believed that what they were doing was in the nation's interest" and served the cause of American academia as well. Cherished concepts of "intellectual independence so prized by American academics simply did not extend to the United States government," she adds in her analysis of academia's response to charges of disloyalty among its ranks.[34] Here, within the narrow confines of the SPD—a microcosm of things to come—the manifest reluctance to defend beleaguered colleagues implicated the program's faculty as accomplices in this travesty of justice. In many ways the trials and tribulations of the accused SPD faculty members presaged a much larger loyalty controversy that would affect American society in general, and institutes of higher learning in particular.

As for the SPD, the loyalty purges created a climate of deceit and fear. Scheming, politically motivated prisoners were quick to take advantage of the dark clouds hanging over the program. The PMG began receiving written protests from prisoners who had been expelled from the School Center, all of whom complained of a leftist conspiracy within the program. On October 12, 1945, eight members of a group of twelve expelled POWs delivered a letter to the PMG protesting that they had been dismissed from the Administrative School at Fort Wetherill because they were ardent anti-Communists. They claimed that they had been falsely implicated as Nazis by the service company, the German POW auxiliary staff at the school that was, they claimed, "a secretly trained" and "politically active communistic committee."[35] In a series of individual letters addressed to the intelligence officer at Fort Dix, to which these twelve POWs had been removed, the expelled candidates elaborated upon their charges. These POWs claimed to have heard strains of the "International" coming from the service company mess hall, or to have been subjected to dogmatic Communist lectures. All of the rejected inmates maintained that their only fault was their vocal and consistent arguments with pro-Communist service company inmates.[36]

Lt. Colonel Alpheus Smith, the commandant of the Schools Center, refuted these accusations in great detail. Most of the twelve had been released because of their persistent espousal of National Socialism, pan-Germanism, or militarism. Another had been released because of "sexually abnormal" behavior, one due to his violent personality, and another because "he was suffering from kleptomania which is a habit not desirable in a policeman," Smith drily observed.[37]

It is safe to assume that at this point, Alpheus Smith's explanations did not resolve suspicions of a Communist underground within the schools project, because he, himself, was a major target of the loyalty investigations. In fact, Alpheus Smith had been implicated by one of his peers. On August 2, 1945, Chaplain John Dvorovy, the officer in charge of the SPD's religious branch, approached an intelligence officer at the PMG's branch headquarters in New York. "It was plain to see that something was bothering the Chaplain, and he asked the undersigned if he could have a personal and private 'chat,'" the intelligence officer wrote in his report.

> The Chaplain thinks that the management of . . . [the schools] under Lt. Col. A[lpheus] W. Smith, is not being carried out in the best interests of the Provost Marshal General; that the "civilians in uniform" are injuring the entire program; and that the "leftist" leanings of Lt. Col. A. W. Smith and Major Henry L. Smith [the linguistics expert] are becoming quite apparent. . . . The Chaplain stated, "Something is very rotten."[38]

Captain Dvorovy went on to accuse Major Maxwell McKnight of leaning "over backward toward the left." McKnight's sympathies, Dvorovy informed the intelligence officer were irrefutably "pro-communism in scope."[39] The Chaplain, a marginal and disgruntled officer in the SPD, had never been able to convince his fellow officers to accept religious activities as a bona-fide tool for reeducation. Whatever other motives he might have had for indicting his colleagues, the climate of fear created by innuendos of disloyalty allowed Dvorovy to settle old scores with some of his fellow officers and, perhaps, to gain some sort of favored status in the eyes of his superiors in the OPMG. His designs were thwarted by Major General Lerch's reassignment to Korea, and Edward Davison's return to the helm of the SPD.

Davison used Lerch's departure to save the heads of Henry Lee Smith and Alpheus Smith who, together with McKnight, had been accused of disloyalty; both Smiths retained their jobs. Davison was, however, swiftly confronted with another unsettling crisis. Even before the dust of the loyalty purge had settled, the SPD found itself fending off a mutiny of sorts among the prisoner rank and file. The policy of diverting all senior members of the SPD from their previous duties to the schools, and the funneling of most resources toward the reeducation of a small group of prisoners at the expense of other inmates aroused resentment within the camps.

The new crisis was sparked by press reports concerning plans to transfer American-based POWs to France as labor brigades. An urgent memorandum from Major Paul Neuland, the chief of the Field Service Branch of the SPD, stated that these reports had "practically blown the reorientation program."

> The prisoners of war are stunned by the report. . . . They have become indifferent to many impacts of American ways of life afforded them through the re-orientation program and have developed a decided turn toward leftist and communist attitudes. The old Nazi die-hards are laughing at the ones who had begun to develop a saner viewpoint and are saying 'I told you so' to them with great satisfaction and very harmful results.[40]

The initial reaction of American officials to this implicit rebellion merely alienated the rank and file further. Some camp commanders and field representatives of the SPD informed the dismayed prisoners that "this change in policy is not a real infringement of their rights because they are not free citizens in their present status and as such are not entitled to the full realization of democratic principles."[41] Other officials chose to deny the rumors, informing the prisoners that "they must not be so quick to believe that reports found in American newspapers are official because our newspapers do not always reflect governmental decisions but are sometimes merely private conjectures on the part of the newspapers."[42]

When pressed for a more meaningful solution, the SPD sought to regain the confidence of POWs by expanding its school policy and opening its gates to a larger cross section of the camp population. Successful completion of a school program, as all prisoners knew, entailed swift repatriation without having to experience the way-station of the French labor brigades. The dangling of such a carrot before the rank and file promised to mend the fences between the SPD and a significant portion of the prisoners. A more extensive school program provided as well an excellent forum for the faculty to elaborate their views on American values and the role of education in the pending new world order.

CHAPTER NINE

The Democracy Seminars: Preparation for "One World"

ON AUGUST 26, 1942, former Republican presidential candidate Wendell Willkie launched a memorable world tour as special emissary of his one-time rival, President Franklin D. Roosevelt. During the course of forty-nine days, thirty of which were spent on the ground in meetings and tours with the leaders of Allied nations, Willkie logged a total of 31,000 air miles, a figure "which still impresses me and almost bewilders me," he recalled.[1]

While the contraction of distance brought on by aviation technology amazed Willkie, the overall impressions generated by the trip were quite predictable. Willkie observed that the soaring angle of vision offered by flight did not generate a sense of "distance from other peoples, but of closeness to them." Peering at the world from above produced impressions of geographical continuity and political sameness rather than division and diversity. "If I had ever had any doubts that the world has become small and completely interdependent," Willkie added in acknowledging his internationalist preconceptions, "this trip would have dispelled them."[2]

> There are no distant points in the world any longer. I learned by this trip that the myriad millions of human beings of the Far East are as close to us as Los Angeles is to New York by the fastest train. . . . When you fly around the world in forty-nine days, you learn that the world has become small not only on the map, but also in the minds of men. All around the world, there are some ideas which millions and millions of men hold in common, almost as if they lived in the same town.[3]

Willkie was, of course, well aware of lingering resistance to the politics of a common global destiny in the United States. "Today . . . America is like a beleaguered city that lives within high walls through which passes only an occasional courier to tell us what is happening outside those walls," Wendell Willkie wrote in *One World*. "I have been outside those walls. And I have found that nothing outside is exactly what it seems to those within," he added.[4]

From within, it appeared that American political values were unique. From outside—or actually from above—the differences in political orientation between an American citizen, "a veiled woman in ancient Baghdad," a "weaver of carpets in legendary Persia," a "strong-limbed, resolute factory worker in Russia . . . or a Chinese soldier at the front" were as insignificant as the minute differences in topography and land-scape as seen from the soaring heights of Willkie's airplane.[5] "Continents and oceans are plainly only parts of a whole, seen, as I have seen them, from the air. England and America are parts. Russia and China, Egypt, Syria and Turkey, Iraq and Iran are also parts" of one comprehensive picture rather than discrete unrelated units.[6]

Wendell Willkie was the son of German immigrants. As such, it was appropriate that his book, *One World*, provided the framework for the last-ditch effort to indoctrinate a large group of German POWs prior to their departure from the United States. The book offered guidelines for dispelling the notion of incompatible differences between Germans and Americans by proposing a canopy of internationalist thought. Moreover, Willkie's simplistic and reductionist presentation of geopolitics and culture was written in simple prose. *One World*, the central text of the new phase of reeducation, contrasted sharply with the restrictive intellectual level of much of the Special Project Division's (SPD) program up to this point.

The SPD scuttled its preceding didactic strategy for prosaic reasons. Repatriation was imminent and the SPD was under tremendous pressure to produce tangible results from reeducation. Therefore, in late September 1945, the SPD lowered its expectations and modified its designs. Instead of intellectual exercises, reeducation officials resorted now to learning programs catering to the low- and middlebrow. Rather than relying solely on intellectual persuasion, the SPD abandoned its disproportionate funneling of energy, funds, and resources toward a small elite of intellectuals and technocrats. As part of this final concerted effort to familiarize certain "positive elements within the POW population" with the new global order, some twenty-three thousand inmates endured a six-day crash course centered around the gospel of internationalism as propounded in *One World*.

Even prior to the initiation of these short seminars, the SPD had already begun to pay greater attention to the rank and file within the camps. As of September 1945, reeducation officials introduced standard methods of mass propaganda to get their message through to the vast majority of the POWs. Overt propaganda implied a certain disillusionment with the assumption that time and conducive surroundings would allow the prisoners to discover on their own the benefits of the American system and, conversely, the evils of National Socialism. To encourage the process of self-discovery of democracy and its benefits, the SPD had tolerated in the past a large degree of freedom of expression, even among

POW opponents of reeducation. By late 1945, however, the SPD began curtailing expressions that contradicted its mission.

The most prominent forums for POW defiance were the local camp newspapers. The original tone of the eighty camp newspapers had been decidedly hostile. During the first eight months of 1945, the Factory monitors reported that twenty-five newspapers "were Nazi," eight were "violent Nazi," while only three were anti-Nazi; the rest were neutral.[7] By fall 1945 the Factory reported a dramatic change in the politics of camp newspapers. Twenty-four of the eighty camp papers demonstrated "democratic tendencies"; thirty-two were "nonpolitical"; eighteen "strongly anti-Nazi"; three were religious; one "camouflaged Nazi"; and two were "militaristic."[8]

Such a striking turnabout resulted, in part, from the realization of defeat. Yet no less important was the new activist policy of the SPD. The surrender of Germany as well as the imminent repatriation of the POWs encouraged the SPD to intervene and censor camp newspapers. New regulations sent out to SPD field representatives instructed them to "discourage" a long list of trappings of German and Nazi solidarity in camp newspapers, including the use of "Nazi symbols, slogans, or catchwords. Titles of camp newspapers in emulation of well-known Nazi papers. . . . Eulogies of military or political heroes, living or dead. . . . Glorification of *Kameradschaft* to promote political solidarity. . . . Elaborate commemoration of political holidays and party festivals. . . . Pseudophilosophical articles, based upon the persecution theme, attempting to justify German aggression and brutality. . . . Self-pity in any form, including complaints about living or working conditions."[9]

In addition, the SPD "recommended" and presumably enforced the nomination of "impartial and objective" editors for the newspapers, as well as "balanced" reporting based on the reprinting of approved articles from *Die Auslese*/The Selection, a new magazine published by the Idea Factory. This new forum for the dissemination of SPD views published preapproved articles criticizing "Nazi doctrines and practices" or praising "the positive aspects of pre-Hitler Germany" and American democracy. The revised policy for POW newspapers set aside all pretense of "truth rather than propaganda," and scuttled the self-discovery strategy of reeducation. By winter of 1945, the SPD showed no qualms at dictating the content of the local camp publications.

Reeducation officials demonstrated other signs of abandoning the facade of noncoercion and a voluntary exposure to the American message. In addition to the manipulation of camp newspapers, the SPD encouraged prisoners to listen to the European shortwave broadcasts of the Office of War Information (OWI), as well as to Allied-controlled radio stations broadcasting from occupied Germany. Following V-J Day, camps with public address systems began broadcasting prepackaged propaganda recordings of other government agencies, thereby compelling all inmates to confront an official American interpretation of events. These broadcasts relied heavily on OWI material prepared for occupied Germany, such as the German version of Norman Corwin's "On a Note of Triumph"—a CBS Radio poem to victory and its consequences. Other recorded programs from the OWI included music performances with spoken interludes on "American life."[10]

The principal goal of this new phase of reeducation was to combat negative views on American cultural achievements. According to the SPD, the portrayal of America as an underachiever had been a major weapon in the hands of reeducation adversaries among the POWs. Such views were inadvertently strengthened by the sometimes bungling and uncoordinated actions of camp commanders. The historical monograph of the SPD included the story of a local camp commander who "brought in a group of photographs to advertise American movies of the cheapest sort and instructed a prisoner of war artist to copy these pictures on the walls of the officer's club. Consequently, a familiar saying of the prisoners in the camps was, 'America has no culture. Why do you want to destroy Germany, the seat of all culture?'"[11]

The SPD attempted to combat such anti-American cultural prejudices by downplaying the most conspicuous elements of mass-culture, in particular movies, and underscoring, by contrast, high-culture forms of artistic expression. Music figured prominently in these designs.

> It was obvious that one of the best ways to show the German prisoners how false their racial supremacy ideas were would be to let them compare the quality of a so-called "Aryan" performer with a Jewish or Negro performer. Also if the German prisoners could hear the quality of American symphony orchestras and performers they might lose a little of their supreme belief in Germany as the seat of all culture.[12]

SPD authorities devised a list of symphonic recordings by American orchestras "to impress the prisoners with the fact that music is universal and not national as the Nazis proclaimed."[13] American interpretations of important German classical compositions, as well as the presentation of classical music with American themes, such as the works of Aaron Copland and Anton Dvorak, acquainted the "German prisoners with the benefits of a democratic way of life as revealed in the cultural growth and freedom of expression in American symphony orchestras."[14] This music program judiciously ignored the work of iconoclasts, including the works of the famous German-Jewish exile, Arnold Schoenberg. His dismissal of conventional tonality had been damned in Nazi Germany as a cancerous

"Jewish" infection of a classical tradition best left untouched. Rather than challenge the musical prejudices of their audience, the SPD limited itself to proving that Americans of all backgrounds were as equally competent, if not better than Germans, at mastering conventional classical music.

The potential advantages of such new and more direct forms of propaganda were, however, rendered useless by the rumors of forced repatriation to France. The plans for a massive and indiscriminate transfer of all POWs to European labor brigades contradicted an essential aspect of indoctrination: the rewarding of the cooperative prisoner. A strong protest to the Provost Marshal General (PMG) brought about policy revisions. SPD officials received permission to single out about 10 to 15 percent of the most cooperative prisoners for direct repatriation to Germany. The ultimate objective of this shift in policy was the "selection, indoctrination, and direct repatriation of some twenty thousand prisoners" of modestly positive credentials whose presence would serve as a modifying influence on the civilian population in Germany. In addition, the plan acknowledged somewhat vaguely the possible use of these prisoners to serve in some capacity in the Allied military government in Germany. On December 15, 1945, following the completion of the last classes in the Administrative and Police Schools at Getty and Wetherill, the SPD began transferring both staff and equipment from these locations to the Eustis site in Virginia. On January 4, 1946, the school initiated the first of its twelve six-day orientation cycles.

Having already siphoned off the cream of the POW population during the course of Project II, and given the limited amount of time available for intensive indoctrination in the new project, the SPD revised its criteria for sifting through the POW population. Following the departure of Major General Archer Lerch, and the subsequent subsiding of the internal loyalty purges, the SPD dropped its strict "anti-communistic" criteria. Leftist political leanings no longer qualified as a valid reason for blacklisting a potential candidate for rehabilitation. The new directive sought more broadly potential candidates among "cooperative prisoners favorably inclined toward democracy . . . who had proven their sincerity by attitudes and actions while confined in this country."[15]

The identification of committed anti-Nazis was a comparatively simple task. These were inmates who, in one way or another, had attracted their guardians' attention during the early period of captivity. The more general rummaging for reliable noncommitted inmates proved to be a much more difficult feat. Once the finality of Germany's defeat had registered in the minds of the POWs, the camps witnessed an abrupt and massive presence of "March Violets": the opportunistic abandonment of former loyalties, and a reflexive acceptance of the New Order by prisoners who hitherto had remained faithful to the old German cause.[16]

Given this sudden blooming of March Violets, the SPD attempted to sort through the masses of instant converts by evaluating the prisoners' political history. The criteria, drawn up by the Idea Factory's prisoner-workers, focused on the inmates' associational ties with the Nazi establishment. All members of "Nazi military, semi-military, political, religious, and affiliated organizations" were immediately disqualified.[17] The prisoners who survived the first round of selection then filled out a detailed questionnaire "designed to determine whether they had ever belonged to any Nazi or anti-Nazi organizations, or were ever persecuted by the Nazis." The questionnaires were checked by the German prisoner staff at the Factory, "many of them former concentration camp inmates who had had extensive experience with Nazi organizations and were highly skilled in detecting the subterfuge by which Nazis attempted to conceal their political connections and attitudes." This screening led to the division of prisoners into three categories: white, gray, and black. The whites qualified immediately for the new program, the blacks were returned to the camps, while the grays underwent further screening. All in all, 23,142 prisoners qualified for the six-day intensive "orientation" seminars held at Fort Eustis, Virginia.[18]

The quality of those who passed the screening process left much to be desired, as they represented a very narrow segment of the POW population. The very broad definition of negative associational ties during the Third Reich automatically disqualified over 70 percent of the prisoners from the Eustis seminars. In one way or another, job security, government employment, and organized youth activities had entailed membership in Nazi-affiliated organizations. The new rules abandoned the search for those who had at least demonstrated a pattern of latent objections to National Socialism, even though for one reason or another they might have been members of some party or state organization.

Aside from religious and clandestine groups, all associations in the Third Reich had been tied to the state and, by implication, to the party. Consequently, the strict screening criteria rejected everyone except the marginal men. Such a group included bona-fide anti-Nazis. The bulk however, did not fall into this category. Most acceptable candidates were either economically marginal, undereducated, or socially detached. Toward the end of the Eustis program, the SPD revised its rules and began to admit those whose only affiliations had been with the Hitler Youth or the Labor Front. Nevertheless, marginality remained the major measure for selecting candidates for the Eustis seminars, a feature that, by Henry Ehrmann's own account, led to "a considerable lowering of the average educational level of the prisoner-student group."[19] The screening process, then, undermined the ultimate objective of reintroducing a cadre of rehabilitated and well-adjusted prisoners into mainstream Germany.

The fortunate inmates who somehow survived this screening process were served by a well-seasoned faculty and staff that included most of the Projects' faculty, the American personnel of the Idea Factory, a selected group of SPD liaison officers from various camps, sixteen "safe" prisoners who had graduated from Projects II and III, eleven veteran Factory workers, and five graduates from Howard Mumford Jones's Experimental School. Having weathered the loyalty controversy in late 1945, the commanding officers of the School Center, Colonel Alpheus Smith, the Northwestern University professor of physics, and his second-in-command, Major Henry Lee Smith of Brown University, retained their positions as commanding officers of the SPD's Schools Projects Division.[20]

The Eustis project had its own director, who held full responsibility for its ideological content. The director of the Orientation Branch, the official name of the Eustis project, was a newcomer, Commander Edwin R. Casady, a navy man who in civilian life had been a professor of linguistics at Brown University. Casady was assisted by the University of Chicago's Colonel T. V. Smith, who now served in an advisory capacity. Henry Ehrmann, the only civilian on the staff, was the director of the Presentation Branch—the equivalent of supervising faculty member—in addition to serving as lecturer of the German history courses. Captain William G. Moulton, the German-language expert from Cornell, now taught T. V. Smith's American civilization courses.

The eclectic assembly of POWs of all ranks and services who arrived at Fort Eustis from a variety of camps furnished the Eustis faculty with an unusually favorable didactic climate. Diversity neutralized many of the fundamental barriers between wardens and inmates. In the POW camps, the SPD had run up against group loyalties and a sometimes resilient esprit de corps. At Fort Eustis the prisoners were significantly more vulnerable and more likely to at least listen to, if not to internalize, new ideas. Upon entering Eustis, these soon-to-be-released prisoners boarded, lodged, and studied with only a few signs of familiar frames of reference. The sudden milling together of thousands of prisoners from a wide variety of camps and from all services effectively removed the trappings of military life from the prisoners' routine, thereby destroying their primary, and hitherto sole, form of association.

To further this goal, the prisoners were required to remove all signs of military association and rank, a tactic that the SPD had tried with some success in the preceding school projects. The program directors hoped that the absence of military regalia and the random grouping of prisoners would eliminate some of the unyielding "status consciousness" of the prisoners. Failing this result, the school administration anticipated that the lack of familiar military frameworks would at least funnel the innate German respect for authority toward the instructors as symbols of American supremacy.[21]

The Eustis program, basically a simplification of the curriculum originally written by Henry Ehrmann and Howard Mumford Jones and revised by T. V. Smith, offered the fortunate handpicked prisoners a six-day whirlwind presentation of the most salient features of the school projects. Because of its short duration, the Eustis program incorporated a broader multimedia approach to reeducation. In addition to the extensive lecture courses on democracy, the new German history, and American institutions, the POW cadets spent hours watching approved movies, listening to music, and mulling through magazines. The objectives of this "six-day bicycle race" were restructured and modified. Rather than focusing on the unrealistic objective of training the inmates in democracy in less than a week, the program concentrated on two significant issues: a positive portrayal of American society as a political model, and the presentation of alternatives for Germany's political future.

Perhaps the greatest asset of the Eustis experience was the prisoners' ignorance. As far as American society was concerned, the students at Eustis arrived with the tunnel vision typical of inmates. Their knowledge of American society was confined to daily encounters with their wardens, the occasional experience with agricultural life during work details outside the camps' perimeters, and exposure to limited information as passed down through SPD-sponsored media.

Selective knowledge also appeared to be the most conspicuous element of the inmates' awareness of their own cultural roots. Henry Ehrmann reported that the prisoners were quite uninformed about contemporary German history. Even the cream of the crop among the prisoners of war, those who had qualified for Project II—the "graduate school" of the last-minute crash courses—had lacked basic knowledge of their recent past.

> 50 percent were unable to identify either the Paulskirche in Frankfurt, symbol of the revolution of 1848, or Virchow, the liberal antagonist of Bismarck (31 and 40 percent, respectively among the university graduates); 35 percent revealed complete ignorance of the German Peasants' Revolt; 50 percent neither had heard of Karl Schurz nor could they name a single Social Democratic Leader of the period before World War I (41 and 51 percent, respectively, among the university graduates). When tested about their knowledge of . . . the period of the Weimar Republic, the prisoners made hardly a better showing; 57 percent could not identify Hugo Preuss, the "father" of the constitution

(64 percent of the university graduates), several prisoners attributing the authorship of the constitution to Hindenburg; . . . 29 percent of the prisoners between thirty and forty years of age, and 39 percent of those over forty were unable to mention the names of three chancellors of the Weimar Republic.[22]

Such ignorance encouraged the faculty to attempt to subvert the prisoners' preconceptions of Germany's past through the presentation of new information rather than head-on confrontation. The courses on German history circumvented the historical myths perpetrated by the Third Reich. A new interpretation of Germany was devised by focusing on issues and persons which the Nazis had merely ignored rather than vilified. Based upon the experience from Projects II and III, these exercises in discovering a usable past for Germany's future focused on historical issues of which the POWs had only vague knowledge and no solid opinions. By avoiding clashes with any prior information or misconception, the instructors lowered the resistance of their students and evaded troublesome debates concerning objectivity and historical veracity.

By the same token, the program basically disregarded what little knowledge the prisoners had of American society. The SPD disarmingly accepted the hypocrisy and faults that prisoners found in American society, such as American racial prejudices. In fact, in order to present an approachable image of American culture, the SPD deliberately avoided a presentation of the United States as a nation of saints. Instead, the program attributed American accomplishments and power to a technical issue: Americans were successful because in their political development they were not crippled by unbending principles. Politics in the United States was based upon a series of working assumptions rather than upon rigid beliefs.

The American part of these seminars in democracy sought to remove the country's political system from the realm of the history of ideas. The opening lecture of the six-day cycle, "The Democratic Way of Life," hammered home the message that American democracy was not derived from the intellectual abstractions of great minds.[23] The lectures on democracy deliberately avoided name-dropping. With the exception of Washington and Hamilton, who received passing mention in the lecture on the development of political parties in the United States, the lectures gave no credit to the historical force of great men and great ideas.

The pivotal opening lecture, written jointly by the entire senior staff at Fort Eustis, meticulously avoided using ideological terms when describing the tenets of democracy. American democracy was based on "assumptions" rather than principles, or beliefs in "absolute and final truth."[24] The Eustis students were informed that the American political system was a political version of folk values, "an attitude of mind." No elaborate philosophy had created this way of life other than the acceptance of compromise and the rejection of unyielding principles as the working assumption of the American version of democracy. "Differences of opinion are natural, inevitable . . . but honest conviction must not be allowed to turn into blind stubbornness," the course outline stated.

> At first glance it would appear that compromise offers to every side only a second best solution. Actually, however, it is the only course of unified action possible; and in the long run, that course of action on which the greatest number of people agree brings the most "goods" to the most people. . . . Through the use of compromise, differences of opinion are built into real advantage, since they enable men to examine a problem from many sides and to understand all alternatives involved in making a choice.[25]

Two subsequent lectures on the American political system suggested that the U.S. Constitution was in essence a reflection of this common folk wisdom of compromise.[26] The checks and balances embodied in the Constitution assured the primacy of the mechanism of compromise. Accommodation, the lecture on political parties stated, had led to the development of two parties that could "hardly be distinguished from one another." Given the inbred impulse to compromise, "almost all interests and elements of the population" were represented in both parties. The POWs were informed that in other political systems with multiple small parties, "each party represents so few interests, and the party platform is so narrowly conceived, that it [compromise] cannot possibly be realized." Equally detrimental results accompanied the one-party system, where "the many different interests which we mortals have must be suppressed; and that is, of course, quite the opposite of democracy."[27]

This first series of lectures used the film *Abe Lincoln in Illinois* (RKO, 1940), an adaptation of Robert Sherwood's much-acclaimed play, to illustrate the mechanism by which a way of life produced democratic leaders and a democratic political system, strong enough even to weather the impending storm of civil war.[28] Both the movie and the complementing lecture material implied that the resilience of American democracy did not involve a set of clear, articulate, and distinct ideas. Instead, it was a product of the entire body of experience of ordinary people, evolving from a vast mass of mundane experiences rather than a few lofty principles.

The American series in the cycle ended with two lectures on "examples of democratic methods" in everyday life: the American school system and American economic life. The lecture on education stated that, in addition to the imparting of knowledge, the school system prepared the young for a society of multiple opinions. Schools acclimatized the young to democratic attitudes, in particular through the "encouragement of free expression" and the mechanism of accommodation inherent in a classless educational structure. A public school system that opens up its gates to all strata of American society, the lecture stated, produced uniform respect for the opinions of others, as well as an awareness of the importance of compromise.[29]

Two lectures on American economic life presented competition as the economic equivalent of multiple opinions. The role of government was to encourage accommodation between various economic activities, and to discourage efforts to limit access of individuals to the system. The lectures suggested that much like the rejection of ideological monoliths in politics, the renunciation of monopoly in the American economy was the primary reason for the spread of wealth. Consequently, the impact of cheap land and abundant raw material on American prosperity received only marginal attention in these presentations.

Were rich and abundant natural resources the key to America's flourishing economy? the lecture asked rhetorically. "In part, yes; but there are other countries, also rich in land and natural resources, which have nevertheless remained economically poor. . . ." The key, then, was in equitable distribution of economic assets, the lecture noted, sweeping aside any troubling questions regarding the incorporation of American economic life. The lack of large land estates, and consistent efforts to open up the land to all strata of American society, fostered a "feeling of equality and a lack of class consciousness." The survey of American economic development ended with this statement:

> Americans are, of course, not all economically equal; but the maintenance of a maximum of free and open competition gives everyone an equal opportunity to improve his economic status. . . . Since all Americans had equal political and economic rights, many were able to work their way up in a country which was growing so rapidly.[30]

At this point, and in concluding the economic portion of the course, the prisoners saw *An American Romance* (MGM, 1943), a movie that sang the praises of American free enterprise. This film was particularly attractive because of its high technical quality. As one of the first movies to be filmed in Technicolor, it was "greatly admired by the prisoners" and therefore seen as a tool for impressing upon the inmates the great technological prowess of the United States. The crux of the film, the rise of a Czech immigrant from rags to riches, from unskilled immigrant to great auto magnate, was a powerful depiction of the myth of equality of opportunity. Under the supervision of the OWI's movie watchdog, the Bureau of Motion Pictures, the final script of *An American Romance* had been transformed from an antilabor paean to rugged individualism into a story that culminates with a New Deal–style celebration of management-labor cooperation.[31] The SPD thought the film's lauding of entrepreneurship demonstrated "clearly why many American businessmen objected for so long to any kind of social or labor legislation—an objection which many Germans find hard to understand."[32]

Following the screening of *An American Romance*, the prisoners began the lecture series on military government in Germany, the starting point for the German section of the six-day course. To a large degree the German section followed the outlines developed by Henry Ehrmann in Projects II and III. Three consecutive lectures devoted to democratic traditions in Germany and the rise and fall of the Weimar Republic identified the existence of indigenous democratic trends in Germany, particularly in local government and labor unions. The central theme of this portion of the Eustis seminar was the rejection of "the theory that the Germans are racially incapable of a democratic life." The Eustis faculty hoped that their presentation of German democratic traditions would "relieve the students from the fear that they could ever rightfully be regarded as 'Quislings' of the western democracies."[33] Relying heavily on the material presented in the American lectures, the German survey sought to illustrate how the "escapism" of German intellectual traditions and the breakdown of the mechanism of "compromise" had undermined the political fortunes of democracy in Germany.

The Eustis lectures went one step further, and addressed the sensitive issue of collective guilt. The lecture on weak democratic traditions in Germany laid the blame squarely on the shoulders of ordinary citizens. For a variety of reasons, the material declared, Germans had historically placed low priority on freedom and democracy. In an unusually frank tone the lecture notes stated that

> The German people have shown therefore, that they were indeed incapable of overcoming the difficulties confronting the development toward a democratic state and society. Nations as well as individuals may be unlucky. Germany was unlucky and the whole world must suffer for this. Misfortune of nations, like all misfortune, is partly brought about by one's own fault and partly by external circumstances. . . . (T)he German . . . best take for granted that many of his historical weaknesses were brought about by his own fault.[34]

To drive this point home, the German section of the six-day course included a compulsory viewing of the movie version of Anna Segher's novel, *The Seventh Cross* (MGM, 1943), the story of an anti-Nazi's escape from a concentration camp and an indictment of German society's acquiescence of totalitarianism.[35] "In many respects this film ran counter to a basic decision made early in the planning stage, namely that instead of focusing on the evils of the Nazis, the orientation should confine itself to . . . mentioning Germany's past only where lessons could be learned or good traditions discovered," the final report of the Eustis project noted.

> This film, however, . . . answers a protestation heard from thousands of Germans: that we were only "little men" and hence were powerless to resist the Nazis, much as they might have liked to. For in this film there is such a "little man," a man who never saw the significance of his factory's switch from manufacturing needles to producing machine guns; a man who asked no questions as long as he got his daily bread and sausage. "And yet, this "little man," once awakened, shows that he *can* resist the Nazis, that he has the courage to help his friend escape even though this means endangering his own life and that of his wife and children.[36]

Following this exceptionally frank attack on the most basic of the German defense mechanisms—the claim of ignorance and powerlessness—the two final lectures abruptly ceased dwelling on the past and turned, instead, to the future, the visionary One World. "The World of today and Germany" and "New Democratic Trends in the World Today" were lifted out of the pages of Wendell Willkie's book; in fact the phrase "One World" appeared repeatedly throughout the lectures.

Much like Willkie, the Eustis staff members espoused Internationalism, the belief that peace and international harmony depended upon the globalization of American liberal tenets, and the development of international policies and supervisory mechanisms to ensure the triumph of these conditions. The global fellowship presented to the prisoners at Eustis foresaw a world dominated and held together by American values. Naturally, the SPD chose American metaphors for its vision of the postwar world. The analogy was that of the thirteen original states, and the "history of the United States from 1783 to 1789." "The world of today is thrown closer together than were the 13 states of 1783. In the interest of a common democratic existence, one might hope that the world stands today where the U.S. stood in 1788, just before its unification (which does not mean uniformity)."[37]

This teleological version of the American experience lay at the basis of the SPD's presentation of world affairs. Just as the thirteen original states had agreed to relinquish some of their rights and part of their sovereignty embodied in the articles of confederation when "it became apparent that the federal government was unworkable because of almost unlimited sovereignty of the states," so the nations of the world would have to "step towards the reduction of national sovereignty" in the quest for "One World."

At this point, toward the end of the Eustis crash course, the lecture material finally came to grips with one of the most conspicuous inconsistencies embedded in the presentation of the universal value of democracy, the American alliance with the Soviet Union. American military and political collaboration with an ambitious totalitarian power contradicted much of the political and intellectual content of the Eustis material. Here once again, the lecture notes were based heavily on *One World*. "Many among the democracies fear and mistrust Soviet Russia," Wendell Willkie had written.

> They dread the inroads of an economic order that would be destructive of their own. Such fear is weakness. Russia is neither going to eat us or seduce us. That is—and this is something for us to think about—that is, unless our democratic institutions and our free economy become so frail through abuse and failure in practice as to make us soft and vulnerable. . . . No we do not need to fear Russia. . . . We need to learn to work with her in the world after the war.[38]

The Eustis program adopted Willkie's rationalization of the east-west alliance, his humanizing of Russia and its leaders, and his allaying of fears concerning the objectives of the Communist creed. The Eustis lecture on the Soviet Union conceded that "attempts to 'define' Soviet Russia as a democracy make little sense. . . . It is beyond doubt that the Russian citizen does not know democratic freedom in the western sense of the word, but does this mean that Russia must be undemocratic in its foreign relations?"

This survey of the Soviet Union's presence in a democratic world discounted the significance of Communism's global aspirations. Stalin, the POWs were informed, was a believer of "Socialism in one country" and his foreign policy was a continuation of Russia's historical geopolitical objectives rather than the precursor of worldwide revolution.

> The Soviet Russia of today is, without doubt, continuing the traditions of Tsarist Russia. That is, Russia striving to gain ice-free ports and to erect a security zone. . . . [of] dependable states as far west as the Oder. But so far there is no indication that, in addition, Russia is seeking to create spheres of influence as a guarantee of economic advantages. . . . not even in Russian occupied Germany west of the Oder. Russia does not need all of this. (Hitler's Germany was a dictatorship which could not exist without imperialistic expansion. Russia is a dictatorship which can maintain itself better the more it concentrates on

the expansion of its internal social accomplishments.) . . . All indications are that Russia has no confidence in revolutions outside its own security zone.[39]

The accuracy of the Eustis depiction of the Soviet Union was, of course, beside the point. Its significance lay in the untiring effort to seek universal versions of American pragmatism—even in such incongruous places as the Soviet Union—as well as the attempt to deny or ignore the motivating power of ideology. The message of Eustis was that Germany had departed from the straight and narrow because its basically sound political structure had malfunctioned; the Soviet Union, irrespective of the sometimes frightening rhetoric emanating from its leaders, displayed a spirit of compromise and pragmatism reminiscent of the American attitude toward politics. In neither case was ideology an issue of great importance.

These themes, repeated frequently in lectures, film, and books, represented the farewell message of the SPD to this first large wave of repatriated prisoners, those whose function it was to serve as goodwill ambassadors for the American cause. Thus, the highlight of the periodic commencement ceremonies for departing POWs was the ceremonial reading of Stephen Vincent Benét's "A Prayer For United Nations."

> God of the free, we pledge our hearts and lives today to the cause of all mankind. . . . Our earth is but a small star in the great universe. Yet all of it we can make, if we choose, a planet unvexed by war, untroubled by hunger or fear, undivided by distinction of race, color or theory. We are all of us children of earth—grant us that simple knowledge. If our brothers are oppressed, then we are oppressed. If they hunger, we hunger. If their freedom is taken away, our freedom is not secure.[40]

Of course, the Eustis faculty was well aware of the inherent limitations of this internationalist vision. The summary of the Eustis project acknowledged that "six short days" was too brief a period for inducing conversion. Moreover, the report added, a sizable portion of the Eustis students had been admitted for all the wrong reasons. "Some of those chosen qualified for negative reasons only; they had not been uncooperative, and they had never been associated with any Nazi organization," the final report of the Eustis program admitted. "Such men are no builders of the future; in all probability, they will never take positive action of any kind, whether for good or for evil." In the same breath, however, the report placed undue expectations on another group of prisoners, the undecided "fencesitters."

> For most of these the orientation was of great value, since it gave them the final push needed to swing them over to the democratic side. No one who was in daily contact with the prisoners at the Special Projects

Center, who watched and talked with them during even six short days, could fail to see this, or could be fooled into seeing something which was not genuinely there.[41]

The SPD's own evaluations suggest the converse; the Eustis experience, like most other aspects of the reorientation, did not appear to have induced any profound change. Prisoner reactions to the most crucial material of the Eustis project brought to the surface a mentality and worldview that the SPD claimed to have weakened, if not eradicated. When momentarily overcome by emotions, as was often the case after viewing the uncomfortable message imbedded in the movie *The Seventh Cross*, the prisoner-cadets at Eustis discarded their roles as docile students. Only 30 percent of the prisoners were willing to profess that "they thought well" of the politics of the movie, in particular its central motif that those who had not resisted had, in effect, collaborated with the vilest of political systems. Fifty-five percent chose a deafening silence; 15 percent were angered enough to express outright objection, although the report passed on by Henry Ehrmann to his commanding officers did not elaborate on the reasons for their disapproval. Perhaps out of discomfort, perhaps trying to salvage something positive from a damaging indicator of limited success, Ehrmann interpreted the silence of the majority of prisoners as "indifference"; he brushed aside the objections of what was, by his own admission, a sizeable minority," as "unimportant" and "contradictory."[42] The Eustis reports discounted those who complained about the content of the program, choosing instead to pass on to SPD headquarters reports of effusive praise.

The authors of such praise were usually chosen to deliver the commencement address at the periodic graduation ceremonies, a ritual that took place every week or so. At the final exercises of Cycle IV, POW Emil Roth delivered a typical shower of compliments upon the Eustis staff and the intellectual content of the program. "Most of us," he stated, "were skeptical when we were told that democratic ways of living and thinking would be explained in six days." And yet, he added, the impossible had happened. A well-directed program and carefully selected topics had imbued the inmates with "democratic ideas."[43]

Now, commencement ceremonies by their very nature are an inopportune time to ruffle feathers. Positive exaggerations are tolerated, even expected. Roth's speech was an unexceptional event in this formal parting of ways between prisoners and educators; nagging doubts were ceremoniously set aside. It was not only at commencement ceremonies, however, that the central issue of the SPD was swept under the carpet. At no time during the course of reeducation was there any serious inspection of the assumptions of the entire program. Was it at all realistic to expect a significant and profound change in the worldview of an adult population during the course of six days, six months, or even six years? If so, how could one develop a successful strategy for such a complex operation? No searching discussion of these central tenets of reeducation ever occurred. It remains, then, to survey alternative approaches to the type of problem facing the SPD, and to discuss the reasons for the restrictive approach to reeducation espoused by the American educators in uniform.

CHAPTER TEN

Variations on the Theme of Reeducation

DURING the spring of 1946, the German POWs in the United States prepared for their long-awaited departure to Europe. For many, however, the final destination was not Germany. Much to their dismay, most prisoners were assigned one final act of penance; they were being shipped to France as members of labor battalions. Home, and the end to their journey through purgatory, had elusively moved out of their grasp.

It was under these circumstances of disappointment and resentment among the POWs that the U.S. Army decided to poll a large sample of over 22,000 prisoners gathered at embarkation centers in order to assess the achievements of the Provost Marshal General's (PMG) ambitious reeducation program. Much to the satisfaction and surprise of the pollsters, the departing prisoners dutifully completed their anonymous questionnaires with politically correct answers. Resentment over their shipment to France did not seem to induce displays of rebelliousness.

The figures appeared to be quite impressive. Seventy-eight percent of the polled prisoners disavowed the idea that individuals existed only to serve the higher authority of the state. They declared acceptance of the "American" concept that the "state exists to serve the people." Only 6 percent still professed that "Germans are a superior master race destined to rule the world"; 79 percent rejected this central premise of Nazi dogma, while the remaining 15 percent chose not to answer. In question after question, an overwhelming majority expressed sympathy for democracy and rejection of National Socialism. Democracy was the preferred form of government, and Germans, they declared, were already prepared for, or at least willing to experiment with, a new political order.[1]

The question, "Knowing what you know *now*, if Germany could fight THE SAME WAR over tomorrow and win, and you know that you would come out alive, would you be for it?" planted in the middle of the poll, induced 83 percent of the prisoners from the 36–40 age group to declare a reluctance to fight another war. The "determined aversion to fight another war" was significantly weaker among the younger prisoners. Twenty-nine percent of the prisoners from the crucial 26–30 age group expressed some degree of willingness to fight the same war all over again. Such inconsistencies left the American authorities undaunted. "Considering the special conditions included in this question," the military authorities stated in their interpretation of the poll, "the favorable percentage is encouraging."[2] These officials declared that reeducation had been a resounding success. They concluded that the Special Projects Division (SPD) had managed to influence the politically susceptible silent majority "by changing 61% [of all inmates] from a neutral to a positive appreciation of democracy."[3]

Optimistic press releases made no mention of other, quite problematic findings, in particular the persistent, nagging residuals of Nazi dogma even as the prisoners professed endorsement of their captors' views on politics and civil rights. The POWs still presumed that "Jews were the cause of Germany's troubles." Fifty-seven percent of all replies placed at least partial blame for Germany's misfortunes leading to the Second World War on the shoulders of Jews. An additional 10 percent failed to answer the question, their choice most probably motivated by prudence; they chose not to antagonize their jailers on the eve of their departure. Only 30 percent accepted as true the reports of concentration camps and Nazi atrocities. The rest dismissed the films, pictures, and booklets which they had been required to view as mere propaganda. Even at Fort Eustis, where POWs with seemingly impeccable anti-Nazi credentials were undergoing special democracy training courses, 10 percent of these "special" inmates still entertained the notion that Jews were partly responsible for their country's calamities.[4] The official SPD interpretation of the poll chose to ignore this puzzling fusion of democracy and remnants of Nazi dogma.

A similar survey carried out by a different military branch suggests a possible reason for the SPD's dismissal of such troubling inconsistencies. In a scholarly article published in July 1945, two social scientists in uniform suggested that the simultaneous espousal of democratic and totalitarian creeds underscored the futility of reeducation projects. Donald McGranahan and Morris Janowitz had administered a poll of young Germans, including a group of German POWs in an American-administered camp in France, that posed strikingly similar questions to those of the SPD survey. Their material demonstrated the same mixture of seemingly conflicting political beliefs. The Germans in the Janowitz poll agreed wholeheartedly with the idea that Germany should become a democracy. They expressed great admiration for the American political system and its ideals. At the same time, they also blamed Jews, at least in part, for Germany's calamities. Moreover, they hesitated "on the question as to whether Hitler himself was bad or whether it was just his advisors who were bad."[5]

In contrast to SPD evaluations, Janowitz and McGranahan warned against isolating the positive replies from their overall context and construing them as "evidence that these youths had changed their basic character and are now young democrats." They argued that their subjects chose Nazi-oriented answers that contradicted their acceptance of democracy when they did not know the "correct" democratic rejoinder to the question. The young men fell back on familiar responses without realizing the inherent conflict between their ingrained views and their professed conversion to democracy.

> They are still totalitarian youth in search of leadership. They now echo what they consider to be the official views of their current masters. In a sense, the very manner in which they quickly pick up and express democratic and pro-American views reveals their totalitarian attitude of implicit and uncritical submission to authority ingrained by Nazi education and German tradition.[6]

Thus, according to the two authors of the questionnaire, the "durability" of German democratic opinions was doubtful. The most meaningful result of the poll was that these youngsters displayed "little critical and independent thinking, but much servility."[7]

McGranahan and Janowitz did acknowledge that the POWs in their study had, indeed, espoused democracy and American ideals more enthusiastically than any other group. "Compared with the civilian youth, they [the POWs in American-administered camps in France] revealed a greater susceptibility to the influence of their new masters." Nevertheless, they cautioned, such pro-democratic answers were more a sign of greater familiarity with the "correct" answers than of any significant change in attitude and ideology. Democratic responses were not a sign of conversion to western ideals. The regime of camp life, in particular the methodic exposure to Allied propaganda, merely allowed the prisoners to anticipate the type of response expected by their captors.

McGranahan and Janowitz did not propose a method for inducing profound democratic change among Germany's young people, nor did they assess the role of education, reeducation, or other means of genteel persuasion in remaking German society. As social scientists they proposed somewhat predictably some form of behavior modification rather than ideological conversion. They rejected the premise that, given the right environment, a captive population could be converted within a relatively short span of time. McGranahan and Janowitz asserted that the fundamental objective of reeducation—the changing of worldviews and the eradication of well-ingrained cultural conventions—was a complicated, if not impossible mission.

Officials charged with the reeducation of German POWs in the United States never expressed such doubts nor did they respond to the reservations of their colleagues from the social sciences. They maintained they had the power to capture both the hearts and minds of the enemy; all findings which suggested the contrary, such as lingering residuals of Nazism among their wards, were politely ignored.

The SPD's claims for successful conversion were never severely challenged. With the departure of German POWs, the policies of prisoner reeducation became a moot point. Questions regarding the accomplishments of military reeducation as well as its ethical foundations were brushed aside as the nation shifted its attention to the more rewarding and immediate issues of peacetime and prosperity.

A mere seven years later, the issues of POW policy and the indoctrination of military captives aroused new, and even passionate, interest. Following the cessation of hostilities in the Korean War, an alarmed American public learned of supposedly spectacular Chinese accomplishments in "brainwashing" American POWs and conversely, the disappointing results of American POW reeducation programs for Korean and Chinese captives.

In 1953, with the return of the four thousand–odd survivors among the many thousands of Americans who had fallen into enemy hands, Americans pondered the significance of a methodic Chinese campaign to indoctrinate American POWs. A group of American officials who had been associated with POW repatriation declared that at least one-third of the prisoners had turned collaborators and many more had been won over by Communist indoctrination. Explanations ranged from accusations of social decay and moral weakness among young Americans to allegations of torture and inhumane brainwashing by the Chinese.[8]

In 1963, following a decade of acrimonious controversy, the sociologist Albert Biderman completed the most comprehensive scholarly investigation of this Chinese campaign of "ideological reform" for American POWs. Biderman found little evidence of endemic weaknesses in the American national character, nor did he accept the premise of conversion via brainwashing.[9] The Chinese had indeed employed extremely harsh physical deprivation and actual abuse of the prisoners. However, Biderman claimed, the key to the Chinese operation had been a skillful understanding of military group dynamics. To begin with, the Chinese captors had separated the enlisted prisoners from their leaders, the officers and the NCOs. Deprived of traditional frames of reference, the rank and file became particularly vulnerable to a combination of physical coercion and psychological pressure, as well as to a massive indoctrination campaign exerted by their captors. At the same time, the Chinese focused most of their attention on American officers, hoping to convert and then return them to the camps as indoctrinated role models.[10]

In addition, the Chinese created masterful confusion by spreading rumors that key figures in the various camps had agreed clandestinely to collaborate and had informed on their fellow prisoners. This campaign of disinformation produced mistrust within the ranks and undermined attempts to resist the psychological persuasion campaign of Chinese captors.

Given this description of methodic, well-planned tactics of indoctrination, Biderman's final assessment of Chinese efforts was quite astounding. Having completed a study of the prisoners after their repatriation, the American sociologist argued that the Chinese campaign had achieved nothing more than a short-term modification of behavior. Driven by the will to survive, American prisoners had collaborated, but upon returning home they exhibited no meaningful change in their worldview. Indoctrination, as the instilling of new and well-anchored values, had failed.

The Chinese were not the only ones engaged in campaigns of indoctrination during the Korean War. American authorities launched their own "education" program among enemy POWs, both Chinese and Korean. The island of Koje, off the southwest coast of mainland Korea, was the site for a series of American-administrated prisoner-of-war camps for some 163,000 Chinese and North Korean soldiers and civilian internees. Approximately 1,500 American officers and an additional contingent of civilian personnel were charged with administering the camps. The educational staff consisted of twenty-six American officers, eighty American enlisted men, and a large auxiliary staff of South Korean and Taiwanese civilians.

As point of departure, the educational staff attempted to exploit traditional enmities between Chinese and Koreans, to separate the impressionable young—the camps held some twelve hundred juveniles under the age of seventeen—and to employ native teaching officers who were more attuned to the subtleties of Korean and Chinese cultures.[11] Given the fact that 24 percent of the Koreans and 60 percent of the Chinese were illiterate, the educational program focused on basic learning skills. The political dimension of this project sought to shatter the narrow political and cultural horizons of prisoners. A reeducation official recalled:

> The primary phase of the program was basic social studies, later known as Education in Citizenship, in which historical data, both past and present, were presented with the objective of giving the POW some basic knowledge and understanding of events that led to the present world conditions. It included the History of Korea, Democracy, Totalitarianism, Labor, The Farmer, The United Nations, European Nations, Latin-American Countries, Asia, Conservation, Education, and Agriculture.[12]

Reeducation officials would later point toward high percentages of POWs refusing repatriation as a sign of success. American authorities claimed that 75 percent of the Chinese and over half of the North Koreans declined repatriation.[13] However, the correlation between repatriation rates and the success of reeducation is problematic. A variety of other reasons, ranging from peer pressure and family ties, to the loss of face associated with POW status, presumably affected the decisions of the inmates. Perhaps a good indication of the program's limited achievements was the fact that American commanders were unable to break the hold of an obdurate, underground, anti-American leadership in many of the compounds. To the very end, some of the POW compounds were basically off-limits to the American reeducation staff. In fact, Koje Island was plagued by violent confrontations and mutinies which left hundreds of prisoners dead. In the most audacious incident of all, the United Nations camp commander, Brigadier General Francis T. Dodd, was held hostage by Communist prisoners.[14] Any attempt to claim success for American POW reeducation in Korea, is, then, belied by these incidences.

Curiously, the many analyses and historical accounts of American reeducation and Chinese "thought reform" during the Korean War lack a historical dimension. The efforts of the SPD during World War II were conspicuously absent from both official reports and the public debate. As far as both the scholars and protagonists of the Korean POW experience were concerned, the German POW presence in the United States and the subsequent reeducation program had never existed.

There are several possible explanations for this lack of concern for precedent. To begin with, the Korean POW controversy was dominated by social scientists, in particular sociologists and psychologists, who demonstrated little interest in historical analogies. Historicism was not fashionable in the social sciences community of the 1950s; the pioneering works of World War II sociologists such as Edward Shils, Morris Janowitz, and Donald McGranahan, while listed in some of the more exhaustive bibliographies of the many scholarly books and articles on POWs in Korea, were never produced as evidence by either side in the debate. Contemporary social scientists presumed that they were dealing with new forms of psychological manipulation for which there were no meaningful historical precedents.

Yet even if there had been more interest in historical analogies, it is doubtful that the experience of the SPD would have provoked much discussion. Social scientists had been deliberately excluded from the reeducation project for German POWs. As far as they were concerned, reeducation in the 1940s was an unknown and esoteric enterprise at best. In the aftermath of the war, SPD officials rarely bothered to describe their experiences in academic journals. The few articles published after the dismantling of German POW reeducation had been anecdotal. Only one review, an exercise in self-praise written by Henry Ehrmann, appeared in a scholarly journal of the social sciences.[15]

Unsubstantiated claims of success provided an additional reason to ignore the SPD precedent. Most SPD studies of the POWs' worldviews held little value for social scientists because they did not meet their methodological criteria. The most important investigation of all, the poll of departing POWs which claimed to have changed "61% from a neutral to a positive appreciation of democracy" was of little use because the prisoners had not undergone a similar polling of their beliefs before being exposed to reeducation.[16] In addition, American authorities initiated only one follow-up study of SPD graduates, the results of which were not very encouraging.

The principal investigator in this follow-up survey was Captain William Moulton, the former instructor of language and American studies at Kearney and Eustis. In 1947, he contacted about five hundred graduates from the school projects who resided in large cities in the American zone. The substance of Moulton's account revealed fundamental caveats in the SPD's declarations of success. The program, he implied, had not achieved the ambitious objective of creating a cadre of democratically oriented leaders for postwar Germany.

While attempting to provide an upbeat report for the War Department, Moulton confided in a letter to his former colleagues at the SPD that even the most democratically inclined elements among the former POWs were a dispirited lot. The former prize students of the SPD—the graduates of Project II at Fort Getty—had experienced "a terrific letdown when they discovered that the Military Government knew nothing of them, and was not particularly interested in them," Moulton wrote. The POWs expressed a host of other reasons for disappointment. However, Moulton intimated that the main reason for their despondence was a fundamental sense of alienation. His informants dismissed postwar German politics as "pseudo-democracy" and felt that Germany did not exhibit any sign of meaningful reform "in the economic, political, or any other fields." They described the American military government as a "military dictatorship" and they were annoyed with the idea that it was their task to explain the benefits of allied supervision of German reconstruction. "The whole picture is the curious one of a democracy trying to run a dictatorship to teach the Germans about democracy. Although most of our PWs understand the inevitability of this situation, they resent it, and feel embarrassed when they have to explain to other Germans that the Americans 'aren't really like this.'"[17]

Moulton's letter revealed one of the fundamental flaws of reeducation, the reliance on marginal men as catalysts for change. The SPD had deliberately sought students who were outside of the mainstream in the camps. They were marginal men in the POW stockades, and, not surprisingly, they retained their sense of alienation upon returning home.

Indifference to the SPD project of World War II, was, then, a combination of lack of exposure, ambiguous results, and irreconcilable differences between the humanist approach of SPD officials and the academic precepts of social scientists. To a certain degree the invisibility of the SPD experience illustrated the estrangement between rival branches of academic research in the immediate postwar years. Nevertheless, such plain disinterest in the work of others was not a problem peculiar to the social scientists of the 1950s. One should note that during the final phases of World War II, SPD officials demonstrated an equally narrow vision. There were numerous avenues of comparison available to the humanist faculty of reeducation but the files of the Office of the Provost Marshal General (OPMG) indicate that staff of the SPD paid no attention to ongoing research in the areas of reeducation, indoctrination, and other related fields.

Perhaps due to their humanist background, SPD officials appeared to have been unaware of important related research that existed in the twilight zone between psychology, sociology, and education. The most influential contributor in this field was the German-born, MIT social psychologist, Kurt Lewin. In 1945, during the middle of the American reeducation program, Lewin and his associate Paul Grabbe published their assessment of reeducation in the *Journal of Social Issues*. "The difficulties encountered in efforts to reduce prejudices or otherwise change the social outlook have led to a realization that reeducation cannot be merely a rational process," Lewin and Grabbe contended. Therefore, "lectures or other similarly abstract methods of transmitting knowledge are of little avail in changing" the subjects' outlook and worldview. "Even extensive first-hand experience," they added, "does not automatically create correct concepts (knowledge)."[18]

Lewin and Grabbe gave the example of a liberally minded white American soldier stationed in England observing, and instinctively disapproving of a black colleague fraternizing with a white woman. Such an individual "may feel that he should not mind—and he might consciously condemn himself for his prejudices. Still he may frequently be helpless in the face of his prejudice since his perception and emotional reaction remain contrary to what he knows they ought to be."[19] Thus, they noted, "re-education is frequently in danger of reaching only the official system of values, the level of verbal expression and not of conduct."[20] In other words, intellectual persuasion as the singular means of reeducation had no chance of inducing any significant modification in the worldview of the target population.

The publication of Lewin's findings in a journal of the social sciences may have hindered access to this very relevant material. Nevertheless, the SPD demonstrated a pattern of avoiding analogies. SPD files indicate no interest in the POW indoctrination policies of either allies or enemies. The American reeducation program for German POWs ignored, for example, a similar educational project aimed at another prisoner population held during the same years within the borders of the continental United States. Between 1942 and 1945, over 110,000 Americans of Japanese origin and their alien parents were forcibly removed from their homes and incarcerated in ten internment camps in desolate areas of the American west. Within the confines of these so-called relocation camps, American authorities devised an educational procedure with all the trappings of reeducation, focusing, in particular, on the impressionable and intellectually vulnerable youth.

It is difficult, and even painful to equate success with one of the most blatant instances of racism and violation of civil rights in modern American history. Nevertheless, the internment of West Coast Japanese in the United States was accompanied by a mostly effective campaign to undermine traditional bonds and allegiances among the young, and to encourage acceptance of unequivocal standards of Americanization, this despite the adverse setting of barbed wire and imprisonment, as well as a general atmosphere of bitterness, betrayal, and alienation.[21] The body charged with the running of the Japanese internment camps, the War Relocation Agency (WRA), required all camp children between the ages of six and eighteen years to attend school from 8 A.M to 4 P.M., thereby effectively removing the young and impressionable from family and communal guidance for most of their waking hours. In his study of the educational system in the camps, Robert Mossman notes that the WRA instructed its staff to utilize these extended periods of separation between the young and their parents to promote an "understanding of American ideals and loyalty to American institutions" and to create an "appreciation of the English language and American democracy."[22] Acceptance of American values, usually measured by the students' endorsement of official interpretations of internment, was rewarded in numerous ways, including highly prized appointments to student councils, yearbook and student newspaper staffs, valedictorian awards, and, of course, access to colleges for deserving graduating seniors.

At the same time, the WRA undermined traditional authority by refusing the issei, the Japanese-born parents, any form of influence or prestige in the camps. Ethnographer Christie Kiefer has noted the many faces of this deliberate elimination of the stature of the issei, including barring these elders from internal elective offices, and denying them job opportunities outside the camps. Without the familiar economic and social trappings of prestige the issei parents could not maintain their traditional authority. Kiefer observed that the "shame-oriented" issei abstained from disciplining their children in the communal dining halls as well as in the thin-walled barracks.[23] This decrease in the prestige of traditional authority figures reinforced a competing subculture of youth and weakened the hold of familial piety. All positions of self-government and authority within the camps were diverted to the American-born nisei who, in one way or another, had replaced loyalty to their family with allegiance to other, outside institutions.

While there are no statistical measurements of the Americanization campaign among the nisei youth, the many written impressions of inmates and supervisors indicate a certain degree of success. Frances Cushman, a guidance director at a camp high school, reported that upon asking students of the junior class "What personal adjustments have you found most difficult since coming to Poston?" she received some surprising answers. School, where the process of Americanization and desensitizing to primary cultural allegiances took place, was the most important institution for about a quarter of this typical group of students. "Twenty-five indicated study conditions, thirty school conditions, five—lack of libraries, three—teachers. In other words, almost twenty-five percent reflected concerns over schools."[24]

The most influential competing source of identity, the family, could not rival the lure of school and its rewards. "Our family, like most Japanese families prior to evacuation was very close," wrote Kaizo Kubo, a high school student at one of the camps. And yet, "today, after these years of communal living, I find myself stumbling over words, as I make vain attempts to talk to my father. I don't understand him; he doesn't understand me."[25]

The indoctrination strategy of the WRA had its share of unexpected problems as well as erroneous assumptions. The destruction of family caused severe morale problems in some camps. The undermining of traditional frameworks and the subsequent freedom of the young led, at times, to juvenile gang activity or, in some cases, to the rise of secret Japanese nationalist peer societies among the nisei. Nevertheless, the relevance of this project to the issue of reeducating POWs is quite clear. Contrary to the erratic policy of the SPD, the WRA demonstrated a methodic system of awards, as well as a single-minded dedication to the destruction of competing forms of allegiance, in this case, the Japanese family.

One could argue, of course, that it is only after the fact, that the Japanese example seems relevant. During the heat of battle, it is conceivable that there was neither time to contemplate, nor immediate awareness of the role of education within relocation camps. Nevertheless, evidence of the SPD's unwillingness to learn from others is not limited to this particular example. American reeducation officials apparently paid no attention to analogous military projects either. There is no documental evidence of interest in the reeducational efforts of either friend or foe.

Of course, some of the other reeducation programs during the war were so modest as to not warrant attention. German POW authorities never initiated any systematic form of indoctrination, although their efforts were still quite interesting. The Germans limited their venture to the publication of a magazine, known as *O.K.*, or the *Overseas Kid*. This periodical assured its readers that its purpose was to report the "news, good or bad, in a simple and straightforward manner." But, as David Ford observes in his study of American POWs in Germany, the *O.K.* never moved much beyond standard "Nazi invectives against Jews and Negroes along with the usual biases against Russia and Britain." The editors of the *O.K.* did, however, realize the need to lure readers, and so they peppered their publication with such popular subjects as sports and other forms of light reading.[26]

Among the Allied nations, the British approach to reeducation for German POWs was the most intriguing. British authorities studiously avoided the ambitious, intellectually oriented American scheme. Over four hundred thousand German military personnel were interned in the British Isles; the last POWs were released as late as the spring of 1948. The specialists charged with the reeducation of prisoners of war—the Prisoner of War Division of the Foreign Office (POWD)—were civilians and they began their operations only after the end of the war. Up to that point, British authorities had not considered reeducation a feasible alternative because they feared that the most suitable candidates for rehabilitation would buckle under peer pressure.

At first glance, the POWD appeared to have a familiar agenda. In a pamphlet distributed among camp commandants, British reeducation officials stated that their ultimate goals were:

1. To eradicate from the minds of the prisoners belief in the military tradition and the National Socialist ideology . . .
2. To impart to the prisoners an accurate understanding and a just appreciation of the principles of democratic government . . .
3. To present the British Commonwealth of Nations as an example of a democratic community in action, while avoiding the projection of Britain as a model to be slavishly copied.
4. To remove German misconceptions about European history of the last 50 years and especially about the origin, conduct, and results of the two world wars.[27]

While these guidelines appeared quite unexceptional and not much different from the American scheme, the POWD's actual implementation of its program had little in common with the efforts of the SPD. To begin with, the POWD never pursued radical change in the worldview of the prisoners. Instead it sought to discredit the hold of Nazi ideology by encouraging debate of any sort. The undermining of group conformity was the ultimate aim. The POWD, therefore, tolerated any form of dissension and expression of opinion, not only democratic sentiments.[28] The British aim was to induce behavioral, and not ideological changes among the POWs; the POWD surmised that more profound conversion would follow changes at the behavioral level.

To hasten these goals, the POWD removed from the camps the most intractable elements of the prisoner population by means of the familiar screening process which divided the prisoners into whites, grays, and blacks. But here, too, the British approach was quite different from that of their American counterparts. The British segregation officers showed little concern for previous ties with Nazi organizations. They were not concerned with politics but with locating "men capable of initiating new norms," and, conversely, with ferreting out conformist personalities, those who showed the greatest potential for hindering the acceptance of dialogue and debate. "The interest of the Segregation Officers was in the outlook and attitudes acquired from family and social conformity" which appeared to motivate "attitudes towards other groups." They were not concerned with political persuasion per se.[29]

The POWD modified other familiar trappings of reeducation in order to accomplish its own particular agenda. Like the Americans, the POWD published a weekly newspaper, *Die Wochenpost*/The Weekly Post. This newspaper, however, never pretended to be anything else than the work of POWD staff officers. In a marked departure from the highly intellectualized contents of the American *Der Ruf*, the British journal assigned the two front pages to straight news items from Germany rather than commentary or polemics. At least two additional pages were devoted to the concerns of the rank and file: sports, local news items from camps, and an all-important "search corner" for those seeking lost comrades.

The British also initiated a training center similar to the American special schools project. The Wilton Park center ran fifteen courses for about four thousand prisoners, approximately 1 percent of the entire German POW population in Great Britain. This special camp, which began its official operations in January 1946 and was disbanded in June 1948, sought foremost candidates of outstanding "intelligence, personality and activity." As for political credentials, the POWD limited its criteria to what was disarmingly called "near whiteness," a concept that emphasized the current ideological leanings of the candidate rather than his political affiliations prior to incarceration. Seventy-five percent of the student body at Wilton Park were well-educated, natural candidates for leadership positions—a marked contrast to the high percentage of marginal men who graduated from Fort Eustis, the American equivalent of the British project.

But perhaps the most significant departure of the British approach was that the graduates of Wilton Park were not repatriated. Instead, Wilton graduates were sent back to the camps where, British authorities hoped, they would take upon themselves leadership roles. Instead of the very ambitious American objective of using crash courses in democracy to prepare a cadre of democratically inclined leaders and potential civil servants for Germany, the British sought only to use the graduates of Wilton to change the atmosphere within the limited confines of the camps.

The most meaningful difference of the British approach to reeducation was the use of a new form of screening based on age. Working under the assumption that age was a cardinal factor in defining the political attitudes of POWs, the British authorities designed a special, separate approach to the younger element among the prisoners. Young POWs, those between the ages of seventeen and twenty-six, had been below the age of what the POWD defined as "social awareness" when Hitler seized power. "To them, Hitler, National Socialism, as a political system, and the awareness of being a German, was a single concept," POWD director Henry Faulk noted in his chronicles of the program. "Their group concepts were categoric, because in their world no deviation from or even discussion of the prescribed answers to political questions had been tolerated, and every other form of state organization had been proscribed as decadent and un-German."[30]

As a partial solution to this particularly obdurate segment of the POW population, the POWD established the Youth Camp, where some seven thousand young Germans were exposed to a didactic regime of work and rehabilitative instructional programs. Situated near Cambridge, the Youth Camp sought partial rehabilitation of "black" youth, those "young men who would have nothing to do with re-education, because of defiance, a faithful-unto-death attitude, resentment, stubbornness, despair or apathy."[31] The camp functioned like all working camps, the only exception being that all inmates spent one day a week attending classes. Given the uneven educational level of the young prisoners, the course work focused mostly on the modification of behavior rather than intellectual persuasion. The idea was to demilitarize the inmates, by instructing them in Western etiquette or, in the words of one of the educational advisors, to teach them to be "decent human beings." Instead of indoctrination, the emphasis was on "encouraging decent, unselfish behavior, consideration for one's neighbors, and respect for other people's opinion rather than on politics."

The most important pedagogical experience at the Youth Camp was a fourteen-week class on citizenship characterized by a minimal number of lectures, a daily press review, and many hours of group discussion. In another departure from the American mode, the educational staff at the

Youth Camp was comprised entirely of democratically inclined German POWs who, the British surmised, would have a better chance at inducing change among the youthful inmates than German-speaking British personnel. Beginning in January 1947, the Youth Camp challenged the inmates' harsh views on British society by initiating a policy of fraternization with the local population. The inmates received permission to spend part of their leisure hours in surrounding villages where, unsupervised, they could meet British citizens.

The success of the British experience in the Youth Camp as well as in other facets of this experiment in reeducation is quite difficult to assess. Henry Faulk's summary of the work of the POWD offers various measurements, none of which are very enlightening because of the vacillating composition of the POW population in Britain. As of late 1945, the local POW camps absorbed growing numbers of German prisoners from Canada, the United States, and Belgium, all of whom arrived at the British camps with their own set of grievances, preconceptions, and political views. Under these circumstances, measurements of political tendencies were tenuous at best. Nevertheless, a revealing report emanating from the British repatriation center indicated that some change in worldview had probably taken place in the British surroundings. "POWs expressed dissatisfaction at the treatment of German Officer POW," the report noted.

> They considered that War Guilt should rest more on the shoulders of the officers than anyone else and that they form a greater source of potential danger in the future by virtue of their militaristic past. It therefore seemed logical to the POW that officers should not be treated preferentially but rather that they should be subject to much greater supervision. Reference to the Geneva Convention was of no avail and the view was expressed that perhaps Britain was trying to curry favor with the Officer Class in Germany with an eye to the future clash with Russia.[32]

This indication of erosion in group solidarity had appeared among the rank and file as early as 1946. Whether such dissension and undermining of solidarity within the camps was the result of successful reeducation or other factors such as "the search for scapegoats to alleviate the guilt sense" following defeat or, perhaps, fundamental tensions between officers and enlisted personnel, is a matter of contention. Nevertheless, the fact remains that the Americans never made similar inroads into the loyalties of other ranks and the prestige of officers. The British, by contrast, had managed to persuade many ordinary soldiers in the POW camps "that the officers had access to information on the real nature of Hitlerism, but did nothing about it."[33]

In sum, the British policies of separating treatment for the young, the reintroduction of graduates from prestige courses back into the camps, and the editorial guidelines for their POW newspaper, *Die Wochenpost*, indicated a sophisticated understanding of the limits of reeducation. At face value, British reeducation appears to have been significantly more attuned to the mission at hand.

Nevertheless, before assigning grades to the two different Allied programs, it is important to acknowledge the irrelevance of reeducation as a tool for reforming German society. Neither British nor American reeducation officials were able to secure pivotal government positions for their graduates. There is no evidence of large numbers of POWs from either program serving as apostles of democracy in their home country. Ironically, Germany did appear to change quite dramatically, but change had nothing to do with the infusion of hundreds of thousands of reeducated POWs into postwar Germany.

The reasons for German transformation were quite clear to Captain Robert Kunzig, the executive officer of the SPD who, in the spring of 1946, had accompanied the first shipload of Eustis graduates on their journey back home. During the course of this mission he witnessed a traumatic event that highlighted the real impetus for significant change among his wards in particular, and German society in general. After landing in the French port of Le Havre, Kunzig joined the former inmates on a train bound for Germany.

> As our train approached the border, in the Saar region, I was conscious of a tenseness in the men. I could see it their eyes. They crowded to the doors for that first glimpse. Then they saw. They saw, and they'll remember for all time. Ruin, desolation, and destruction were framed in that open door. The only sound was the lonely shriek of the engine far ahead.
>
> Standing next to me, Hans____ watched and waited. His home was in the next little town on a small side street near the tracks. We rounded a bend, and I heard him gasp. I knew the reason. His home wasn't there. It couldn't be, because the town wasn't there. Nothing but mounds of rubble piled high.[34]

The high-minded objectives of reeducation appeared superfluous given Germany's utter destruction. Nazism could never survive in the smoldering ruins. A new Germany would be built for which both the physical and ideological rubble of the former Reich would be of little consequence. Kunzig attempted to illustrate this point by relating the story of "Otto W." who, upon returning home to Cologne, discovered that a "bomb had wiped out his father, mother, two sisters, brother, and grandparents." Otto would not be a disciple for democracy and the American way. But by the same token he would not resort to former ways either. "He wasn't bitter," Kunzig noted, "just numb."[35] Physical destruction, not a new enlightenment, had obliterated the complex social conditions and ideological values that had nurtured National Socialism.[36]

For Hans Werner Richter, recently returned to Germany from his American prison, the ruins signified the finite destruction of past experiences. "The sign of our times is the ruins. They surround our lives. They line the streets of our cities. They are our reality. In their burned-out facades there blooms not the blue flower of romanticism but the demonic spirit of destruction, decay, and the apocalypse."[37]

The crater-filled landscape of postwar Germany was inhabited by the disoriented and the dazed. "The ruins live in us as we in them," Richter explained; whatever it meant to be a German would have to be built from scratch. He did not expect the mythical phoenix of Germany's recent past to rise out of the twisted, smoldering ruins.

Many historical accounts of the Allied war effort have consistently rejected this notion that indiscriminate destruction induced German political and cultural transformation. The economist John Kenneth Galbraith, a member of a distinguished team sent to Germany to assess the impact of the strategic bombing campaign on Germany's military-industrial complex is quoted in Studs Terkel's *The Good War* as saying that "strategic bombing was designed to destroy the industrial base of the enemy and the morale of its people. It did neither."[38] The literary critic and historian Paul Fussell, apparently basing his findings on Galbraith's testimony, states that the U.S. Strategic Bombing Survey "ascertained, among other findings, that German military and industrial production seemed to increase—just like civilian determination not to surrender—the more the bombs were dropped."[39]

In actual fact, the reports of the Strategic Bombing Survey claimed the opposite. Galbraith's mission had been to establish the damage to Germany's economic infrastructure, and there is no reason to doubt his recollections that such damage had been overrated. But his statement about the negligible effect on German morale conflicts with the findings of his colleagues charged with investigating this particular aspect of the strategic bombing campaign. In an exhaustive sociological survey undertaken during the first months of occupation, a group of American social scientists from the Morale Division of the Strategic Bombing Survey ascertained that "bombing did not stiffen morale" and that the "hate and anger it aroused" tended to be directed against "the Nazi regime which was blamed for beginning air warfare and for being unable to ward off Allied air attacks."[40]

In addition to basing its conclusions on a representative polling of Germans after the occupation, the Morale Division found ample confirmation of its findings in the official intelligence reports of the many internal security agencies of Nazi Germany, the Propaganda Ministry, as well as other government and party agencies. From mid-1943 and onward these reports demonstrated a decline in morale and belief in victory, all of which had damaging political implications for the popular support of the Third Reich. By March 1944, a security service report admitted freely that morale was dangerously low. Resentment had not been translated into action, according to the report, because of "authoritative pressure" and "the fear of punishment which precludes especially severe expressions against the state leadership."[41] The Morale Division found that the Allied air raids were mentioned as the principal cause of low morale for every month from May 1943 though May 1944. The Normandy invasion replaced strategic bombing in the reports of June–August 1944, only to reappear in September and October as the most important factor affecting morale. Thus, the researchers stated in their summary:

> Bombing seriously depressed the morale of German citizens. Its main psychological effects were defeatism, fear, hopelessness, fatalism, and apathy. War weariness, willingness to surrender, loss of hope for German victory, distrust of leaders, feelings of disunity and demoralizing fear were all more common among bombed than unbombed people.[42]

In perhaps their most controversial statement, the social scientists of the survey claimed that "the morale effects of bombing may thus prove to have had even more importance for the denazification of Germany than for hastening military defeat."[43]

The verification of such a finding remains beyond the scope of this study. However, there is little doubt that the horrendous effects of indiscriminate bombing of civilian targets, whatever negative moral implications one might associate with such an action, destroyed the will and undermined the positive self-image of a hostile enemy population. Such harsh actions, together with the dismemberment of Prussia as well as the ruthless economic and physical destruction of the Junker elite, rendered the German populace quite unable to resist the imposition of not just one, but two foreign political systems in their country.

As fate would have it, then, the limited results of the reeducation program for German POWs were, in historical terms, of little importance. Upon returning home, the repatriated POWs—numerically insignificant and never privy to key political and educational positions in the new German government as the SPD had hoped—were swept away by the same current of events that affected the remaining civilian population in Germany.

When viewed against the background of physical destruction and the harsh treatment of Germany's civilian population during the final phases of the war, the fate of enemy POWs in the United States was decidedly benign. They experienced no meaningful attempts to annihilate their old familiar world. Their primary reference groups, their sense of national pride, as well as their esprit de corps as soldiers in the German Armed Forces, had never been challenged. Worldviews, as nurtured before captivity, had remained intact. There were no manifestations of coercion, intimidation, or single-minded destruction of elites in the POW camps. Quite the opposite had been the case. American reeducation authorities rejected severe forms of manipulation and indoctrination. Consequently, and with the partial acquiescence of their captors, the German prisoners resurrected familiar frameworks with relative ease. For the vast majority of POWs—in particular those who were not accepted for the crash courses on democracy on the eve of repatriation—the social and ideological concepts that had sustained their beliefs prior to prison life in the United States remained unaltered.

There was, of course, no intrinsic need for heavy-handed methods to induce at least short-term shifts in the mentality of POWs. A mere curtailing of the internal chain of command together with the mixing up of units and service branches would have probably sufficed. But as long as camp authorities permitted a large degree of self-rule among the inmates, the lectures, reading material, and other forms of "intellectual diversion" had little impact on the rank and file. When judged on its own terms, and irrespective of the decisive turning of Germany's political and social tides at the end of the war, the SPD's seemingly poor choice of pedagogical policy demands an explanation.

Why did American officials address the issue of reeducation in such a narrow manner? How could these professors in uniform have claimed resounding success for an operation which clearly had little effect on the culture and politics of POWs? It is tempting to dismiss the SPD program as a combination of naiveté and superficiality. Such an answer is in itself superficial. The architects of the reeducation were intelligent individuals; it is doubtful that their claims for success stemmed from ignorance of what had actually transpired in the POW camps. An intentional presentation of false, misleadingly positive results seems equally unlikely.

The final task of this study, then, is to suggest a possible explanation for the discrepancy between claims of success and the manifest lack of change in the worldview of German POWs who were exposed to reeducation. Perhaps the mission for which SPD officials claimed success was not a mere uplifting of the enemy, but something more intricate and more personal.

CHAPTER ELEVEN

Reeducation and the Decline of the American Dons

IN THE spring of 1943, prior to the commencement of the reeducation program, Wendell Willkie published an impassioned plea for supporting the liberal arts in modern America. "Clearly in a technological age like ours, a great deal of training is necessary," he wrote. However, he argued, no technical skill could be considered "true education." Willkie, who was to a large degree the spiritual mentor of POW reeducation, declared that the "onrush of what we call modern civilization has obscured this essential truth that enduring national greatness was not the result of technical proficiency but the result of what we call the liberal arts . . . to know for the sheer joy of understanding; to speculate, to analyze, to compare, and to imagine." Willkie maintained that the most ominous threat to American freedom was not the military might of an outside enemy, but the demotion of a liberal arts education from necessity to indulgence.

> People—some of them in very high places—have openly disparaged the liberal arts. You are told that they are of little help to a man in earning his living or in making a contribution to his fellow men. The thing to do, you are told, is to get trained: learn an occupation: make yourself proficient in some trade or profession. Of course, this advice is sound as far as it goes. But the inference, and sometimes the outright declaration that frequently follows it, strikes at the very roots of our society. The liberal arts, we are told, are luxuries. . . . They are mere decorations upon the sterner pattern of life which must be lived in action and by the application of skills. When such arguments gain acceptance then it is the end of us as a civilized nation.[1]

Overspecialization, the emphasis on technical skills, and the subsequent trivialization of the liberal arts, Willkie continued, were un-American traits, imports of the "German university." He argued that German influences on the American academic system "encouraged the sacrifice of methods that make for wide intelligence to those which are concerned only with highly specialized knowledge; it has held that the subject is more important than the student; that knowledge is more important than understanding; that science, in itself, can satisfy the soul of man; and that intelligent men should not be allowed to concern themselves with politics and the administration of state."

The attack on humanities in American academia, according to Willkie, reeked of Fascism; he compared the phenomenon to the rampant anti-intellectualism of the Nazi state. "Burn your books—or, what amounts to the same thing, neglect your books—and you will lose freedom, as surely as if you were to invite Hitler and his henchmen to rule."[2]

Although he, himself, was not a member of the academic community, Willkie was able to capture much of the sense of siege that characterized the humanities in American universities during the 1940s. In this age of total war, in which the most cultured of European nations had produced a terrifying political system, the liberal arts approach to education appeared to many, both within academia and among the general public, to be quite aimless, if not an actual waste of human and material resources. Defenders of the humanities were accused of squandering precious assets on superfluous education and weakening the nation by detracting both talent and capital from more vital sectors of the war effort. Such negative convictions, the historian Richard Hofstadter observed sadly, had actually reversed the prewar trend toward a humanistic revival in American academia.[3] The humanists of the 1940s had been victimized by what the poet Roscoe Pound called "fallacious propositions" that "the social sciences are so far advanced" and so much more accurate for both understanding and predicting the behavior of human beings that the humanities had become obsolete.[4]

The Librarian of Congress and renowned poet Archibald MacLeish was even more blunt in his assessment of the dwindling fortunes of wartime humanities. "There was never a time . . . in the history of this country when learning was held cheaper than it is today," he declared. MacLeish, one of the central figures in the Office of War Information (OWI), another of the war's intellectual enterprises, expressed the common fear of the practitioners of humanism that in America of the early 1940s, "to be an intellectual is to be an object of suspicion in the public mind. To be a professor is to invite attack in any public service, any public undertaking."[5]

The writings of the more verbose faculty members of the Special Projects Division (SPD), both during and following the war, suggest that they, too, were intensely concerned with the diminishing stature of the liberal arts and its bearing on their own personal professional future. In a very typical and emotional defense of his profession Howard Mumford Jones assailed the rival social sciences for "depersonalizing" the human intellect and trespassing in the domain of the humanities. The social sciences,

Jones wrote, had cavalierly disposed of "judgement and rationality" as historical forces. In the post-humanist age, the citizen represented nothing more than "a case" for behavioral analysis.

> The clear light of eighteenth century right reason fades into the murk of libido, the inferiority complex, penis envy, incest, sadism, masochism. . . . Personality traits are made the subject of statistical inquiry, as if people had gone to the wrong clothing stores and had to begin sorting out ill-sorted garments. Such phrases as a "disturbed person," the "well-adjusted (or badly adjusted) person," the "neurotic personality of our time," a "pleasant personality" are the terms in which we now categorize the political heirs of Jefferson and Franklin.[6]

T. V. Smith, Jones's colleague and sometimes ideological rival within the SPD, concurred. He went so far as to suggest that the depreciation of the liberal arts in the United States in the 1930s and 1940s had affected detrimentally the practices of other nations, those who looked up and copied American ways. In an article written in early 1947, Smith paraphrased a response that he had heard frequently during his tenure as member of the task force for the American educational authority in occupied Japan:

> Half a century ago we Japanese thought it was science which defined your superiority to us, insofar as you were superior. So we went after science in a large way. . . . We have sufficiently industrialized our feudal nation so as to hold our own for quite a time at war with the Western giant of technology. We now see, or think we see, that science is not enough. Indeed, we are beginning to suspect that we were on the wrong road. . . . There seems to be something in your type of social organization that is superior to ours. . . . We want you to teach us about equality and to familiarize us with your horizontal, as distinct from our hierarchic approach to one another. We want you to help us democratize our schools so that we may democratize ourselves.[7]

Smith argued that teaching the Japanese the intrinsic benefits of equality and democracy was the domain of the humanities. He declared that a humanistic edification of the Japanese would transform this former enemy into a trusted ally. He also suggested that had the United States adopted such a strategy before World War II, had the country exported its liberal arts and not only its technology, the war with Japan might never have occurred.

The issue at hand, however, was somewhat more complex than merely persuading the American government and public to recognize the value of the intellectual commodities manufactured in the libraries and lecture halls of the humanities. Advocates of the liberal arts were not only battling what Duke University's literary scholar, Norman Foerster, called "the indifference and frivolity of the public" or the demeaning attitude of colleagues from the social sciences. There was a cancer within. Foerster identified "a want of conviction and vision prevailing among those who are active" in the humanities. Historians, he complained, "preferred facts to interpretation," while "literary and other artists, together with academic professors of literature and the arts, have been largely content with problems of technique or the amassing of closely observed facts."[8] The concept of a useable past, or the weaving of a relationship between humanism and contemporary problems was, he implied, in danger of disappearing from the agenda of the scholarly community.

It is within this context of upheaval in academia and the subsequent attempts by defenders of the humanities to prove their usefulness, that the seemingly capricious approach to the reeducation of enemy POWs in the United States begins to make sense. The program addressed the uplifting of German POWs only in passing because SPD instructors were conceivably distracted by the much more personal question of the future of their academic careers. The architects of reeducation seemed to seize upon this program to prove, perhaps to themselves, perhaps to the American public, that the humanities had a meaningful role to play in the impending new world order, and that total war and its political consequences had not rendered them obsolete. Here, then, lies a possible explanation for both the overtly intellectual approach to reeducation and for the insistent refusal to integrate the behavioral sciences into the project. Reeducation was the domain of humanists, who presumably were seeking to validate their canon before a skeptical audience. The reeducation curriculum was a vicarious form for waging battle against rival divisions within the academic community in preparation for the impending turf disputes of the postwar years.

Bearing such an assumption in mind, the many anomalies of the SPD appear to make sense. The apparent irrelevance of much of the curriculum occurred because, in the eyes of the architects of reeducation, their mission was not a narrow effort to reshape the German mind. It was, instead, a more complex attempt to sketch an outline for "applied humanities" on the eve of the impending restructuring of American academia. The reeducation of POWs disregarded fundamental premises of military life, such as the internal cohesion and esprit de corps of the prisoners, because a successful remaking of the prisoners was only the nominal goal. The university faculty of the SPD drew almost exclusively upon the analogy of the college teacher-pupil relationship because this was the model they intended to develop. Their eyes were set on fashioning the future form of the liberal arts, and not on the education of transient foreigners. As such, they adopted, with very few modifications, an educational format with no direct reference to the dynamics of a prison camp.

Given the context of diminishing prestige within the academic community, the humanist SPD officials demonstrated low tolerance for an interdisciplinary breaching of the walls separating the robust social sciences from the struggling humanities. A striking representation of the humanists' bristling defensiveness was their deliberate rejection of contemporary social science theories, ranging from social stratification to an economic understanding of political developments. "Economic man" had not written Hamlet or painted the Sistine Madonna, and no contemporary social theory could "explain the style of Emerson or the wide appeal of the 'Gettysburg Address,'" wrote Howard Mumford Jones.[9] Such poor assessments of the value of social sciences for explaining human developments governed the didactic strategy of the reeducation program. Mere behavior modification was out of the question. The tenuous status of humanists required an intellectual strategy for reeducation which denied any positive assessment of the contributions of the social sciences.

Any design for education other than rational persuasion was rejected for moral reasons, as well. The concept of indoctrination—the imparting of a set of fundamental beliefs without reliance on reason—had a distinct totalitarian ring about it. In fact, indoctrination as an educational strategy had already suffered a serious setback in the United States prior to World War II. Progressive educators, led by John Dewey, had rejected the idea of "education by imposition" of even the most fundamental of societal values. Progressive educational theorists had argued that imbuing values by fiat, even among children or the ignorant, did not produce durable results; ideas inculcated by imposition rather than through reason were easily dislodged.[10]

The American educators who made up the staff of the SPD were allied with anti-indoctrination progressive educators. Their familiarity with the manipulative propaganda techniques of totalitarian countries presumably strengthened their suspicion of all pedagogical strategies other than rational persuasion. However, as the educational philosopher Willis Moore has pointed out, "in associating 'indoctrination' with authoritarian political philosophy and practice," particularly as these were exemplified in the Nazi regime of Germany, "American liberals so stigmatized the term that none of them was willing to admit that this method of teaching had any legitimate use whatsoever."[11] Their endorsement of logic rather than authority produced an intellectual master plan for rational reeducation in the camps even though reason and abstract thought had no meaningful bearing on life in the POW camps as Total Institutions. The oppressive frameworks of the camps placed little premium on, indeed, discouraged, any form of individuality and rational thinking.

These liberal arts educators had, as well, ample intellectual reasons for insisting upon rational education and rejecting indoctrination. They were spiritual heirs to Rousseau and Locke; philosophically, they rejected the idea of original sin, the pessimistic view of man born with a propensity for evil. While contemporary social theory focused on the irrational, on perversion, and on the pathological behavioral traits that had produced Nazism, these humanists sought otherwise. In a world dominated by violence and irrationality they clung to the well-ordered universe of Plato and Kant, insisting that the horrors surrounding them were but temporary deviations from the rational, positive path of western progress.

Whether the staff of the SPD had imbibed these views from the American progressive movement of their youth, or whether they had imbued these thoughts in the European countries of their origin is inconsequential. What is important is that both the American-educated and the European-born architects of reeducation assumed that the aggression and violence of individuals and nations were the result of unfortunate social irregularities—poor leadership or poor luck—and not an inevitable by-product of some innate evil strain in human nature. "I disbelieve very strongly in man's inherent evil and brutality," Walter Schoenstedt wrote. "I do not see any more beastly components in the German people than in any other people. In these days of destruction and propaganda it is easy to condemn the carriers of the disease without trying to find the origin of the bacteria," he added in a statement that represented an important article of faith for the entire reeducation program.[12]

In one very crucial aspect, the SPD instructors did resemble their colleagues in the social sciences. Somewhat paradoxically, these men of ideas endorsed a negative analysis of the role of doctrines and ideology as a historical force. In both its literature and lectures, the SPD damned the distorting effects of visionary movements of all political persuasions in governing human affairs. In a variety of forms and fashions the curriculum of the SPD stated that the German worldview had been perverted not by Nazism per se, but by an uncritical acceptance of rigid principles; Americans, on the other hand, had managed to avoid the pitfalls of all-consuming political postulates. While at times Americans may have been gullible or misguided, the SPD lectures declared, they had never been ideologically dogmatic; they had never been tied down by overriding worldviews.

The diplomatic historian Michael Hunt has suggested that such pervasive suspicions of ideology were the result of a remarkable cultural stability, which allowed Americans "to leave their ideology implicit and informal." As such they "tended to regard as unusual if not aberrant most other ideologies," especially those that were "couched in explicit, formal, even formulaic terms."[13] While obviously affected by such general national attitudes, SPD officials had, as well, some very specific reasons for discounting ideology. Their immediate task during the war years was to present America as a utopia fulfilled. As advocates of a society which espoused classlessness and political consensus, the officers of the SPD were ill equipped to deal with social, economic, or ideological divisions as significant historical forces.

This dismissal of ideologies had unforeseen results when SPD officials found themselves in the uncomfortable position of having to prove that they, too, were ideologically free persons. For all the will and energy invested in advocating free speech and democracy, SPD educators were trapped by the logic of their own condemnations of all ideological movements. As was the case in their universities during this same period, these professors in uniform were unable or unwilling to reject the intrusion of politically minded administrators into purely intellectual debates. The hunt for fellow travelers among the faculty of the SPD, more the result of the obsessions of an ambitious Provost Marshal General than anything else, clearly illustrated the inherent weaknesses of their humanistic approach to the affairs of the world.

University politics and academic controversies were reflected in other crucial aspects of the program as well, such as the SPD's distinct preference for educating elites, their enamoration with German high culture, and the continuous search for respectable paradigms of American cultural greatness. The architects of reeducation were aligned with a predominant elitist faction within the universities who opposed contemporary calls for the democratization of higher learning. "Excessive vocationalism" and the broadening access to higher education were condemned for the lowering of standards and trivialization of the educational process. Historian Richard Hofstadter, an eloquent spokesman for this position, complained that "democracy in education . . . had been invoked as an excuse for the vulgarization of the educational system."[14] The elitist slant in the curriculum for reeducation suggests that, like Hofstadter, these professors in uniform had little tolerance for the lowering of academic standards which had accompanied the diminishing stature of the humanities. The development of a reeducational strategy catering, as much as possible, to intellectuals, was in many ways another means for maintaining some semblance of self-respect during tough times.

Within the realm of this intellectual strategy, there was, of course, a certain logic to the SPD's particular fascination with German poets, writers, and philosophers. Literary scholar Michael Hamburger has observed that "philosophical and literary ideas have permeated German policies and institutions to an extent that has no parallel" in the western world. "Who would think of including Blake or Keats in a study of British political thought?" Nevertheless, reeducation officials' fixation with the great minds of German culture went beyond mere recognition of their special status in German society. Both the American and the German-born educators of the SPD admired the German musical geniuses, great philosophers, and outstanding writers of the nineteenth and early twentieth centuries because they believed that these artists had defined the parameters of a common culture shared by all men of education, regardless of nationality. "What fool would look to find the so-called 'German Spirit' in the music of Beethoven and Mozart, Mendelssohn or Bach?" Walter Schoenstedt asked rhetorically in a lecture before the faculty of the U.S. Army School For Orientation and Education. "Their work belongs to humanity," adding sadly that "everything we have known as German culture was destroyed, and in its place the Nazis put their own 'culture.'"[15] As devoted admirers of German high culture and its inherent universalism, SPD educators presumed that by resurrecting German cultural achievements of the nineteenth century, they could neutralize the mesmerizing hold of Nazism and reorient their German students toward their rightful place within the fold of liberal Western nations.

Classic German culture was not the only source of inspiration for this universalist creed. The staff of the SPD found useful tenets in American culture as well. They endorsed what Robert Bellah has called an American Civil Religion, the endowing of the American political creed with quasi-religious, mystical, and universal significance. These educators harped, in particular, upon the multinational significance of the American political experience. T. V. Smith explained that "though our announced aim and our prevailing policy is simply the negative one of purifying our enemies militarily and ideologically it is but natural, and certainly not unwholesome, for us to hope that what we have that has kept us peaceable, what we have that has kept us tolerant, and what we have that has made for prosperity may find a home with other nations."[16] After all, Howard Mumford Jones argued, the American system of liberal republican government had "outlasted every European government save two"; such inherent stability was reason enough for emulation.[17]

This preaching of American exceptionalism was somewhat more complex than a mere manifestation of intellectual provincialism. These educators sensed that the future of the humanities in American academia, and, by implication, their own professional standing, hinged upon the construction of an attractive portrayal of their country's contemporary good fortune. Howard Mumford Jones argued that the drift of gifted students away from the humanities was "symptomatic of a deeper malady than the urge for vocational study." Disenchantment reflected "the profound fact that the undergraduate wants to understand his own country and that the humanities have mainly failed to show him how they could help him to comprehend it." Jones explained that it was self defeating to "insist that humane values are found everywhere but in the United States." After all, "Goethe did not become a Hellenist first and a German afterwards."[18] There was nothing wrong in singing the praise of the American system so long as it was true. Humanists would only benefit from declaring that they had discovered the intellectual formula of American greatness, and that they held the key to a usable American past.

There is, then, little doubt that the SPD reeducation program reflected some very personal concerns and professional objectives which had little to do with the actual tutoring of POWs. If the staff of the SPD confused their POW wards with their students, and their universities with the POW camps, they reflected an understandable human tendency to tackle their own problems first, and to seek out the familiar in strange and foreign terrain. When viewed as an extension of contemporary academic issues in America rather than as a narrow experiment to uplift an enemy, much of the seemingly ineffectual defining of objectives and strategies of the SPD seems reasonable. In fact, the expansion of liberal arts in the postwar years, and the rise of government-ordained academic exchange programs with heavy emphasis on the humanities suggests that the SPD's declarations of success were not entirely unfounded. The humanities had held their ground in the battle against some very powerful forces within the academic establishment.

Sometime during the early war years, Lt. Colonel Edward Davison wrote a poem that is somewhat indicative of the convergion of the SPD's national, military task with the private, professional concerns of the program's architect. "In Times of Discouragement" represented Davison's understanding of the predicament of the humanist in a turbulent age:

> Night blackens to the core. Poet, awake!
> The worst, the darkest hour of your heart's ache
> Begins . . .
> So keep your little inch of that great field
> Where Shelley fought and died, and never yield:
> Let your short sword the little while it shines
> Strike at the army of the Philistines.[19]

Given *Webster's Dictionary*'s definition of "Philistine" as a "crass, prosaic, often priggish individual guided by material rather than intellectual or artistic values," one is left with the impression that the enemies in Davison's world were not necessarily the totalitarian regimes who challenged Western democracies from without, but perhaps those detractors of liberal arts and the humanities who threatened the personal, professional domain of Davison and his fellow humanists.

Notes

Introduction

1. John Morton Blum, *V Was For Victory: Politics and American Culture during World War II* (San Diego, 1976), 190–91.

2. Jeanne Hill, "Our Unlikely Thanksgiving," *Reader's Digest* (November 1992), 96–99.

3. Barry M. Katz, *Foreign Intelligence: Research and Analysis in the Office of Strategic Services, 1942–1945* (Cambridge, Mass., 1989), xi.

4. The conscripted academics of the Division of Research and Analysis in the Office of Strategic Services (OSS), many of whom were on the cutting edge of their profession, provide a stark contrast to the state of affairs among reeducation officials. See Barry M. Katz, *Foreign Intelligence*, and Robin Winks, *Cloak and Gown: Scholars in the Secret War, 1939–1961* (New York, 1987). See also Allan M. Winkler, *The Politics of Propaganda: The Office of War Information, 1942–1945* (New Haven, 1978), for an interesting study of another war project dominated by academics.

5. *New York Times*, February 13, 1945, 7.

6. Headquarters Army Service Forces, *Handbook for Work Supervisors of Prisoner of War Labor* (Washington, D.C., 1945), 4, Library of Congress Microfilms, L.C. 51437, Reel 2; Major General Archer L. Lerch, "The Army Reports on Prisoners of War," *American Mercury* 60 (May 1945), 536–47.

7. The War Department's final tabulation of POWs incarcerated in the continental United States appears in the *New York Times*, August 8, 1947, 19.

8. Arnold Krammer, "Japanese Prisoners of War in America," *Pacific Historical Review* 52 (February 1983), 67–91. Predictably, a half-hearted attempt to devise a reeducation program for these prisoners sputtered to a halt at a very early stage. See Richard Paul Walker, "Prisoners of War in Texas during World War II" (Ph.D. diss., North Texas State University, 1980), 328–44.

9. Louis E. Keefer, *Italian Prisoners of War in America, 1942–1946: Captives or Allies?* (New York, 1992), 56.

10. Ibid., 142.

11. George Gallup, *The Gallup Poll: Public Opinion, 1935–1971*, vol. 1 (New York, 1972), 370. See also Richard W. Steele, "American Popular Opinion and the War Against Germany: The Issue of Negotiated Peace, 1942," *Journal of American History* 65 (December 1978), 704–23.

12. *The Gallup Poll*, 337.

13. *Handbook for Work Supervisors of Prisoner of War Labor*, 1.

14. Henry W. Ehrmann, "An Experiment in Political Education; The Prisoner-of-War Schools in the United States," *Social Research* 14 (September 1947), 319.

CHAPTER ONE

1. Emily Rosenberg, *Spreading the American Dream: American Economic and Cultural Expansionism, 1890–1945* (New York, 1982), 85.

2. The spread of educational and other philanthropic endeavors in the early twentieth century are surveyed in Frank Ninkovich, *The Diplomacy of Ideas: U.S. Foreign Policy and Cultural Relations, 1938–1950* (New York, 1981), 8–34.

3. Ibid., 35–60.

4. Lothar Kettenacker, "The Planning of 'Re-Education' during the Second World War," in Nicholas Pronay and Keith Wilson, eds., *The Political Reeducation of Germany after World War II* (London, 1985), 71.

5. Helen Peak, "Some Psychological Problems in the Re-education of Germany," *Journal of Social Issues* 2 (August 1946), 28.

6. Ibid., 29.

7. Kenneth S. Davis, *FDR: The Beckoning of Destiny, 1882–1928* (New York, 1971), 92. See also Robert Edwin Herzstein, *Roosevelt and Hitler: Prelude to War* (New York, 1989), 45–120.

8. Warren F. Kimball, *Swords or Ploughshares? The Morgenthau Plan for Defeated Nazi Germany, 1943–1946* (Philadelphia, 1976), 31.

9. On Wilson and the prospects of democracy in Germany see Klaus Schwabe, *Woodrow Wilson, Revolutionary Germany, and Peacemaking, 1918–1919* (Chapel Hill, N.C., 1985).

10. Richard M. Brickner, *Is Germany Incurable?* (Philadelphia, 1943), 31–32.

11. Ibid., 35–37.

12. Ibid., 308.

13. For a good selection of negative reviews on Brickner's work, including Fromm's article, see "What Shall We Do With Germany? A Panel Discussion of *Is Germany Incurable?*" *Saturday Review of Literature* 24 (May 29, 1943), 4–10.

14. Henry V. Dicks, "Personality Traits and National Socialist Ideology: A War-Time Study of German Prisoners of War," *Human Relations* 3 (1950), 111–54.

15. H. L. Ansbacher, "Attitudes of German Prisoners of War; A Study of the Dynamics of National-Socialistic Followership," *Psychological Monographs* 62 (1948), 22.

16. Sigfried E. Hartmann, "German P/W Newspapers" (January 6, 1945), Record Group 389, Records of the Provost Marshal General, National Archives, Washington, D.C. (hereafter, RG 389), box 1616.

17. Major General Allen W. Gullion to Chief of Staff, Army Service Forces, "Orientation of Enemy Prisoners" (June 24, 1943), Edward Davison Papers, Beinecke Library, Yale University, box 9.

18. Special War Problems Division, State Department, "Indoctrination of German Prisoners of War" (March 2, 1944), RG 389, box 1603.

19. Talcott Parsons, "The Problem of Controlled Institutional Change," in Parsons, *Essays in Sociological Theory* (rev. ed., Glencoe, Ill., 1954). This article, originally published in 1945, summarizes much of Parson's views on the problems of the ideological reorientation of German society which he expressed throughout the early 1940s.

20. *The Memoirs of Cordell Hull*, vol. 2 (New York, 1948), 1606.

21. For a brief biographical sketch of Lerch, see *Current Biography: Who's News and Why* (New York, 1945), 345–47.

22. Department of State, Special War Problems Division, "Indoctrination of German Prisoners of War" (March 2, 1944), RG 389, box 1603.

23. Ibid.

24. Ibid.

25. James F. Tent, *Mission on the Rhine: Reeducation and Denazification in American-Occupied Germany* (Chicago, 1982), 6–8.

26. State Department, Special War Problems Division, "Comments on the Proposed Program for Reorientation of German Prisoners of War" (August 28, 1944); "Memo on the Revision of Major Davison's Report on Reorientation of Prisoners of War" (October 4, 1944), Stephen Farrand Papers, Hoover Institute, Stanford University, box 2.

27. See interview with Maxwell McKnight in Judith Gansberg, *Stalag USA: The Remarkable Story of German POWs in America* (New York, 1977). McKnight's recollections are the only source of information concerning Mrs. Roosevelt's concern and personal intervention. Her autobiography and numerous biographies make no mention of this incident.

28. F. G. Alletson Cook, "Nazi Prisoners Are Nazis Still," *New York Times Magazine* (November 21, 1943), 12, 38.

29. James H. Powers, "What To Do With German Prisoners: The American Muddle," *Atlantic Monthly* 174 (November 1944), 46–50.

30. Ibid.

31. Henry Cassidy, "What To Do With German Prisoners: The Russian Solution," ibid., 43–45. Both the Cassidy and Powers article were reprinted in the December 1944 edition of *Reader's Digest*.

32. Anonymous U.S. Army Chaplain, "PWs" *Life*, January 10, 1944, 50.

CHAPTER TWO

1. Hans Werner Richter, *Beyond Defeat/Die Geschlagenen*, translated by Robert Kee (New York, 1950), 182.

2. Erving Goffman, "Characteristics of Total Institutions," in Maurice Stein, Arthur Vidich, and David Manning White, eds., *Identity and Anxiety: Survival of the Person in Mass Society* (New York, 1960), 449–79. See also Arthur J. Vidich and Maurice R. Stein, "The Dissolved Identity in Military Life," in ibid., 493–505; and Robert K. Merton and Paul Lazarsfeld, eds., *Continuities in Social Research: Studies in the Scope and Method of "The American Soldier"* (Glencoe, Ill., 1950).

3. Vidich and Stein, "The Dissolved Identity of Military Life," 498. Vidich and Stein's observations were derived from a Marine boot camp but apply equally well to most military inductions.

4. J. Glenn Gray, *The Warriors: Reflections on Men in Battle* (New York, 1959), 103.

5. Erving Goffman, "Characteristics of the Total Institution," 449–79.

6. George Gaertner, *Hitler's Last Soldier in America* (New York, 1985), 55.

7. Helmut Hörner, *A German Odyssey: The Journal of a German Prisoner of War*, translated and edited by Allan Kent Powell (Golden, Colo., 1991), 107–8.

8. Hörner, *A German Odyssey*, 92.

9. Gaertner, *Hitler's Last Soldier in America*, 57.

10. Daniel Costelle, *Les Prisonniers* (Paris, 1975), 29–30, cited in Arnold Krammer, *Nazi Prisoners of War in America* (New York, 1979), 162. Italics are mine.

11. For an example of the celebration of Hitler's birthday, see Hörner, *A German Odyssey*, 257–58.

12. For an example of these covert methods for enforcing discipline, see Richter, *Beyond Defeat*, 181–284.

13. See, for example, Thomas R. Buecker, "Nazi Influence at the Fort Robinson Prisoner of War Camp during World War II," *Nebraska History*, 1992 (73), 32–41.

14. "Prison Camps Rid of Nazi Terrorism," *New York Times*, January 16, 1945, 1, 13; Judith Gansberg, *Stalag USA: The Remarkable Story of German POWs in America* (New York, 1975), 53.

15. War Department, *What About the German Prisoner?* W.D. Pamphlet 19–1, attached to OPMG, "Notes Memoranda and War Department Publications: Conference at Fort Slocum, N.Y." (November 1944), in Record Group 389, Records of the Provost Marshal General, National Archives, Washington, D.C. (hereafter, RG 389), box 1606.

16. "Poll of German Prisoner of War Opinion" (n.d.), 17: RG 389, box 1603.

17. Edward Shils and Morris Janowitz, "Cohesion and Disintegration in the Wehrmacht in World War II," *Public Opinion Quarterly* 12 (1948), 280–315. See also Tamotsu Shibutani, *The Derelicts of Company K: A Sociological Study of Demoralization* (Berkeley, 1978) for a similar assessment of behavioral traits among soldiers.

18. For some advocates of the theories of Shils and Janowitz, see Richard Holmes, *Acts of War: The Behavior of Men in Battle* (New York, 1985), and William C. Bradbury, Samuel M. Meyers, and Albert D. Biderman, eds., *Mass Behavior in Battle and Captivity: The Communist Soldier in the Korean War* (Chicago, 1968), in particular the discussion of defiant manifestations of Communist symbols among Chinese POWs, even though many revealed long-term disaffection with the precepts of Chinese Communism. For a conflicting opinion, one which places greater emphasis on ideology as opposed to military discipline, see Omer Bartov, *Hitler's Army: Soldiers, Nazis and War in the Third Reich* (New York, 1991). A brief summary of the book appears in Bartov's "Soldiers, Nazis, and War in the Third Reich," *Journal of Modern History* 63 (March 1991), 44–60.

19. Bartov, *Hitler's Army*, 7.

20. Hörner, *A German Odyssey*, 182–83.

21. Armando Boscolo cited in Louis Keefer, *Italian Prisoners of War in America, 1942–1946: Captives or Allies?* (New York, 1992), 79–80.

22. Pierre Boulle, *The Bridge over the River Kwai*, translated by Xan Fielding (New York, 1954), 9–10.

23. Spivey cited in Arthur A. Durand, *Stalag Luft III* (Baton Rouge, 1988), 149.

24. Ibid., 87.

25. Douglas Collins, *POW* (New York, 1968), 54–55.

26. The United States Strategic Bombing Survey, Morale Division, *The Effects of Strategic Bombing on German Morale* (Washington, D.C., 1947), 2:38.

27. "Report on Poll Taken Among 1191 German Prisoners of War at Prisoner of War Camp, Atlanta, Neb.," RG 389, box 1603. The report has no date, but the introduction states that the poll was administrated prior to the political segregation of prisoners. The report describes Camp Atlanta as typical, with 30 percent of its population composed of committed Nazis.

CHAPTER THREE

1. Howard Mumford Jones, "Patriotism—But How?" *Atlantic Monthly* 162 (November 1938), 585–92.

2. Axton Clark, "Edward Davison's Collected Poems," *New York Times Book Review*, May 26, 1940, 3.

3. Edward Davison, *Collected Poems 1917–1939* (New York, 1940), 47.

4. "Kill or Get Killed," unpublished poem in the Edward Davison Papers, Beinecke Library, Yale University (hereafter, EDP), box 10.

5. The German POW experience in Canada is discussed in John Melady, *Escape From Canada! The Untold Story of German POWs in Canada, 1939–1945* (Toronto, 1981).

6. "In Times of Discouragement," in Davison, *Collected Poems*, 139.

7. Karl-Heinz Schoeps, "The 'Golden Cage' and the Re-education of German Writers in American POW Camps: Hans Werner Richter and Alfred Andersch," in Heinz D. Osterle, *Amerika! New Images in German Literature* (New York, 1989), 40–41.

8. Egbert Krispyn, *Anti-Nazi Writers in Exile* (Athens, Georgia, 1978), 10.

9. Walter Schoenstedt, *In Praise of Life*, translated by Maxim Newmark (New York, 1938), 360.

10. Walter Schoenstedt, *The Cradle Builder* (New York, 1940).

11. Howard Mumford Jones, *An Autobiography* (Madison, Wisc., 1979), 212–20.

12. Howard Mumford Jones, *They Say the Forties* (New York, 1937), 41.

13. Ibid.

14. Howard Mumford Jones, *Violence and the Humanist* (Middlebury, Vt., 1967), 7.

15. Jones, "Patriotism—But How?" 591.

16. Jones, *Violence and the Humanist*, 20.

17. For a list of Ehrmann's many publications as well as his contribution to the comparative studies of constitutional issues, see Fred Edlin, ed., *Constitutional Democracy: Essays in Comparative Politics: A Festschrift in Honor of Henry W. Ehrmann* (Westview, Conn., 1983).

18. For a brief history of this fascinating institution, see Peter M. Rutkoff and

William B. Scott, *New School: A History of the New School of Social Research* (New York, 1986).

19. Henry W. Ehrmann, *French Labor: From Popular Front to Liberation* (New York, 1947), 111. This study is an adaptation of Ehrmann's earlier work and dissertation.

20. Ibid., 194.

21. Henry W. Ehrmann, "Prenationalism," *New Republic* 111 (May 29, 1944), 742.

22. Ibid.

23. Henry Ehrmann, "Washington's Plan For Germany," *New Republic* 108 (May 3, 1943), 585–87; id., "No Peace With the German Generals!" *Current History* 3 (December 1942), 273–79.

24. See Ehrmann's "No Peace With the German Generals!" and "Croce's Confession," *New Republic* 111 (September 1944), 285.

25. Ehrmann, "Prenationalism," 741–42.

26. M. Whitcomb Hess, "Philosopher to Politician: A Personal Appraisal of T. V. Smith," *School and Society* 52 (September 28, 1940), 246–52.

27. T. V. Smith, *The Democratic Way of Life* (Chicago, 1926); id., *The American Philosophy of Equality* (Chicago, 1927); id., "The Unknown Soldier and the Ideal of Honor," *Yale Review* 33 (December 1943), 225–37; id., *The Reeducation of Germany, Italy, and Japan* (Claremont, Calif., 1947); id., *The Ethics of Compromise and the Art of Containment* (New York, 1956).

28. Smith cited in Hess, "Philosopher to Politician," 249.

29. Howard Mumford Jones, "Tribalism," *Atlantic Monthly* 170 (October 1942), 87–93.

30. John Brown Mason to Bernard Gufler, "Memorandum Concerning the Special Projects Branch of the Office of the Provost Marshal General" (December 16, 1944), Stephan Farrand Papers, Hoover Institute, Stanford University, box 2.

31. Howard Mumford Jones, "The Relation of the Humanities to General Education," in William S. Gray, ed., *General Education: Its Nature, Scope, and Essential Elements* (Chicago, 1934), 45–46.

32. OPMG, "Historical Monograph: Re-education of Enemy Prisoners of War" (November 1945), 5–10, Office of the Chief of Military History, Department of the Army, Washington, D.C.

33. "Notes on Staff Meeting" (May 20, 1945), EDP, box 9.

34. Mason to Gufler, "Memorandum Concerning the Special Projects Branch," 2.

35. Jones, *An Autobiography*, 217.

CHAPTER FOUR

1. Daniel Lerner, *Psychological Warfare Against Nazi Germany: The Skywar Campaign, D-Day to VE Day* (Cambridge, Mass., 1971), 67–69. See also Barry Katz's fascinating study, *Foreign Intelligence: Research and Analysis in the Office of Strategic Services, 1942–1945* (Cambridge, Mass., 1989).

2. Captain Walter Schoenstedt to director SPD, "Subject: Captain Jessen"

(January 20, 1945), Record Group 389, Records of the Provost Marshal General, National Archives, Washington, D.C. (hereafter, RG 389), box 1616.

3. For a list of Idea Factory workers, see Captain Walter Schoenstedt to Director, Prisoner of War Special Projects Division, "Repatriation" (October 10, 1945), RG 389, box 1616.

4. Oskar Wintergerst, "'Why We Fight' Series and Reeducation of the German Prisoners of War" (February 16, 1945), RG 389, box 1616.

5. Eginhard von Lieberman, "Suggestions and Ideas for Radio Programs in Post-War Germany" (February 20, 1945), RG 389, box 1616.

6. Karl Kuntze, "Reaction of Our Group on Filmstrip #86—Boy and Girl Scouts" (August 25, 1945), RG 389, box 1605.

7. Memo written by Captain Meyer attached to ibid.

8. Dr. Gustav R. Hocke, "The Press in Germany" (n.d.), RG 389, box 1605.

9. Hans Werner Richter, *Beyond Defeat*, translated by Robert Kee (New York, 1950), 186–87. The British edition of this book, published during the same year, was entitled *The Odds Against Us*.

10. Alfred Andersch, "The Cherries of Freedom," in *My Disappearance in Providence and Other Stories*, translated by Ralph Manheim (New York, 1978), 193–223.

11. Ibid., 197, 200, 204–5.

12. Andersch, "My Disappearance in Providence," in *My Disappearance in Providence*, 131–57.

13. Hans Werner Richter, *They Fell From God's Hands*, translated by Geoffrey Sainsbury (New York, 1956), 187–93.

Chapter Five

1. Transcript of telephone conversation between Colonel Davison, Captain Schoenstedt, and Major Kreze, First Service Command (March 12, 1945), Record Group 389, Records of the Provost Marshal General, National Archives, Washington, D.C. (hereafter, RG 389), box 1597.

2. Colonel Davison to Captain Schoenstedt, "Attached Editorial for Der Ruf" (February 2, 1945), RG 389, box 1616.

3. "The Inner Powers," *Der Ruf* 1 (March 1, 1945), 1–2.

4. Transcript of conversation between Colonel Davison, Captain Schoenstedt, and Major Kreze (March 12, 1945).

5. Captain Raymond A. Speiser, Assistant Executive Officer (AEO), Camp Aliceville to Office of the Provost Marshal General (OPMG), "PW Reaction to Der Ruf" (March 14, 1945), RG 389, box 1599.

6. Davison to Schoenstedt "Attached Editorial for Der Ruf."

7. Speiser, "PW Reaction to Der Ruf."

8. Comments on speech by Captain Walter Schoenstedt, "Prisoner of War Newspaper" (May 19, 1945), RG 389, box 1599.

9. Peter Demetz, *Postwar German Literature: A Critical Introduction* (New York, 1970), 49–50.

10. Memorandum for Chief, Special Projects Division, "Proposed POW News Magazine" (November 4, 1944), RG 389, box 1596.

11. Comments on Speech by Captain Walter Schoenstedt.

12. Oron J. Hale, *The Captive Press in the Third Reich* (Princeton, N.J., 1964), 1–63, provides many insights into the structure of the German press before 1933.

13. "Open Letter to the Editors of 'Querschmitt,' Prisoner of War Camp, Okelika, Alabama," *Der Ruf* 7 (June 15, 1945), 8.

14. Ibid.

15. Memorandum for Chief, Special Projects Division, "Proposed POW News Magazine" (November 4, 1944), RG 389, box 1596.

16. *Der Ruf* 12 (September 1, 1945), 2.

17. "Germans or Jews?" *Der Ruf* 9 (July 15, 1945), 3.

18. Egbert Krispyn, *Anti-Nazi Writers in Exile* (Athens, Ga., 1978), 94–97; Peter Demetz, *Postwar German Literature*, 47–49; Ronald Taylor, *Literature and Society in Germany, 1918–1945* (Brighton, Great Britain, 1980), 266.

19. Thomas Mann quoted in *Der Ruf* 9 (July 15, 1945), 2.

20. Friedrich Meinecke, "The Guilt of the Regime," *Der Ruf* 12 (September 1, 1945), 3.

21. Stephen Jenard, "The Agreement," *Der Ruf* 4 (May 1, 1945), 4.

22. "The Spiritual Powers," *Der Ruf* 17 (November 15, 1945), 4.

23. Richter cited in Daniel Costelle, *Les Prisonniers* (Paris, 1975), 225–26.

24. This "influential member of *Der Ruf*'s editorial board" is cited in Hermann Jung, *Die deutschen Kriegsgefangenen in amerikanischer Hand, USA* (Munich, 1972), 223–24.

25. *Der Ruf* 15 (October 15, 1945), 4.

26. "The Voice of Reason," *Der Ruf* 9 (July 15, 1945), 1.

27. "Democrats and Republicans," *Der Ruf* 12 (September 1, 1945), 7.

28. "Parties in Germany," ibid., 5.

29. "The New Home," *Der Ruf* 12 (September 1, 1945), 3.

30. *Der Ruf* 15 (October 15, 1945), 5.

31. The article appears in the English translation of *Der Ruf*, together with a laconic note mentioning its deletion from the German language edition. See English translation of *Der Ruf* 17 (November 15, 1991), 4, RG 389, box 1597.

32. Karl Kuntze to the PMG through Captain Walter Schoenstedt, "Camp Elections" (November 15, 1945), RG 389, box 1616.

33. "Endangered Youth," *Der Ruf* 17 (November 15, 1945), 5.

34. *Der Ruf* 16 (November 1, 1945), 8.

35. Frederick Joseph Doyle, "German Prisoners of War in the Southwest United States During World War II: An Oral History" (Ph.D. diss., University of Denver, 1978).

36. Helmut Hörner, *A German Odyssey: The Journal of a German Prisoner of War*, translated and edited by Allan Kent Powell (Golden, Colo., 1991), 287.

37. Alfred Andersch, "The Cherries of Freedom," in *My Disappearance in Providence and Other Stories*, translated by Ralph Manheim (New York, 1978), 199.

38. Andersch, "My Disappearance in Providence," in *My Disappearance in Providence*, 152.

39. Memorandum from Brigadier General Edward S. Greenbaum to Major General Lerch, "Prisoners of War" (April 20, 1945), RG 389, box 1597.

40. Comments of Captain Walter Schoenstedt, "Prisoner of War Newspaper."

41. Kurt Hesse, "Expression of Opinion Concerning the War Prisoner Periodical *Der Ruf*" (August 13, 1945), RG 389, box 1597.

42. "Comments on 15th April issue of 'Der Ruf,'" attached to Memorandum from Brig. General Edward S. Greenbaum to Major General Lerch (April 20, 1945), RG 389, box 1597.

43. Ibid.

44. Memorandum on *Der Ruf* from Lt. Col. Ben H. Powell, Acting Director, SPD to Major General Lerch (July 23, 1945), RG 389, box 1597.

45. Comments of Lerch attached to ibid.

CHAPTER SIX

1. Major Maxwell McKnight to Major General Bryan, "Books for Prisoners of War" (June 5, 1945), Record Group 389, Records of the Provost Marshal General, National Archives, Washington, D.C. (hereafter, RG 389), box 1646.

2. "Selection of Books," in OPMG, "Notes, Memoranda, and War Department Publications: Conference at Fort Slocum, N.Y." (November 1944), RG 389, box 1650.

3. Ibid.

4. Ibid.

5. Lt. Colonel Edward Davison to Major General Bryan, "Memorandum from State Department Concerning Censorship of Books for Prisoners of War" (May 10, 1945), RG 389, box 1647.

6. "Censorship of Books" attached to memorandum from McKnight to Bryan "Books for Prisoners of War."

7. Karl Kuntze, "Report on *Children in the U.S.A.* (January 1, 1945), RG 389, box 1616.

8. Henry Ehrmann to Chief, Review Branch, "Flugschriften zur Weltpolitik" (March 28, 1945), RG 389, box 1652. Ehrmann was probably commenting on Nathaniel Micklem's *National Socialism and the Roman Catholic Church* (New York, 1939).

9. Reports on Emil Ludwig, *The Moral Conquest of Germany* (July 3, 1945), RG 389, box 1645.

10. Henry Ehrmann, "Factory Review of German Text-books to be Reprinted" (n.d.), RG 389, box 1652.

11. Captain Michael Ginsburg to Lt. Colonel Edward Davison, "Beards' *Basic History of the United States*" (December 23, 1945), RG 389, box 1645.

12. Ibid.

13. Henry Ehrmann to Lieutenant Schrekinger, "Schoenmann—*Geschichte der Vereinigten Staaten*" (April 21, 1945), RG 389, box 1645.

14. Howard Mumford Jones, "Writers and American Values," *New York Times Book Review* 50 (August 5, 1945), 2.

15. Howard Mumford Jones, "Literature as an Aid to Intercultural Under-

standing" in Lyman Bryson, Louis Finkelstein, R. M. Maciver, eds., *Conflicts of Power in Modern Culture: Seventh Symposium of the Conference on Science, Philosophy, and Religion* (New York, 1947), 313.

16. Ibid.

17. Ibid., 315.

18. Henry Ehrmann to Chief, Review Branch, "Justification of the Selection for the First Series of the *Buecherreihe Neue Welt*" (April 3, 1945), 1, RG 389, box 1645.

19. Ibid., 1–2.

20. Wayne Kvam, *Hemingway in Germany: The Fiction, the Legend, and the Critics* (Athens, Ohio, 1973), 4.

21. Max Dietrich cited in ibid., 7.

22. *Time* 36 (October 21, 1940), 94–95.

23. Howard Mumford Jones, "The Soul of Spain," *Saturday Review of Literature* 23 (October 26, 1940), 5, 19. For some other very favorable reviews by eminent American intellectuals, see Edmund Wilson, "The Return of Ernest Hemingway," *New Republic* 103 (October 28, 1940), 591–92; Malcolm Cowely, "For Whom The Bell Tolls," *New Republic* 114 (January 20, 1941), 89–90.

24. T. V. Smith, "Behind The Barbed Wire," *Saturday Review of Literature* 29 (May 4, 1946), 7.

25. Wallace Stegner, "Saroyan's Wonderful People," *New York Times Book Review*, February 28, 1943, 28.

26. William Philips, "The Cult of Innocence," *Nation* 153 (February 27, 1943), 318–19.

27. William Saroyan, *The Human Comedy* (New York, 1943), 72–73.

28. Ehrmann, "Justification of the Selection for the First Series," 2–3.

29. See Dr. Wolfgang Hildebrandt, "The Magic Mountain and the POWs: an Open Letter to Thomas Mann," *Der Ruf* 14 (October 1, 1945), 4.

30. Lore B. Foltin, "Franz Werfel's Image of America," in John M. Spalek and Robert F. Bell, *Exile: The Writer's Experience* (Chapel Hill, N.C., 1982), 300–310.

31. See Helmut F. Pfanner, *Exile in New York* (Detroit, 1983), 122.

32. Ibid., 152–53.

33. Ibid., 159.

34. Curt Sanger, "The Experience of Exile in Joseph Roth's Novels," in Spalek and Bell, *Exile: The Writer's Experience*, 258–66.

35. Herbert Lehnert, "Thomas Mann, Berthold Brecht, and the 'Free Germany' Movement," in Spalek and Bell, *Exile: The Writer's Experience*, 198.

36. Ronald Taylor, *Literature and Society in Germany, 1918–1945* (Brighton, Great Britain, 1980), 126.

37. "Reactions to *Buecherreihe Neue Welt*," OPMG, "Re-education of Enemy Prisoners of War: A Historical Monograph," Office of Chief of Military History, Department of the Army, Washington, D.C.

38. Ibid.

39. Major E. D. Law to Commanding Officer, Camp Forrest, Tennessee, "Censorship Control in Library Block 26, Prisoner of War Camp Forrest, Tenn., by Prisoner of War Karl Fritz Weise" (March 14, 1945), RG 389, box 1647.

CHAPTER SEVEN

1. Major General Archer L. Lerch to Chief of Staff, Army Service Forces, "Reorientation of German Prisoners of War" (August 23, 1944), 3–4, in SPD, "Historical Monograph: Re-education of Enemy Prisoner of War" (November 1, 1945), Office of Chief Military History Branch, Department of the Army, Washington, D.C.

2. Department of State, Special War Problems Division, "Indoctrination of German Prisoners of War" (March 2, 1944), Record Group 389, Records of the Provost Marshal General, National Archives, Washington, D.C. (hereafter, RG 389), box 1603.

3. Dr. Wilhelm Th. Doerr, "The Movies in Post-War Germany" (March 11, 1945), RG 389, box 1616.

4. Hans Werner Richter cited in Daniel Costelle, *Les Prisonniers* (Paris, 1975), 233.

5. SPD, "Historical Monograph of Film Branch" (November 5, 1945), RG 389, box 1649.

6. Harry Warner to Lt. General W. D. Styer (April 26, 1945), RG 389, box 1605.

7. On the clash between the Senate Interstate Commerce Committee and Hollywood, see "Propaganda or History?" *Nation* 153 (September 20, 1941), 241–42.

8. On Warner Brothers' projection of contemporary social values, see Nick Roddick, *A New Deal in Entertainment: Warner Brothers in the 1930s* (London, 1983).

9. Lawrence Levine and Robert Middlekauff, eds., *The National Temper: Readings in American Culture and Society* (New York, 1972), 303. These remarks appear in the introduction to Robert Warshow, "The Gangster as Tragic Hero," *Partisan Review* 15 (February 1948), which was reprinted in this anthology.

10. Major Maxwell McKnight to Major Gemmill, "Analysis of Motion Pictures Appearing on the Film Circuit from Warner Brothers" (June 8, 1945), RG 389, box 1605.

11. Ibid.

12. Ray Allen Billington, *Land of Savagery, Land of Promise: The European Image of the American Frontier in the Nineteenth Century* (New York, 1981), 54–56. See also Joseph Wechsberg, "Winnetou of der Wild West," *The American West* 1 (summer 1964), 32–39.

13. Jan-Christopher Horak, "Luis Trenker's *The Kaiser of California*: How the West Was Won, Nazi Style," *Historical Journal of Film and Television* 6 (1986), 181–95; Robert Edwin Herzstein, *Roosevelt and Hitler: Prelude to War* (New York, 1989), 34–35.

14. SPD, "Historical Monograph of Film Branch," 10.

15. Ibid., 25.

16. Ibid., 10.

17. Synopsis of *G.I. Joe*, RG 389, box 1605. For an interesting analysis of this movie, see Clayton R. Koppes and Gregory D. Black, *Hollywood Goes to War:*

How Politics, Profits, and Propaganda Shaped World War II Movies (New York, 1987), 304–9.

18. Synopsis of *The Sullivans*, RG 389, box 1605.

19. Erwin Leiser, *Nazi Cinema*, translated by Gertrud Mander and David Wilson (New York, 1974), 30–31.

20. Ibid., 33.

21. Synopsis of *Gung-Ho*, RG 389, box 1605.

22. Cited in Leiser, *Nazi Cinema*, 32.

23. Synopsis for *So Proudly We Hail*, RG 389, box 1605. See Koppes and Black, *Hollywood Goes to War*, 98–104, for a description of OWI attempts to manipulate the screenplay of this movie for propaganda purposes.

24. Synopsis of *Happy Land*, RG 389, box 1605.

25. Synopsis of *Human Comedy*, RG 389, box 1605.

26. Synopsis of *Going My Way*, RG 389, box 1605.

27. Synopsis of *Wells Fargo*, RG 389, box 1605.

28. Synopsis of *Young Mr. Lincoln*, RG 389, box 1605.

29. Synopsis of *Valley of Decision*, RG 389, box 1605.

30. See the appropriate synopses in RG 389, box 1605.

31. Synopsis for *Roughly Speaking*, RG 389, box 1605.

32. Synopsis for *What a Woman*, RG 389, box 1605.

33. Captain Otto Englander to Acting Director, PW Special Projects Division, "War Themes in Motion Pictures For Prisoners of War" (August 2, 1945), RG 389, box 1605.

34. Ibid.

35. Brigadier General B. M. Bryan to Chief Signal Officer, "Deglamorization Film for Prisoners of War" (May 5, 1945); Lt. Colonel Edward Davison to Brig. General B. M. Bryan, "Production of Two Films" (April 17, 1945), RG 389, box 1605. The James E. Stewart mentioned here was not Jimmy Stewart the actor, who served in the Navy during the war.

36. David Culbert, "American Film Policy in the Re-Education of Germany after 1945," in Nicholas Pronay, ed., *The Political Re-Education of Germany and Her Allies After WWII* (London, 1985), 173–201.

37. SPD, "Historical Monograph: Re-education of Enemy Prisoners of War," 69–70.

38. Ibid., 69.

CHAPTER EIGHT

1. On the role of the survey course in American Education during this period, see Patricia Beesley, *The Revival of the Humanities in American Education* (New York, 1940), 80–84.

2. SPD, "Report on the Experimental Administrative School for Selected German Prisoners of War, Fort Kearney, Rhode Island May 7 to July 7, 1945" (n.d.), 1–12, Office of the Chief of Military History, Department of the Army, Washington, D.C.

3. Ibid., 3.

4. Ibid., 4.

5. Henry W. Ehrmann, "On Some implications of the War Department's Re-

orientation Program For German Prisoners of War" (April 17, 1946), 14–15. Edward Davison Papers, Beinecke Library, Yale University (hereafter, EDP), box 10.

6. Ibid., 3.

7. Henry Ehrmann, "Course in German History," in "Report on the Experimental School," 17.

8. Ibid., 20.

9. Ibid.

10. Howard Mumford Jones, "Course in American History and Institutions," in ibid., 26.

11. Ibid., 4.

12. Henry W. Ehrmann, "An Experiment in Political Education: The Prisoner-of-War Schools in the United States," *Social Research* 14 (September 1947), 311.

13. Major Burnham N. Dell, "Course in Military Government," in "Report on the Experimental Administrative School," 13–14.

14. Major Maxwell McKnight, Acting Director, Prisoner of War Special Projects Division to Chief, Field Service Branch, "Screening of German Prisoners of War" (June 7, 1945), attached to "Report on the Experimental Administrative School."

15. Ehrmann, "An Experiment in Political Education," 311.

16. T. V. Smith, "Behind Barbed Wire," *Saturday Review of Literature* 29 (May 4, 1946), 6.

17. Ibid.

18. SPD, "Historical Monograph: Re-education of Enemy Prisoners of War, Projects II and III" (March 1, 1946), 11, Office of the Chief of Military History, Department of the Army.

19. Ehrmann, "An Experiment in Political Education," 314.

20. Howard Mumford Jones to Major General Archer L. Lerch (July 18, 1945), EDP, box 8.

21. Transcript of telephone conversation between Major Gemmill and Major McKnight, Fort Kearney, Rhode Island (July 19, 1945), EDP, box 8.

22. Maxwell McKnight to Edward Davison (July 19, 1945), EDP, box 9.

23. Major W. B. Gemmill to Major General Lerch, "Visit to Fort Kearney and Fort Getty" (August 11, 1945), Record Group 389, Records of the Provost Marshal General, National Archives, Washington, D.C. (hereafter, RG 389), box 1616.

24. Lerch cited in letter from McKnight to Davison (July 19, 1945).

25. *New York Times*, July 19, 1945, 8; July 21, 1945, 24; July 22, 1945, 25.

26. I. F. Stone, "The Army and the Reds," *Nation* 160 (March 3, 1945), 238–39.

27. Gemmill to Lerch, "Visit to Fort Kearney and Fort Getty."

28. On the isolation of anti-Nazis, see POW Friedrich Schiltz to Major Hims, Chief Executive Officer, Camp Campbell, Kentucky, "Memorandum Concerning Treatment of Anti-Nazis" (October 10, 1944), Stephen Farrand Papers, Hoover Institute, Stanford University (hereafter, SFP), box 2.

29. On Lerch's death, see his obituary in the *New York Times*, September 11, 1947, 15.

30. Lerch cited in the *New York Times*, March 21, 1946, 15.

31. On this subject, see Ellen W. Schrecker, *No Ivory Tower: McCarthyism and the Universities* (New York, 1986).

32. T. V. Smith, "Academic Expediency as Democratic Justice," *American Scholar* 18 (summer 1949), 342–46.

33. Ibid., 345.

34. Schrecker, *No Ivory Tower*, 340.

35. Letter to Provost Marshal General from rejected POWs (November 9, 1945), RG 389, box 1142.

36. See, for example, Hermann Joseph Reith to Intelligence Officer, Fort Dix (October 13, 1945); Siegfried Cammann to Intelligence Officer, Fort Dix (October 12, 1945); Thankmar Steuding to Intelligence Officer, Fort Dix (October 11, 1945), RG 389, box 1142.

37. Lt. Colonel Alpheus W. Smith to Lt. Colonel Edward Davison, "Petition from Prisoners of War at Fort Dix, New Jersey" (November 9, 1945), RG 389, box 1142.

38. Second Lt. William R. Hommiller to Acting Director Special Projects Division, "Intelligence Report From Chaplain John Dvorovy, PW Special Projects Division" (August 2, 1945), EDP, box 9.

39. Ibid.

40. Major Paul A. Neuland to Director, SPD, "Effects of Press Reports" (September 17, 1945), RG 389, box 1596.

41. Ibid.

42. Ibid.

CHAPTER NINE

1. Wendell L. Willkie, *One World* (New York, 1943), 1.

2. Ibid.

3. Ibid., 2, 134.

4. Ibid., i.

5. Ibid., 134.

6. Ibid., 173–74.

7. "Report No. 2 about the camp newspapers in the German Prisoner of War camps in the U.S.A." (January 27, 1945), Record Group 389, Records of the Provost Marshal General, National Archives, Washington, D.C. (hereafter, RG 389), box 1599.

8. "Camp Publications," in SPD, "Historical Monograph: Re-Education of Enemy Prisoners of War" (November 1, 1945), 21–30, Office of the Chief of Military History, Department of the Army, Washington, D.C.

9. Ibid., 26–27.

10. Ibid., 71–73.

11. Ibid., 74.

12. Ibid., 75.

13. For a brief overview of music under the Third Reich, see Eric Levi, "Music and National Socialism: The Politicisation of Criticism, Composition and Performance," in Brandon Taylor and Wilfried van der Will, *The Nazification of Art: Art, Design, Music and Film in the Third Reich* (London, 1990), 158–78.

14. "Historical Monograph: Re-education of Enemy Prisoners of War," 75.

15. "Screening of Cooperative Prisoners of War," in SPD, "Historical Monograph: Re-education of Enemy Prisoners of War, Eustis Project" (April 4, 1946), Files of the Chief of Military History, Washington, D.C., tab. 3.

16. Ironically, "*März Veilchen*/March Violets" was the term used by Nazis to describe those who jumped on the Hitler bandwagon after Hitler's rise to power.

17. "Historical Monograph: Re-Education of Enemy Prisoners of War, Eustis Project," 5.

18. Ibid., 5–9.

19. Henry W. Ehrmann, "An Experiment in Political Education: The Prisoner-of-War Schools in the United States," *Social Research* 14 (September 1947), 305.

20. Quentin Reynolds, "Experiment in Democracy," *Collier's* 117 (May 25, 1946), 13, 41.

21. Ehrmann, "An Experiment in Political Education," 311–13.

22. Ibid., 315–16.

23. All lecture outlines, including "The Democratic Way of Life," appear in Special Projects Center, Fort Eustis, Virginia, "Interim Report of the Orientation Branch" (February 28, 1946), RG 389, box 1613.

24. Edwin Casady, "The Basic Assumptions of Democracy as Presented to German POWs," in Lyman Bryson, Louis Finkelstein, and R. M. Maciver, eds., *Conflicts of Power in Modern Culture: Seventh Symposium of the Conference on Science, Philosophy, and Religion* (New York, 1947), 229–46.

25. Lecture notes for "Democratic Way of Life," in "Interim Report of the Orientation Branch," 2.

26. Lecture notes for "The American Constitution," in ibid.

27. Lecture notes on "Political Parties and Elections in America," in ibid.

28. See Allan M. Winkler, *The Politics of Propaganda: The Office of War Information, 1942–1945* (New Haven, 1978), 15, for some interesting comments on the film and play as a metaphor for contemporary political problems.

29. Lecture notes for "The American Education System," in "Interim Report of the Orientation Branch."

30. Lecture notes for "American Economic Life," in ibid.

31. Clayton R. Koppes and Gregory Black, *Hollywood Goes to War: How Politics, Profits and Propaganda Shaped World War II Movies* (New York, 1987), 146–54.

32. "Historical Monograph: Re-education of Enemy Prisoners of War, Eustis Project" (April 4, 1946), 14–15.

33. Ehrmann, "An Experiment in Political Education," 317.

34. Lecture notes for "Democratic Traditions in Germany," in "Interim Report of the Orientation Branch."

35. For a discussion of the movie and its relationship to Segher's original novel, see Jan-Christopher Horak, "The Other Germany in Zinnemann's *The Seventh Cross*," in Eric Rentschler, ed., *German Film and Literature: Adaptations and Transformations* (New York, 1986), 117–31.

36. "Historical Monograph: Re-education of Enemy Prisoners of War, Eustis Project" (April 4, 1946), 16–17.

37. Lecture notes for "The World of Today and Germany," in "Interim Report of the Orientation Branch."

38. Willkie, *One World*, 73.

39. Lecture notes for "The World of Today and Germany."

40. Stephen Vincent Benét, "A Prayer for United Nations," in "Interim Report of the Orientation Branch."

41. "Historical Monograph: Re-education of Enemy Prisoners of War, Eustis Project," 27.

42. Henry W. Ehrmann, Head Presentation Section to Lt. Colonel Alpheus Smith, Commanding Officer Special Project Center, "Critique of Cycles No. 3, 4, and 5 of Orientation Course," in "Interim Report of the Orientation Branch."

43. Address by PW Emil Roth in ibid.

CHAPTER TEN

1. Office of the Provost Marshal General (OPMG), "Poll of German Prisoners of War" (n.d.), Record group 389, Files of the OPMG, National Archives, Washington, D.C. (hereafter, RG 389), box 1603.

2. Ibid., 10.

3. Ibid., 29.

4. Ibid., 9.

5. Donald McGranahan and Morris Janowitz, "Studies of German Youth," *Journal of Abnormal and Social Psychology* 41 (January 1946), 4.

6. Ibid., 5.

7. Ibid., 12.

8. H. H. Wubben, "American Prisoners of War in Korea: a Second Look at the 'Something New in History' Theme," *American Quarterly* 22 (spring 1970), 3–19. The best summary of the moral decay position is to be found in Eugene Kinkead, *In Every War But One* (New York, 1959). For a brief survey on the notions of brainwashing, see Denise Winn, *The Manipulated Mind: Brainwashing, Conditioning, and Indoctrination* (London, 1983).

9. Albert Biderman, *March to Calumny: The Story of American POWs in the Korean War* (New York, 1963), 169.

10. Ibid.

11. John S. Benben, "Education of Prisoners of War on Koje Island, Korea," *Educational Record* 36 (April 1955), 157–73.

12. Ibid., 162.

13. Such claims for high percentages of enemy POWs refusing repatriation have been disputed. See, for example, Jon Halliday and Bruce Cumings, *Korea: The Unknown War* (London, 1988), 179.

14. See Hall Vetter, *Mutiny on Koje Island* (Rutland, Vt., 1965). For two very different interpretations of Koje, see Wilfred Burchett and Alan Winnington, *Koje Unscreened* (Beijing, 1953), and U.S. Army Forces in the Far East, Psychological Warfare Section, *Interviews with 24 Korean POW Leaders Prepared by Research, Analysis and Evaluation Division* (Washington, D.C., 1954).

15. Henry Ehrmann, "Experiment in Political Education: The Prisoner-of-War Schools in the United States," *Social Research* 14 (1947), 304–20.

16. OPMG, "Poll of German Prisoners of War."

17. William Moulton to former colleagues from Forts Kearney, Getty, Wetherill, and Eustis (September 12, 1947), Edward Davison Papers, Beinecke Library, Yale University, box 10. A copy of Moulton's report to the War Department is attached to this letter. For an abstract of this report, see " 'The Cream of the Crop' Two Years Later," in Anna J. Merritt and Richard L. Merritt, *Public Opinion in Occupied Germany: The OMGUS Surveys, 1945–1949* (Urbana, Ill., 1950), 200–201.

18. Kurt Lewin and Paul Grabbe, "Conduct, Knowledge, and Acceptance of New Values," *Journal of Social Issues* 1 (1945), 53–63, reprinted in Kurt Lewin, *Resolving Social Conflicts* (New York, 1948), 60.

19. Ibid., 63.

20. Ibid.

21. On the American rationalization of these internment camps, see Richard Drinnon, *Keeper of Concentration Camps: Dillon S. Myer and American Racism* (Berkeley, Calif., 1987).

22. Robert A. Mossman, "Japanese-American War Relocation Centers as Total Institutions with Emphasis on the Educational Program" (Ph.D. diss., Rutgers University, 1978), 52–71. See also Thomas James, *Exile Within: The Schooling of Japanese Americans, 1942–1945* (Cambridge, Mass., 1987).

23. Christie Kiefer, *Changing Cultures, Changing Lives: An Ethnographic Study of Three Generations of Japanese Americans* (New York, 1974), 29.

24. Frances S. Cushman cited in ibid., 102.

25. Kaizo Kubo cited in ibid., 100.

26. David A. Foy, *For You the War is Over: American Prisoners of War in Nazi Germany* (New York, 1984), 86–87.

27. Henry Faulk, *Group Captives; The Re-education of German Prisoners of War in Britain, 1945–1948* (London, 1977), 58.

28. Ibid., 61.

29. Ibid., 82.

30. Ibid., 95–96.

31. Ibid., 98.

32. Report from POWD No. 4 (Repatriation) Camp, March 1948 in Faulk, *Group Captives*, 187.

33. Ibid., 186.

34. Robert Lowe Kunzig, "360,000 P.W.'s—The Hope of Germany," *American Magazine* 142 (November 1946), 134.

35. Ibid., 135.

36. On Germany's decimation by Allied bombings, see Earl R. Beck, *Under the Bombs: The German Home Front, 1942–1945* (Lexington, Ky., 1986).

37. Hans Werner Richter cited in Jeffry M. Diefendorf, *In The Wake of War: The Reconstruction of German Cities after World War II* (New York, 1993), 13.

38. Galbraith cited in Studs Terkel, *"The Good War": An Oral History of World War Two* (New York, 1984), 209.

39. Paul Fussell, *Wartime: Understanding and Behavior in the Second World War* (New York, 1989), 16.

40. The United States Strategic Bombing Survey, Morale Division, *The Effects of Strategic Bombing on German Morale, Volume 1* (Washington, D.C., 1947), 1. The survey was carried out from March to July 1945. See also Ronald Schaffer, *Wings of Judgment: American Bombing in World War II* (New York, 1985), and "American Military Ethics in World War II: An Exchange," *Journal of American History* 68 (June 1981), 85–92.

41. *The Effects of Strategic Bombing on German Morale*, 43.

42. Ibid.

43. Ibid.

CHAPTER ELEVEN

1. Wendell L. Willkie, "Freedom and the Liberal Arts," in Norman Foerster, ed., *The Humanities After the War* (Princeton, N.J., 1944), 1–2. The article was published originally in the Spring 1943 issue of *American Scholar*.

2. Ibid., 4–5.

3. Richard Hofstadter, "The Development of Higher Education in America," in Richard Hofstadter and C. DeWitt Hardy, eds., *The Development and Scope of Higher Education in the United States* (New York, 1952), 54.

4. Roscoe Pound, "Humanities in an Absolutist World," in Foerster, *The Humanities after the War*, 19. The article appeared originally in the October 1943 issue of *The Classical Journal*.

5. Archibald MacLeish, "The Attack on the Scholar's World," *Saturday Review of Literature* 25 (July 18, 1942), 5.

6. Howard Mumford Jones, *One Great Society: Humane Learning in the United States* (New York, 1959), 44–45. The book was derived from a report on the state of the humanities prepared for the Commission on the Humanities of the American Council of Learned Societies in the early 1950s.

7. T. V. Smith, "American Democracy: Expendable and Exportable," *Virginia Quarterly Review* 23 (spring 1947), 162–63.

8. Norman Foerster, "A University Prepared For Victory," in Foerster, *The Humanities After the War*, 29–30. This article appeared originally in the June 1943 issue of *The Journal of Higher Education*.

9. Howard Mumford Jones, "The American Scholar Once More," *Harvard Alumni Bulletin* 39 (March 19, 1937), 738.

10. Willis Moore, "Indoctrination and Democratic Method," in I. A. Snook, ed., *Concepts of Indoctrination: Philosophical Essays* (London, 1972), 94.

11. Ibid., 96. See also Benjamin Floyd Pittenger, *Indoctrination for American Democracy* (New York, 1941).

12. Walter Schoenstedt, "Totalitarian Education" (n.d.), Walter Schoenstedt Papers, University of California, Davis (hereafter, WSP), box 9.

13. Michael Hunt, *Ideology and U.S. Foreign Policy* (Yale, 1987), 13.

14. Richard Hofstadter, "The Development of Higher Education in America," 107.

15. "Fifteen Minute Speech delivered by Lieutenant Walter Schoenstedt at the U.S. Army School of Orientation and Education" (November 18, 1943), WSP, box 9; Schoenstedt, "Detail Outline for Lecture on Germany" (n.d.), 4, Stephen Farrand Papers, Hoover Institute, Stanford University, box 2.

16. Smith, "American Democracy," 162.

17. Jones, "The American Scholar Once More," 736.

18. Ibid., 736, 739.

19. Edward Davison, "In Times of Discouragement," in Edward Davison, *Collected Poems* (New York, 1940), 139.

Note on the Sources

The following description of primary sources covers the framework of this study. For additional sources please consult the notes.

DOCUMENTARY COLLECTIONS

This study of the German POW experience in the United States relies heavily on the files of U.S. Army Provost Marshal General, Record Group 389, at the National Archives, Washington, D.C. These files contain a full record of routine business and curriculum development of the Special Projects Division (SPD) charged with the reeducation of German POWs within the continental United States. Given the fact that most of the SPD's faculty were not proficient in German, this collection includes English language translations of most German material used in the reeducation program.

The files of Edward Davison, at Yale University's Beinecke Library are of special importance for understanding the internal politics among the SPD staff, as well as the significance of the "Red Scare" that rocked the program in 1945. Davison's papers include numerous unpublished poems, some of them quite revealing of his personal politics.

The Walter Schoenstedt papers, at the special collections library, University of California, Davis, provide a comprehensive documentary record of the ideological inclinations of this important team member of the SPD. Among his many duties, Schoenstedt was responsible for the content of the POW newspaper, *Der Ruf*, as well as the selection of POW collaborators for the Idea Factory.

Stephen Farrand was a legal advisor in the office of the Provost Marshal General. His files at the Hoover Institute, Stanford University, include the exchange of letters between the War and State Departments regarding the establishment of the SPD, personnel evaluations of the SPD staff written by State Department officials, censors' reports based on the mail received and sent by POWs, as well as a large collection of local camp newspapers.

The Office of the Historian of the Army provided me with a full record of the SPD monographs which were written by the American faculty toward the final stages of the program. These historical accounts include staff evaluations of the various schools projects. All monographs are accompanied by appendixes containing important original documents used at various stages of the program.

The library of the University of California, Berkeley, has collected all issues of *Der Ruf*. This newspaper is also available at the National Archives.

AUTOBIOGRAPHIES AND RECOLLECTIONS

Numerous German POWs who were incarcerated in the United States during the war have published their memoirs, several of which are available in English. George Gaertner, *Hitler's Last Soldier in America* (New York, 1985) is the story of a POW who managed to escape and disappear into a German neighborhood in Chicago. Arnold Krammer, the author of *Nazi Prisoners of War in America* (1979)—the definitive work study of German POW camps in the United States—edited this book which contains a fascinating study of life behind barbed wire. Allan Kent Powell has translated and edited the diaries of former POW Helmut Hörner, *A German Odyssey: The Journal of a German Prisoner of War* (1991).

As for the Reeducation program itself, the numerous German writers who were employed in the Idea Factory have, of course, invoked their experiences in their various novels. Hans Werner Richter alluded to the POW experience in general, and the reeducation program, in particular, in *Beyond Defeat* (1950). His colleage, Alfred Andersch recalled the impact of the war, incarceration, and reeducation in *My Disappearance in Providence and Other Stories* (1978).

As for the American officials of reeducation, their written accounts of the program are surprisingly sporadic. SPD director Edward Davison, never published anything on this subject. His published work, in particular *Collected Poems 1917–1939* (New York, 1940), provides a fleeting glimpse of his political beliefs and understanding of the role of liberal arts in American higher education.

Howard Mumford Jones has mentioned the program in passing only in his biography. During and immediately after his tenure at the SPD he did, however, publish some thinly veiled accounts and critiques of reeducation, including, "Writers and American Values," *New York Times Book Review* 50 (August 5, 1945), and "Literature as an Aid to Intercultural Understanding," in Lyman Bryson et al., eds., *Conflicts of Power in Modern Culture: Seventh Symposium of the Conference on Science, Philosophy, and Religion* (1947). The prolific Jones published numerous journalistic articles concerning his understanding of the ideological dimensions of the war, including "Patriotism—But How?" *Atlantic Monthly* 162 (November 1938), and "Tribalism," *Atlantic Monthly* 170 (October 1942). *Primer in Academic Freedom* (1949), a postwar reader edited by Jones, provides a glimpse of his couragious stand on this issue.

Walter Schoenstedt's novels written prior to joining the SPD are indispensable for understanding this very complex character, and his vision of the "new" German who would rise out of the ashes of war and economic despair. *In Praise of Life* (1938) and *The Cradle Builder* (1940) are both autobiographical accounts and vivid political manifestos.

Henry W. Ehrmann's *From Popular Front to Liberation* (New York, 1947); "Prenationalism," *New Republic* 111 (May 29, 1944), 742; and "Washington's Plan For Germany," *The New Republic* 108 (May 3, 1943), 585–87 are good sources for understanding his political views during the war years. "An Experiment in Political Education: The Prisoner-of-War Schools in the United States," *Social Research* 14 (September 1947) is the best published account of the school phase of reeducation.

T. V. Smith's most direct analysis of his work in the SPD appears in "Behind the Barbed Wire," *Saturday Review of Literature* 29 (May 4, 1946). *The Reeducation of Germany, Italy, and Japan* (Claremont, Calif., 1947) discusses Smith's understanding of the role of education in furthering the United States' foreign policy objectives. The most lucid discussion of the doctrine of compromise which underscored all of his efforts at the SPD appears in *The Ethics of Compromise and the Art of Containment* (New York, 1956). For Smith's stance on the loyalty purges in academia, see "Academic Expediency as Democratic Justice," *American Scholar* 18 (Summer 1949).

The most interesting articles written by other, minor members of the SPD staff are Edwin Casady, "The Basic Assumptions of Democracy as Presented to German POWs," in Lymon Bryson et al., eds., *Conflicts of Power in Modern Culture: Seventh Symposium of the Conference on Science, Philosophy, and Religion* (New York, 1947), and Robert Lowe Kunzig, "360,000 P.W.s—The Hope of Germany," *American Magazine* 142 (November 1946).

Index

Numbers in italics refer to illustrations.